JOURNAL FOR THE STUDY OF THE NEW TESTAMENT SUPPLEMENT SERIES
78

Executive Editor
Stanley E. Porter

Editorial Board
Richard Bauckham, David Catchpole, R. Alan Culpepper,
Joanna Dewey, James D.G. Dunn, Robert Fowler, Robert Jewett,
Elizabeth Struthers Malbon, Dan O. Via

JSOT Press
Sheffield

The Function of Suffering
in Philippians

L. Gregory Bloomquist

Journal for the Study of the New Testament
Supplement Series 78

BS
2705.2
.B66
1993

Copyright © 1993 Sheffield Academic Press

Published by JSOT Press
JSOT Press is an imprint of
Sheffield Academic Press Ltd
343 Fulwood Road
Sheffield S10 3BP
England

Typeset by Sheffield Academic Press
and
Printed on acid-free paper in Great Britain
by Biddles Limited
Guildford

British Library Cataloguing in Publication Data

Bloomquist, L. Gregory
   Function of Suffering in Philippians.-
   (JSNT Supplement Series, ISSN 0143-5108;
   No. 78)
   I. Title II. Series
   227

ISBN 1-85075-383-0

CONTENTS

Abbreviations 9
Introduction 13

PART I
HISTORY OF THE INTERPRETATION OF SUFFERING IN PHILIPPIANS

Chapter 1
THE MARTYROLOGICAL APPROACH 18
1. The Earliest Martyrological Texts 18
2. Developments 21
3. Continuation 26
4. The Martyrological Approach in the Critical Period 31
5. Conclusion 33

Chapter 2
FROM THE ORIGINS OF CHRIST-MYSTICISM TO SCHWEITZER 35
1. Christ-Mysticism 35
2. Schweitzer and his Followers 42
3. Conclusion 48

Chapter 3
ALTERNATIVE APPROACHES 50
1. Ernst Lohmeyer and Martyrology 50
2. Ernst Käsemann and the Epiphanic Role of Suffering 54
3. Karl Barth and Suffering as an Apostle 57
4. Daniel Patte and Structural Semiotics 65
5. Conclusion 69

6   *The Function of Suffering in Philippians*

PART II
EPISTOLARY STRUCTURE AND RHETORICAL FUNCTIONS

Chapter 4
LETTER-WRITING AND RHETORIC IN ANTIQUITY   72
   1. Letter-Writing in Antiquity   72
   2. Rhetoric in Antiquity   84
   3. Conclusion   96

Chapter 5
THE INTEGRITY AND EPISTOLARY STRUCTURE OF PHILIPPIANS   97
   1. The Integrity of Philippians   97
   2. The Epistolary Conventions in Philippians and the
      Structure of the Letter   104
   3. Conclusion   116

Chapter 6
THE RHETORICAL FUNCTIONS OF PHILIPPIANS   119
   1. The Rhetorical 'Genus' of the Letter   119
   2. The Rhetorical Features of the Letter   120
   3. Conclusion   137

PART III
EXEGETICAL AND THEMATIC STUDIES

Chapter 7
THE THEME OF SUFFERING IN THE *PREPARATIO*   140
   1. Epistolary Prescript (1.1-2)   140
   2. *Exordium* (1.3-11)   145
   3. *Narratio* (1.12-14)   147
   4. *Partitio* (1.15-18a)   150

Chapter 8
THE THEME OF SUFFERING IN THE *ARGUMENTATIO*, PART I   152
   1. *Confirmatio* (1.18b-26)   152
   2. *Exhortatio* (1.27–2.18)   157

Chapter 9
THE THEME OF SUFFERING IN THE *ARGUMENTATIO*, PART II   173
    1. *Exempla* (2.19-30)   173
    2. *Reprehensio* (3.1-16)   178
    3. *Exhortatio* (3.17–4.7)   183

Chapter 10
THE THEME OF SUFFERING IN THE *PERORATIO*   187

CONCLUSION   191

Appendix: The 'Opponents' of Paul at Philippi   198

Bibliography   202
Index of References   221
Index of Authors   232

ABBREVIATIONS

AcBib	Actualidad bíblica
AGJU	Arbeiten zur Geschichte des antiken Judentums und des Urchristentums
AnBib	Analecta biblica
AUS7TR	American University Studies, Series VII: Theology and Religion
BAGD	W. Bauer, W.F. Arndt, F.W. Gingrich and F.W. Danker, *A Greek–English Lexicon of the New Testament*
BBB	Bonner biblische Beiträge
BDF	F. Blass, A. Debrunner and R.W. Funk, *A Greek Grammar of the New Testament*
BEB	Biblioteca de estudios bíblicos
BeO	*Bibbia e Oriente*
BETL	Bibliotheca ephemeridum theologicarum lovaniensium
BHSE	Biblioteca Herder, Sección de Sagrada Escritura
Bib	*Biblica*
BibLeb	*Bibel und Leben*
BJRL	*Bulletin of the John Rylands University Library of Manchester*
BK	*Bibel und Kirche*
BNTC	Black's New Testament Commentaries
BO	*Bibliotheca orientalis*
BT	*The Bible Translator*
BTh	Bibliothèque théologique
BTN	Bibliotheca Theologica Norvegica
BTod	*Bible Today*
BWANT	Beiträge zur Wissenschaft vom Alten und Neuen Testament
BZ	*Biblische Zeitschrift*
BZHT	Beiträge zur historischen Theologie
BZNW	Beiheft zur *ZNW*
CBC	Cambridge Bible Commentary
CBQ	*Catholic Biblical Quarterly*
CE	Le champ éthique
CH	*Church History*
CJT	*Canadian Journal of Theology*
CNT	Commentaire du Nouveau Testament
ConBNT	Coniectanea biblica, New Testament
CSEL	Corpus scriptorum ecclesiasticorum latinorum
CTMB	Calver theologische Monographien, Series B: Systematische Theologie und Kirchengeschichte

DBSup	*Dictionnaire de la Bible, Supplément*
DLZ	*Deutsche Literaturzeitung*
Echter	Das Neue Testament—Echter Bibel
EHPR	Etudes d'histoire et de philosophie religieuses
EKKNT	Evangelisch-Katholische Kommentar zum Neuen Testament
EstBíb	*Estudios bíblicos*
ETL	*Ephemerides theologicae lovanienses*
ETR	*Etudes théologiques et religieuses*
EvQ	*Evangelical Quarterly*
ExpTim	*Expository Times*
FB	Forschung zur Bibel
FCLD	Forschungen zur christlichen Litteratur- und Dogmengeschichte
FFNT	Foundations and Facets: New Testament
FGLP	Forschungen zur Geschichte und Lehre des Protestantismus
FKD	Forschungen zur Kirchen- und Dogmengeschichte
FRLANT	Forschungen zur Religion und Literatur des Alten und Neuen Testaments
FZPT	*Freiburger Zeitschrift für Philosophie und Theologie*
GBSNTS	Guides to Biblical Scholarship, New Testament Series
GCS	Griechischen christlichen Schriftsteller
GL	*Geist und Leben*
GTA	Göttinger theologische Arbeiten
HKNT	Handkommentar zum Neuen Testament
HNT	Handbuch zum Neuen Testament
HTKNT	Herders theologischer Kommentar zum Neuen Testament
HTR	*Harvard Theological Review*
HTS	Harvard Theological Studies
IB	*Interpreter's Bible*
ICC	International Critical Commentary
Int	*Interpretation*
JBL	*Journal of Biblical Literature*
JQR	*Jewish Quarterly Review*
JR	*Journal of Religion*
JSNTSup	*Journal for the Study of the New Testament* Supplement Series
JTC	*Journal for Theology and Church*
JTS	*Journal of Theological Studies*
JTSA	*Journal of Theology for Southern Africa*
LD	Lectio divina
LEC	Library of Early Christianity
MBT	Münsterische Beiträge zur Theologie
MeyerK	H.A.W. Meyer, Kritisch-exegetischer Kommentar über das Neue Testament
MNTC	Moffatt NT Commentary
MScRel	*Mélanges de science religieuse*
NA	Neutestamentliche Abhandlungen
NCB	New Clarendon Bible
NCBC	New Century Bible Commentary
NF	Neutestamentliche Forschungen

NICNT	The New International Commentary on the New Testament
NIDNTT	C. Brown (ed.), *The New International Dictionary of New Testament Theology*
NovT	*Novum Testamentum*
NovTSup	Supplements to *Novum Testamentum*
NRT	*La nouvelle revue théologique*
NST	*Nouvelle serie théologique*
NTD	*Das Neue Testament Deutsch*
NTS	*New Testament Studies*
NumSup	Studies in the History of Religion: Supplements to *Numen*
PG	J. Migne (ed.), *Patrologia graeca*
PL	J. Migne (ed.), *Patrologia latina*
PNTC	The Pelican New Testament Commentaries
PTMS	Pittsburgh Theological Monograph Series
RArchC	*Rivista di archaeologia cristiana*
RB	*Revue biblique*
RBen	*Revue bénédictine*
RCT	*Revista Catalana de Teologia*
RE Supp	G. Wissowa (ed.), *Paulys Real-Encyclopädie der Classischen Altertumswissenschaft*, Supplement
REA	*Revue des études augustiniennes*
REB	Recueil d'études bibliques
RelSRev	*Religious Studies Review*
ResQ	*Restoration Quarterly*
RevExp	*Review and Expositor*
RevQ	*Revue de Qumran*
RGG	*Religion in Geschichte und Gegenwart*
RHPR	*Revue d' histoire et de philosophie religieuses*
RHR	*Revue de l' histoire des religions*
RivB	*Rivista biblica*
RPTK	*Realencyklopädie für protestantische Theologie und Kirche*
RSPT	*Revue des sciences philosophiques et théologiques*
RSR	*Recherches de science religieuse*
RVDCG	Religionsgeschichtliche volksbücher für die deutsche christliche Gegenwart
SANT	Studien zum Alten und Neuen Testament
SBLDS	SBL Dissertation Series
SBLSPS	SBL Seminar Papers Series
SBS	Stuttgarter Bibelstudien
SBT	Studies in Biblical Theology
SCJ	Studies in Christianity and Judaism
SJT	*Scottish Journal of Theology*
SNTU	Studien zum Neuen Testament und seiner Umwelt
SNTSMS	Society of New Testament Studies Monograph Series
SS	Semeia Studies
Str-B	H. Strack and P. Billerbeck, *Kommentar zum Neuen Testament*
TBNT	Theologische Bücherei, Neues Testament

TDNT	G. Kittel and G. Friedrich (eds.), *Theological Dictionary of the New Testament*
TF	*Theologische Forschungen*
TGI	*Theologie und Glaube*
TH	*Theologie historique*
THNT	*Theologischer Handkommentar zum Neuen Testament*
ThS	*Theologiske Studier*
TLZ	*Theologische Literaturzeitung*
TNTC	Tyndale New Testament Commentaries
TRev	*Theologische Revue*
TTod	*Theology Today*
TTZ	*Trierer theologische Zeitschrift*
TU	Texte und Untersuchungen
TZ	*Theologische Zeitschrift*
UNT	Untersuchungen zum Neuen Testament
VC	*Vigiliae christianae*
VD	*Verbum domini*
VIEGM	Veröffentlichungen des Instituts für Europäische Geschichte Mainz
VP	*Vivre et Penser*
VS	Verbum salutis
WBC	Word Biblical Commentary
WMANT	Wissenschaftliche Monographien zum Alten und Neuen Testament
WTJ	*Westminster Theological Journal*
WUNT	Wissenschaftliche Untersuchungen zum Neuen Testament
ZBNT	Zürcher Bibelkommentare, Neues Testament
ZKG	*Zeitschrift für Kirchengeschichte*
ZNW	*Zeitschrift für die neutestamentliche Wissenschaft*
ZTK	*Zeitschrift für Theologie und Kirche*

INTRODUCTION

All readers of Philippians are struck by the presence of suffering in the letter. For example, throughout the first chapter of Philippians Paul writes of his imprisonment as potentially life-threatening. In 3.10 he states that it is his desire to share Christ's suffering. So, too, Paul's co-workers, Timothy and Epaphroditus, suffer, as evidenced by Paul's words in 2.19-30. Moreover, Paul alludes in the letter to the Philippian Christians' own suffering, as evidenced by their financial support and (perhaps) their undergoing of persecution. Finally, in what is probably the best-known fragment of Paul's letter to the Philippians, the so-called hymn of 2.6-11, the one whom God made Lord is spoken of as suffering. Suffering, therefore, clearly runs through this letter like a scarlet thread.

Yet, in spite of the centrality of suffering in this letter, no specialized study of suffering in Philippians has appeared to date. This is all the more remarkable in that there is an abundance of commentaries on the letter and treatments of Paul's view of suffering generally. My work purports to examine the specific issue of suffering in Philippians.

I will begin to do so by investigating in Part I of this book how interpreters have understood suffering in Philippians. In Chapter 1 I set out a history of interpretation of the suffering texts in Philippians from Ignatius of Antioch to representative Reformation authors. The question posed in this chapter is what are the main lines of interpretation that appear during the pre-critical period with respect to the role or function of suffering in Philippians?

Then, in Chapters 2 and 3 I will turn to modern commentators in order to understand how the Philippians suffering passages have been understood in the critical period of New Testament studies. Specifically, I will examine in Chapter 2 those authors who have been influenced by the Christ-mysticism approach and by Schweitzer's seminal work on Paul, while in Chapter 3 I will examine those modern authors who have followed other trajectories. In these chapters, while

I will be seeking the main lines of interpretation as I do in Chapter 1, I will also be asking the question, do trajectories of interpretation from the pre-critical period continue into the critical period, or do we discover new approaches to Philippians that affect our understanding of the role that suffering plays in the letter?

The history of interpretation concludes with the most recent studies of Philippians and Paul. In these studies it becomes clear that a radical methodological shift is taking place in this last half of the twentieth century. Indeed, in recent years Pauline studies have been radically challenged and stimulated to a re-examination of the apostle not in terms of his theology, as was the case in most Pauline studies up to the mid-twentieth century, but in terms of the very way Paul chose to communicate with his readers. Consequently, New Testament scholarship has begun to be forced to grapple with the very structure of Paul's letters themselves.

Believing that this new emphasis on Paul's letters themselves may enable us to understand Paul's enigmatic treatment of suffering in Philippians, I will turn to the letter itself in Part II in order to ask about the structure of letters in antiquity and about how letters were intended to have been read. So in Chapter 4, by means of a brief overview of pertinent points of epistolography and rhetoric in antiquity, I will examine the way letters in antiquity were understood. Then, in Chapters 5 and 6, I will attempt to draw insights from this overview in order to explain the epistolary structure and function of the different epistolary elements within Philippians (Chapter 5)—prefaced by a discussion of the arguments for and against the integrity of Philippians—as well as its rhetorical functions (Chapter 6).

In Part III, I will turn to a discussion of the function of suffering itself in Philippians, allowing my findings in Part II to govern the discussion. Thus, in Chapter 7 I will discuss the theme of suffering in the *preparatio* (viz. the epistolary prescript, the *exordium*, the *narratio* and the *partitio*—1.1-18a). In Chapter 8 I will discuss the theme in the first part of the *argumentatio* (viz. the *confirmatio* and the *exhortatio*—1.18–2.18). In Chapter 9 I will discuss the theme of suffering in the second part of the *argumentatio* (viz. the *exempla*, *reprehensio* and *exhortatio*—2.19–4.7). Finally, in Chapter 10 I will discuss the theme of suffering in the *peroratio* (4.8-20).

My conclusion will draw together the various insights of the exegesis by setting forth the specific functions of suffering in Philippians. It will also contrast our findings with the main lines of the history of interpretation.

PART I

HISTORY OF THE INTERPRETATION OF SUFFERING
IN PHILIPPIANS

Chapter 1

THE MARTYROLOGICAL APPROACH

The early martyrological texts evidence an approach to the suffering passages of Philippians that was widespread among the early Fathers. It was prominent as well throughout the Middle Ages and Reformation, and appears in the critical period.

1. *The Earliest Martyrological Texts*

The earliest patristic references to the suffering passages of Philippians speak of two goals of martyrdom, namely, (1) to bring about the perfection of the martyr, and (2) to witness to those who observe the martyr. The inclusion of suffering passages from Philippians (Phil. 2.17 and 3.10-12) in the letters of Ignatius of Antioch (*Rom.* 2.2 and *Eph.* 3.1, respectively; cf. *Rom.* 6 and 9.2) is a case in point.[1] Ignatius (died about 110) held that only death as a martyr would show him to be, as Paul was, a true disciple of Christ (μαθητὴς ἀληθῶς Ἰησοῦ Χριστοῦ, *Rom.* 4.2; cf. 5.1-2).[2] Apparently Ignatius held that only those who attain to God via martyrdom are truly free (cf. *Rom.* 6.2; *Rom.* 4.3) because they have been perfected.[3] For Ignatius, suffering is part of 'the nature of reality', and for the true disciple the goal of suffering is 'enduring to the end and escaping the ruler of this world'.[4]

   1. Cf. V.P. Pfitzner, *Paul and the Agon Motif* (Leiden: Brill, 1967), p. 147.
   2. So R.F. Stoops, Jr, 'If I Suffer', *HTR* 80 (1987), p. 177; cf. A. Schweitzer, *The Mysticism of the Apostle Paul* (trans. W. Montgomery; New York: Seabury, repr. 1968), p. 146.
   3. So Stoops, 'If I Suffer', p. 171; cf. P. Meinhold, 'Episkope–Pneumatiker–Märtyrer', in Meinhold, *Studien zu Ignatius von Antioch* (Wiesbaden: Steiner, 1979), pp. 1-18; W. Schoedel, *Ignatius of Antioch* (Philadelphia: Fortress Press, 1985), p. 179 n. 14.
   4. Stoops, 'If I Suffer', pp. 172-73; against W.M. Swartley, 'The *Imitatio Christi* in the Ignatian Letters', *VC* 27 (1973), pp. 81-103; although cf. Schoedel,

1. The Martyrological Approach 19

The *Letters of the Churches of Lyons and Vienne* (c. 180, though redacted at some later date) also portray the martyrs' perfection in language familiar to us from Phil. 2.6:

οἳ καὶ ἐπὶ τοσοῦτον ζηλωταὶ καὶ μιμηταὶ Χριστοῦ ἐγένοντο, ὃς ἐν μορφῇ θεοῦ ὑπάρχων οὐχ ἁρπαγμὸν ἡγήσατο τὸ εἶναι ἴσα θεῷ.[5]

Similarly, Polycarp, in his epistle to the Philippians (c. 100–120),[6] writes that Paul's phrase 'enemies of the cross' (Phil. 3.18) refers to those for whom believers pray (i.e. kings, powers and princes, persecutors and those who hate the believers) and notes that believers do so in order to be perfect (*Phil.* 12.3).[7]

In the *Martyrdom of Polycarp* (c. 160)[8] imagery derived from Phil. 2.4 (see *Mart. Pol.* 1.2) is used to depict Polycarp's martyrdom as both perfecting him and as testifying to others of the way of perfection (cf. Polycarp *Phil.* 9.1 on Ignatius). In the *Martyrdom of Carpus, Papylus and Agathonice* Pamfilus echoes the suffering passages of Philippians when he says of his torturers that they are unable to acknowledge his witness because they do not believe: 'These troubles are nothing. I feel no pain since there is one who comforts me [cf. Phil. 4.13]; he suffers in me whom you cannot see [cf. Phil. 3.10].'[9]

Traditionally we have understood Gnostics as echoing such early martyrological writers as Ignatius. They have been understood, for example, as viewing suffering and evil as arising from the natural

---

Ignatius, p. 13. See also K. Beyschlag, 'Das Problem des Leidens in der frühen Christenheit', in his *Evangelium als Schicksal: Fünf Studien zur Geschichte der alten Kirche* (Munich: Claudius, 1979), p. 107.

5. *Letter of the Churches of Lyons and Vienne*, in Eusebius, *Hist. Eccl.* 2.2, cited in *The Acts of the Christian Martyrs* (ed. H. Musurillo; Oxford: Clarendon Press, 1972), p. 82 lines 10-12. See also the reference to Sanctus's martyrdom (Eusebius, *Hist. Eccl.* 1.23, cited in Musurillo, *Martyrs*, p. 68 lines 17-22) and that of Blandina (Eusebius, *Hist. Eccl.* 1.41, cited in Musurillo, *Martyrs*, p. 74 lines 14-20).

6. Concerning the difficulty of dating Polycarp's Epistle, see J.B. Lightfoot, *The Apostolic Fathers* (London: Macmillan, 1889), II.1, pp. 578-603.

7. Though Polycarp here quotes Phil. 3.18, his thinking follows 1 Peter more than Paul. Similarities between Polycarp and 1 Peter have long been noted: e.g., E.G. Selwyn, *The First Epistle of St Peter: The Greek Text with Introduction, Notes, and Essays* (London: Macmillan, repr. 1964), p. 37.

8. Concerning the difficulty of dating the *Martyrdom*, see Lightfoot, *Apostolic Fathers*, II.1, pp. 646-722.

9. *Martyrdom of Carpus, Papylus, Agathonice* 3.6, in Musurillo, *Martyrs*, p. 32 lines 5-8.

order of things.[10] In fact, this approach is widely understood as *the* Gnostic approach to reality.[11] Likewise, the Alexandrian fathers, such as Clement of Alexandria (died about 215), who were apparently influenced by Gnosticism,[12] are held to have viewed suffering not in terms of individual instances of suffering but in terms of a state of the world in which mankind itself is sick and suffering. According to Karlmann Beyschlag, 'Clement of Alexandria was thinking about *the* sickness that envelops all human suffering, about *the* sin that, since Adam, has dragged in its train, like a dragon's tail, all conceivable evil—including sickness, suffering and death'.[13]

Yet while it is true that there are Gnostic texts with interpretations of the suffering passages of Philippians that are comparable to those of the earliest martyrological texts,[14] there is in the Gnostic texts a unique twist to the view of sufferings as perfecting and witnessing. For example, in *Excerpta ex Theodoto* 22.1-2 and *Epistula ad Rheginum* 44.17-21, Phil. 1.21-25 is understood as a call to martyrdom in the sense of remaining in the flesh so as to save the lost psychic, even though release from the flesh, which is the more 'orthodox' understanding of martyrdom, would be much better. In these texts death becomes the equivalent of remaining in the flesh for the sake of unsaved psychics, and Paul is read as encouraging other pneumatics to the same agony as they see in him (1.29-30).[15]

---

10. E. Pagels, *The Gnostic Gospels* (New York: Random House, 1979), pp. 146-47; cf. *idem, The Gnostic Paul* (Philadelphia: Fortress Press, 1975), p. 135; Beyschlag, 'Problem', p. 108. See, e.g., *The Interpretation of Knowledge* 11.1; 12.29-38, in *The Nag Hammadi Library in English* (trans. J.D. Turner; ed. J.M. Robinson; San Francisco: Harper & Row, 1977), p. 431.

11. So, e.g., H.R. Niebuhr, *Christ and Culture* (New York: Harper & Row, 1956 [1951]), pp. 45-55.

12. Cf. S.R.C. Lilla, *Clement of Alexandria* (Oxford: Oxford University Press, 1971), pp. 6-7, 227-34.

13. Beyschlag, 'Problem', p. 94, citing Clement of Alexandria, *Paedagogus* 1.6.2; 100.1, and Origen, *Contra Celsum* 3.75, 86.

14. E. Pagels, 'Gnostic and Orthodox Views of Christ's Passion: Paradigms for the Christian's Response to Persecution?', in *The Rediscovery of Gnosticism* (ed. B. Layton; Leiden: Brill, 1980), p. 271; cf. *idem, Gnostic Gospels*, p. 91, citing *Apocryphon of James* 4.38–6.18, as well as *The Secret Book of James, Second Apocryphon of James* and *Melchizedek*.

15. So Pagels, *Gnostic Paul*, pp. 134-35.

2. Developments

While the view that suffering perfects and bears witness continues to be emphasized by later patristic commentators, a significant shift in the immediate goal of perfection and witness soon occurs. This shift is visible in Tertullian, who employs the Philippian suffering texts to specify that the perfection to be obtained by all Christians is the future resurrection. On Phil. 3.21 Tertullian writes in his Montanist work *Adversus Marcionem* (207–212 CE):[16]

> but if Christ, coming from heaven, will transfigure our humbled body, making it like his glorious body, then this our body, which was humbled by sufferings and was cast down into the earth by this same law of death, will arise.[17]

The implications of this shift soon come to the fore. Marius Victorinus (died after 362), for example, writes that Phil. 1.20 depicts the time of trial as a particularly appropriate time for the preaching of the gospel: 'those of us who believe in Christ endure all sufferings, even those leading to the cross and to death',[18] because, as Victorinus notes, that to which suffering leads is resurrection glory:

> To do all things without being turned aside to another and to suffer all things for him, this is the prize; and this is our agony, namely, the fight and the intention, which leads to the palm of victory and to the crown.[19]

A further shift takes place as later authors deduce from these conclusions that something more than historic martyrdom is being

---

16. For the date and outlines of this work, see J. Quasten, *Patrology* (Westminster, MD: Christian Classics, repr. 1986 [1950]), II, pp. 273-76.
17. *Adv. Marc.* 5.20; CSEL 47, 649, lines 8-11.
18. *Marii Victorini Afri Comentarii in epistulas Pauli ad Galatas, ad Philippenses, ad Ephesios* (ed. A. Locher; Leipzig: Teubner, 1972), p. 102 (1220 B). Victorinus further writes:

> cum meum corpus poenis subiectum omnibus tolerat universa et Christum praedicat nec desistit nec poenis terretur et omnibus poenis non cedit. quid est autem omnibus poenis exposuit subiugendo: *sive per vitam sive per mortem.* si enim tolerando poenas vixero, praedicabitur Christus, sive sub poenis mortuus fuero, magis ac magis praedicabitur, cum videant omnes me nec poenis deterritum nec morte revocatum, sed in evangelio aut vitam cum poenis exegisse aut usque ad mortem poenas tolerasse et tamen in evangelio praedicando perseverasse (75 [1200 A-B]).

19. Victorinus 79 (1203 A-B).

referred to in Philippians. Thus Jerome (died 419 or 420) depicts Christ as the witness who humbles himself unto death 'ut nobis perfectae obedientiae monstraret exemplum'.[20] Christ's example, however, is not just for martyrs understood historically but for all believers, since, according to Jerome,

> God provides the occasion to exercise faith, so that we should not only have the reward of faith but also the prize of the martyr, that is, when God is pleased to provide us temptations so that we can be victorious against them.[21]

Likewise, in his commentary on Phil. 3.10 Jerome borrows from the language of Rom. 8.17: 'If we suffer with him, we shall live with him'.[22]

Such a shift of understanding was picked up and developed in the writings of Augustine (died 430) in a way that had a far-reaching influence. Augustine's popular sermons for the feast days of martyrs reveal his indebtedness to the martyrological interpretation of suffering in Philippians.[23] For example, in sermon 284 (section 3) Augustine appeals to Phil. 1.29 when noting how the martyrs' strength comes from God, not themselves, because the purpose of martyrdom is the conversion of those who witness it.[24] However, Augustine, like Victorinus, also began to move away from a historic, martyrological interpretation of the suffering texts of Philippians to a more ethicized and spiritualized interpretation. In a sermon on Mt. 11.25 Augustine quotes Phil. 2.6-8 to speak of Christ's humility:

> You pay attention to your neighbour's wealth, holdings, pride, and by paying attention to him and by emulating him, you too will be proud. You will not be humble, unless you pay attention to the one who became humble for you. Learn from Christ what you do not learn from man. The standard

---

20. *Commentarii in Epistolam ad Philippenses, PL* 30.845C.
21. *PL* 30.844 B-C, on Phil. 1.29-30.
22. *Commentarii, PL* 30.849B.
23. Sermons 276, 284, 288, 302, 307-308, 317, 328, 333.1-5 are acknowledged as authentic according to the *Clavis Patrum Latinorum* (ed. E. Dekkers; Steenburg: Abbey of St Peter, 1961). On the homiletical exegesis evidenced by these sermons, see M. Pontet, *L'exégèse de saint Augustin prédicateur* (Paris: Aubier, 1944).
24. *PL* 38.1290.

1. The Martyrological Approach 23

of humility is found in Christ, and the one who comes to Christ is first of all formed in that humility so that he may be adorned with rejoicing. Of what kind of humility do I speak? [quote from Phil. 2.6-8 follows].[25]

Or again, in his sermon given in the Basilica Novarum of Hippo on the birth of the Scilitan martyrs Augustine quotes Phil. 1.21 in the context of an exhortation concerning death, not in the stadia, but to self:

> Brethren, let us choose love, let us live in that love innocently, and let us die free from care. When we have chosen this love—since our hearts were bought by it—'to live' will be 'Christ' and 'death will be gain'. And so, by dying, let us avoid what we hate and by dying let us come to what we love.[26]

A similar theme is expressed by Augustine on the occasion of a sermon on the octave of Easter, in which he alludes to Phil. 3.13-14:

> Leaving behind the things of the past and extending yourselves to what lies before you, following on, according to intention, to the palm of victory of your upward calling. . . .[27]

From an understanding of historic sufferings, Augustine has moved to an understanding of the volitional or spiritual intention behind sufferings,[28] for his emphasis is on the direction of the soul once it has been freed from temporality.[29]

The shift from historical martyrdom to spiritualized martyrdom is further picked up in the pseudo-Augustine writings. For example, ps.-Aug. *Sermon 333*, 6, now ascribed to Cesarius of Arles,[30] invokes Phil. 1.29 as an exhortation to humility and a refusal of pride.[31] In *Sermon 304*, 3, the writer adduces Phil. 2.6-8 as a summons to the Christian to pursue humility and flee pride.[32] Or again, *caritas* is the

---

25. *Sermo Mai 126*, 11 (*PL* Supplement, 2, 510).
26. *Sermo Morin Guelferbytanus* 30, 1 (*PL* Supplement, 2, 626).
27. *Sermo Mai 94* (*PL* Supplement, 2, 487).
28. See G.J.P. O'Daly, 'Time as "Distentio" and St Augustine's Exegesis of Philippians 3.12-14', *REA* 23 (1977), pp. 265-71.
29. Cf. O'Daly, 'Time', p. 269.
30. So *PL* Supplement, 2, 402.
31. *PL* 38.1467.
32. *PL* 38.1398.

context for the martyrological expressions of Philippians for the pseudo-Augustine author of *Sermon 169*, 14-15:[33]

> If the love of God were in you, you would share in the sufferings of Christ and you would be a true martyr. The one in whom love is crowned, that one is the true martyr.

The same shift is probably also at work in the homilies of Augustine's Eastern contemporary John Chrysostom. In his homilies on Philippians (387 CE)[34] Chrysostom was also forced to deal with the historical fact that the Philippian Christians had at some point suffered for their faith. Chrysostom, however, does so in a unique way by arguing that the persecutions in Philippi had already ended before Paul wrote to the Philippians. Consequently, Paul's words address a situation other than that of a community then undergoing persecution.[35] The suffering to which Paul's words in Philippians point is the consequence of the hard work of good deeds. Those who aid others daily by doing good works, for example, monks in the deserts and men in church life, are those to whom Chrysostom points as fulfilling Paul's commands in Philippians.[36] Like Augustine and later Augustinians, Chrysostom understands the perfection consequent on suffering in the labour of service to be a perfection of *caritas* from which is derived the συμμορφία with Christ. Commenting on Paul's rejoicing in 1.18 Chrysostom writes:

> τὴν μεγάλην καὶ φιλόσοφον ψυχὴν οὐδὲν τῶν ἐν τῷ παρόντι βίῳ λυπηρῶν δύναται δοκεῖν, οὐκ ἔχθραι, οὐ κατηγορίαι, οὐ διαβολαί, οὐ κίνδυνοι, οὐκ ἐπιβουλαὶ ὥσπερ γὰρ εἰς μεγάλην τινὰ ἀκρώρειαν καταφυγοῦσα, ἄληπτος πασίν ἐστι τοῖς κάτωθεν ἀνιοῦσιν ἀπὸ τῆς γῆς. τοιαύτη ἦν ἡ τοῦ Παύλου ψυχή, πάσης ἀκρωρείας ὑψηλότερον τόπον τὸν τῆς φιλοσοφίας καταλαβοῦσα τῆς πνευματικῆς, τῆς ὄντως φιλοσοφίας.[37]

33. *PL* 38.923-24.
34. John Chrysostom, *In epistolam ad Philippenses commentarius*, *PG* 62.177-898. These sermons were preached early in his long career; see D. Attwater, *St John Chrysostom: Pastor and Preacher* (London: Harvill, 1959), p. 39.
35. *PG* 62.184 (First Homily). Chrysostom says that we know of the Philippians' suffering from Acts.
36. *PG* 62.185. Cf. also *PG* 62.187 on Phil. 1.7 and *PG* 62.209 on 1.30 (citing Gal. 3.4; Heb. 10.32-33; and 1 Thess. 1.9 and 2.1).
37. Third Homily, *PG* 62.197. Cf. also his words on 1.21, *PG* 62.200-201, 266, on which cf. E. Nowak, *Le chrétien devant la souffrance: Etude sur la pensée*

1. The Martyrological Approach 25

The same kind of interpretation is apparent in later writers. Commenting both on how Epaphroditus's brush with death has led to an extension of salvation and on Phil. 3.10, Theodoret of Cyr (died about 466) writes:

σπουδάζω δὲ καὶ κοινωνῆσαι αὐτῷ τῶν παθημάτων, καὶ τὸν σωτήριον αὐτοῦ μιμήσασθαι θάνατον, ἵνα μετάσχω καὶ τῆς ἀναστάσεως.[38]

However, the context within which this participation is to be gained is suffering that provides an occasion to manifest grace and ultimately love.[39] Later Atto of Vercelli (died 961) stressed that Paul's main emphasis in Philippians is on a life lived for others.[40] Undoubtedly this shift from historical martyrdom to a spiritualized one has a concrete, historical occasion. I believe that it confirms the view of those who associate the rise of asceticism[41] with the decline in martyr deaths. As martyr deaths fade into the distant past, reformulation of the martyrological approach in the light of the new reality becomes inevitable. According to G.M. Colombas, as long as martyrdom is a reality, it is considered the supreme expression of evangelical perfection; however,

> since the grace of the martyr is not given to all and persecutions become scarcer, the idea that Christian life lived in generosity and self-denial is itself a confession of faith—a bloodless martyrdom—begins to take root.[42]

The sentiments here are expressed lucidly in the commentary of Lietbert of St Rufus on Psalm 43:

---

de Jean Chrysostome (Paris: Beauchesne, 1973), p. 202.
38. *PG* 82.582 B. Cf. M.F. Wiles, *The Divine Apostle* (Cambridge: Cambridge University Press, 1967), p. 63, on Theodore of Mopsuestia and pp. 20, 25 on Origen.
39. *Interpretatio epistulae ad Philippenses*, *PG* 82.561 B and 568 C-D.
40. *PL* 134 *passim*.
41. See W.H.C. Frend, Review of Elaine Pagels, *Adam, Eve, and the Serpent* (New York: Random House, 1988), *New York Review of Books*, 30 June 1988, p. 28.
42. G.M. Colombas, *El monacato primitivo* (Madrid: Biblioteca de autores cristianos, 1974), I, p. 31.

There are two kinds of martyrdom; one of mind and one of body, one visible and the other hidden. The visible one is when the body is slain for God's sake; the hidden one is when vices are removed out of love of God.[43]

3. Continuation

From the period of the post-Nicene church through the period of the Reformation, the twofold martyrological approach to the suffering in Philippians—namely, that suffering leads one to perfection and witnesses to others—is further spiritualized.

Throughout the Middle Ages the view that the Philippians suffering texts refer to mortification of the flesh becomes, as suggested in the case of Lietbert, increasingly prominent. Thus in a ninth-century commentary, now extant under the name of Haymo, Bishop of Halberstadt,[44] Phil. 1.20 is shorn of all reference to martyrdom and is paraphrased:

> If I sustain torments, all those who hear will say: Great is this God, for whose name his servants are not afraid to die.[45]

Also in the ninth century, Sedulius Scotus comments using the same words as we have seen Jerome use:

> You shall not only have the reward of faith but also the prize of the martyr, that is, when God is pleased to provide us temptations so that we can be victorious against them.[46]

---

43. *PL* 21.819A. The commentary on the first 75 Psalms of David was once attributed to Rufinus of Aquileia (d. 410) (so Colombas, *Monacato*, p. 31), then to Vincent of Gaul; however, it is now believed that the commentary is the work of the Cistercian abbot, Lietbert of St Rufus (D.A. Wilmart, 'Le commentaire sur les Psaumes imprimé sous le nom de Rufin', *RBen* 31 [1914–19], pp. 258-76). According to Wilmart, the commentary was widely read throughout late medieval France and England ('Commentaire', p. 274).

44. *Expositio in epistolam Pauli ad Philippenses, PL* 117.733-54. On the representative nature of this commentary for the period, see A.M. Landgraf, *Einführung in die Geschichte der theologischen Literatur der Frühscholastik unter dem Gesichtspunkte der Schulenbildung* (Regensburg: Gregorius, 1948), pp. 11-12.

45. *PL* 117.738B. Cf. Peter Lombard, *Philippenses, PL* 192.251 C-D, citing Haymo; John Damascene (died about 749), *In epistolam ad Philippenses, PG* 95.857D, on Phil. 1.7; cf. *PG* 95.859C.

46. *PL* 103.213C.

1. The Martyrological Approach 27

Even in the important Victorine school of scriptural interpretation we find the same overarching view. Hugh of St Victor notes that in Philippians Paul intends 'to urge the Philippians to patience against sufferings'.[47] All Christians have become martyrs for they have before them the goal of perfection, namely resurrection.

Thomas Aquinas (died 1274) provides a lucid presentation of this interpretation when, in his commentary on Philippians,[48] he treats the entire letter as an extended exhortation to magnify Christ through the mortification of the body.[49] Aquinas notes how Christ's humility (2.6) and his exaltation and glory (2.9) are intended as examples for all believers:

> Therefore [Paul] says: from the fact that Christ humbled himself and was exalted, you ought to know that if we are humbled we shall be exalted, and this you ought to do, since you always obeyed.[50]

But in that Paul suffered in the same way as Christ did—that is, 'obedienter' ('Since if he did not suffer because of obedience, he would not have been commended, since obedience gives merit to our sufferings'),[51] 'constanter' ('knowing confidently that external sufferings propagate the faith and cause it to increase in the community'),[52] and 'patienter' ('if life gives me this fruit, that Christ should be magnified in it, then life in the flesh is good and fruitful')[53]—Paul, too, is an example to be followed (1.12–2.2), as are Paul's co-workers (2.19-30).

Aquinas does not deny that Paul, unlike believers of Aquinas's day, experienced persecution;[54] however, in a way that reminds us of Augustine's methodological shift from history to intention—using the same text as Augustine used!—Aquinas makes the transition from

---

47. *PL* 175.575C. On the Victorines, see B. Smalley, *The Study of the Bible in the Middle Ages* (Notre Dame, IN: University of Notre Dame Press, 1964), pp. 83ff.
48. *S. Thomae Aquinatis super epistolas S. Pauli lectura: Vol. 2* (ed. R. Cai; Rome: Marietti, 8th edn, 1953). On the difficulty of establishing the date of Thomas's biblical commentaries (many of which were penned by students from notes), see Thomas Aquinas, *Commentary on Saint Paul's Epistle to the Galatians* (trans. F.R. Larcher; Albany: Magi, 1966), p. viii.
49. *Lectura*, p. 116 n. 145, and p. 96 n. 31, on Phil. 1.21.
50. *Lectura*, p. 103 n. 75.
51. *Lectura*, p. 102 n. 65, on Phil. 2.8.
52. *Lectura*, p. 94 n. 21, citing 2 Cor. 1.6, and p. 94 n. 22, citing 1 Pet. 4.15.
53. *Lectura*, p. 97 n. 34.
54. *Lectura*, p. 96 n. 31.

Paul's situation of persecution to the experience of his own day by noting that it is not persecution that makes Paul's sufferings valuable, but rather suffering for Christ. This suffering, insists Aquinas, is an even greater gift than faith itself (1.29), since suffering for Christ imitates Christ's example:

> Whosoever shares in the virtue of divinity through grace and imitates the suffering of Christ will be glorified.[55]

The entrenchment of the spiritualized approach evident in these authors is finally enshrined in the *Glossa Ordinaria*,[56] the body of received interpretation of Scripture during the latter Middle Ages. The *Glossa* preserves Haymo's comment on Phil. 4.18, as well as lexical evidence of the indebtedness of a wide spectrum of medieval commentary to the methodological shift as found, say, in Augustine:

> The odour that is pleasing to God is a good *intention* and the ready will of the one offering the sacrifice. It is not to be thought that the omnipotent Lord delights in the sacrifice of victims, in the smoke of flesh and in the fatness of flesh, but rather in the good *intention* and in the ready will of the one offering the sacrifice.[57]

Here Paul's sacrificial language is understood to refer to a mental or volitional attitude. Similarly, the *Glossa* also preserves Nicholas of Lyra's by now traditional interpretation of ἐταπείνωσεν ἑαυτόν (Phil. 2.8): '"He humbled himself." In order to give you an example. John 13.b: I gave you an example etc.'[58] Clearly, the purpose of Christ's suffering had become a matter of intentional imitation with a view to right living in the world.

John Calvin's commentary on Philippians (c. 1550) stands in the same tradition,[59] for in it we read how believers still suffer for the

---

55. *Lectura*, p. 113 n. 123.
56. See Smalley, *Bible*, pp. 56-64. The *Glossa* contains comments of Patristic and pre-Scholastic writers. The *Glossa Ordinaria* (Antwerp, 1634) used here also contains the commentary of Jerome, Nicholas of Lyra's *Postillae*, and Paul of Burgos's *Additiones*.
57. *Glossa*, pp. 605-606, my emphases.
58. *Glossa*, pp. 583-84. On Nicholas of Lyra's interpretation of Scripture, see B. Smalley, 'The Exposition and Exegesis of Scripture, 3: The Bible in the Medieval Schools', in *The Cambridge History of the Bible*. II. *The West from the Fathers to the Reformation* (Cambridge: Cambridge University Press, 1969), p. 219.
59. *Commentarius in epistolam ad Philippenses*, in *Joannis Calvini opera quae supersunt omnia* (ed. W. Baum, E. Cunitz and E. Reuss; Corpus Reformatorum, 80;

1. The Martyrological Approach

purpose of mortification. The whole of this life is in the image of death:

> This body which we carry about is not an eternal home but a failing tabernacle, which suddenly turns back to nothing. Thus it is subject to miseries on the one hand and subject to shameful weaknesses on the other, such that it may be called destitute of worth and full of baseness.[60]

Persecution, indeed, lies at the heart of the suffering described in Philippians, but Calvin understands persecution as spiritual warfare. Even Epaphroditus's suffering ('a noble example of his fervent zeal')[61] arises from such spiritual persecution:

> In this way he expresses what the condition is of those who minister the gospel: namely, that they are engaged in constant battles. For Satan will certainly not suffer them to advance the gospel without a fight. So let those who prepare for the building up of the church know that Satan has declared and prepared war. It is indeed common to all Christians to earn their wages in the fortresses of Christ since Satan is the enemy of all. But especially is this true of the ministry of the word, that is, of those who carry and bear forth the banner.[62]

This is not to say that life is an unmitigated series of tragedies. Calvin stresses that it is how one *uses* life that makes the difference. One can use life either for the Lord's purposes or for evil. When humanity submits to the flesh, it uses life for evil. Members of Christ, however, use life for good when they follow Christ crucified through tribulations and distresses, until, like Christ, they arrive at the resurrection of the dead through them. Consequently, God permits

---

Braunschweig, 1895), 52.5-76. On the date of the commentary on Philippians, see T.H.L. Parker, *Calvin's New Testament Commentaries* (London: SCM Press, 1971), pp. 1-25. In light of Calvin's commentary on the Philippian suffering texts, one could take issue with Parker's view that 'in the historical books, Calvin never seeks a secondary, spiritual meaning, for the *sensus literalis* is God's own record of the outworking of his purpose in his incarnate Son and is sufficient in itself. . . the account of God's activity within history' (Parker, *Commentaries*, p. 67). Calvin seems much more indebted to medieval exegetical methods of tropology and anagogy than Parker is willing to admit! See H. de Lubac, *Exégèse médiévale* (Paris: Aubier, 1959), II, pp. 549-620 (on tropology) and pp. 621-681 (on anagogy).

60. *Commentarius* 56.
61. *Commentarius* 42.
62. *Commentarius* 40.

suffering in order to prepare believers for heaven and to make God's grace more attractive:

> Rare, indeed, is the person who, when Satan undertakes to increase the bitterness of the cross so that the name of God become repugnant, rests only in the pleasure of the grace of God, with the end result that all trials, pains, cares, and troubles become sweet.[63]

Accordingly, when Paul exhorts his churches to joy and good courage, it is to joy and good courage in the midst of suffering:

> For let the faithful, if they are terrified by persecutions, or chains, or exile, or death, here behold the apostle, the one who although in chains, in the midst of the ardour of persecutions, and in fear of death, is not only happy but also encourages others. The conclusion then is this: in whatever happens, the faithful, who have the reigning Lord on their side, have more than ample reason to rejoice.[64]

Thus because nothing less awaits the believers than resurrection ('hunc perfectionis nostrae scopum...quo enitendum sit tota vita: communicationem habere cum Christo mortis et resurrectionis'),[65] Calvin believes that Paul exhorts believers to die to the flesh, that is, to everything that is apart from Christ.[66]

Martin Luther's homilies on Philippians (1528–45) are perhaps the clearest example of the reformulation of the Philippian suffering texts that began in the pre-Nicene period and found in both Augustine and Chrysostom fertile ground for a new understanding of suffering.[67] Although Luther preached vigorously against the saving nature of good works,[68] he nonetheless believed that Christians must express their faith in loving and selfless service—even to the point of suffering and

---

63. *Commentarius* 43.
64. *Commentarius* 59-60 on 4.4.
65. *Commentarius* 6.
66. *Commentarius* 45.
67. *D. Martin Luthers Epistel-Auslegung*. III. *Die Briefe an die Epheser, Philipper, und Kolosser* (ed. E. Ellwein; Göttingen: Vandenhoeck & Ruprecht, 1973).
68. Believers are those who have received the gift of Christ (his blood and wounds, his death and resurrection) through baptism (*Epistel*, pp. 226-27, sermon on Phil. 3.17-19 [8 November, 1545]; see also his sermon on Phil. 1.3-7, 28 October, 1537 [*Epistel*, pp. 179-85]). What alone counts is that one is baptized, hears the gospel, and is in fellowship with the gospel of Christ (*Epistel*, p. 189, sermon on Phil. 1.3-11 [1 November, 1545]).

1. *The Martyrological Approach* 31

martyrdom—precisely because they are thankful for their salvation.[69] Thus he notes that Paul does not promise believers deliverance from suffering,[70] but rather that Paul exhorts believers to joy even when in prison,[71] for it is only as Christians prove themselves a joyful people that they are able to pour out their lives in thankful service to God and to others.[72] The pattern of service leading to suffering was set by Christ, whose suffering resulted from his obedience to the Father and his redemptive, humble service of people, even to the point of subjection to sin, to death, and to the devil, that is, to the point of suffering death as a worm, as the worst of all conceivable rogues.[73] Believers imitate Christ when obedience characterizes their lives and leads them to sacrificial, loving service.[74]

4. *The Martyrological Approach in the Critical Period*

Various authors have kept alive the spiritualized martyrological approach as it developed in Augustine, Chrysostom and throughout the medieval period. In the critical period of New Testament study, that reformulation is represented in a masterful way in J.B. Lightfoot's Philippians commentary (1868).[75] In Lightfoot, as in the authors discussed above, Paul's suffering included not just persecution but 'all pangs and afflictions undergone in the struggle against sin either within or without'.[76] Suffering was used by God to bring Paul to spiritual perfection, that is, salvation (σωτηρία), by developing spiritual life as 'a pathway to the glories of heaven' and by bringing about the elimination of sin.[77] The Philippians, who were also 'baptized with the baptism of suffering',[78] are thus urged by Paul to continue in the

69. *Epistel*, pp. 226-27, sermon on Phil. 3.17-19 (8 November, 1545).
70. *Epistel*, p. 210, sermon on Phil. 2.5-8 (2 April, 1531).
71. *Epistel*, pp. 253-58, sermon on Phil. 4.4 (20 December, 1545).
72. *Epistel*, pp. 206-207, sermon on Phil. 2.1-8 (5 April, 1528).
73. *Epistel*, pp. 200-201, sermon on Phil. 2.5-11 (esp. 2.8) (Palm Sunday, 1525).
74. *Epistel*, p. 209, sermon on Phil. 2.6 (2 April, 1531) and p. 207, sermon on Phil. 2.5-8 (2 April, 1531).
75. J.B. Lightfoot, *Saint Paul's Epistle to the Philippians* (London: Macmillan, 12th edn, 1896).
76. *Philippians*, p. 151; cf. p. 106, on 1.27.
77. *Philippians*, pp. 58-59, 91, on 1.19.
78. J.B. Lightfoot, 'The Churches of Macedonia', in *Biblical Essays* (London: Macmillan, 1893), pp. 247-48.

same attitude that he reflects towards suffering, that is to say, 'unflinching courage and steady combination'.[79]

Spiritual perfection, which comes about through suffering and leads to resurrection,[80] is to be experienced, on the one hand, in the future. Christ's exaltation to his original place of honour, which follows from his voluntary humiliation (2.9), serves as a type for the exaltation of believers (3.21), who will be transformed into Christ's image of glory. On the other hand, believers already experience the power of Christ's resurrection in so far as they share Christ's sufferings,[81] for this power is 'assurance of immortality (Rom. 8.11; 1 Cor. 15.14 sq.)', 'the triumph over sin and the pledge of justification (Rom. 6.24, 25)', and an assertion of the dignity and an enforcing of the claims of the human body (1 Cor. 6.13-15; Phil. 3.21), all of which quicken and stimulate 'the whole moral and spiritual being (Rom. 6.4 sq.; Gal. 2.20; Eph. 2.5; Col. 2.12)'.[82] According to Lightfoot, then, Christians endure trials and sufferings having been given the assurance of present resurrection power.[83]

Not only does Paul's present experience of resurrection power allow him to choose suffering service rather than martyrdom; it also allows him, as it had Christ, to serve others. Lightfoot, like Augustine, completes the picture of suffering in Philippians by depicting Christ's voluntary and self-imposed suffering in 2.6-11 as analogous to the suffering of believers: as Christ suffered *for* people, so Paul suffers *for* those who believe his gospel, and the Philippians suffer *for* the apostle.[84]

Lightfoot, as well as authors such as J.H. Michael[85] and W. Barclay,[86] represent Protestant adoption of the martyrological reformulation. An

---

79. Lightfoot, *Philippians*, p. 106; cf. p. 164.
80. *Philippians*, p. 150.
81. *Philippians*, p. 156.
82. *Philippians*, p. 150.
83. *Philippians*, pp. 90-91. Although Lightfoot argues that Paul, in 3.11, states 'not a positive assurance but a modest hope' (*Philippians*, p. 151), this does not contradict his reading of the flow of Paul's thought.
84. *Philippians*, p. 120; cf. p. 112.
85. J.H. Michael, *The Epistle of Paul to the Philippians* (London: Hodder & Stoughton, repr. 1958).
86. W. Barclay, 'Great Themes of the New Testament: 1, Phil. 2.1-11', *ExpTim* 70 (1958–59), p. 7.

1. The Martyrological Approach

important exponent from the Catholic side is J.T. Forestell. Forestell argues that

> the power of Christ's resurrection effects a real death in man, over and above the symbolic and mystical death of sacramental baptism. This mortification, in fact, becomes a necessary condition for sharing in Christ's resurrection.[87]

The mystical death or mortification leads the believer to a practice of virtue ('the subjective response in the moral life of the Christian') as well as to 'the lustre of the imitation of Christ and the mystical sharing in his passion and death, in the hope of a physical and corporeal sharing in the glories of his resurrection'.[88] Forestell writes, as did Augustine, that Paul's objective was not only (1) to encourage and foster moral perfection, but also (2) to show that moral perfection in and of itself was harmful unless developed in a context of love.[89]

5. Conclusion

Our examination of the earliest interpretations of suffering in Philippians reveals that two basic positions are taken by early interpreters: (1) that suffering perfects, and (2) that suffering bears witness. The way in which suffering perfects and that to which it bears witness fall into three categories, each of which is a variant on the understanding of union with Christ.

First, in the early martyrological texts, suffering effects union with Christ via martyrdom. The resulting union, expressed variously, but most often as the imitation of Christ, is a union with the suffering, crucified Christ. Thus there is union with Christ in the suffering of martyrs and their resurrection.

Secondly, a subtle twist to this orthodox imitation of Christ through martyrdom appears in those Gnostic texts where suffering perfects as the Gnostic remains in the flesh—which for some Gnostics was martyrdom indeed!—and so witnesses to his redemptive mission in the salvation of the psychics. Even here, however, suffering perfects via martyrdom, and so although the martyrdom is understood as occurring

---

87. J.T. Forestell, 'Christian Perfection and Gnosis in Philippians 3.7-16', *CBQ* 18 (1956), p. 125, against F.W. Beare, *A Commentary on the Epistle to the Philippians* (BNTC; London: A. & C. Black, 1959), pp. 123-24.
88. Forestell, 'Perfection', p. 132.
89. Forestell, 'Perfection', p. 127.

in life rather than in death, it still imitates Christ's salvation.

In these two cases, the earliest forms in which the function of suffering in Philippians is viewed, the interpretation is clearly governed by the historical reality of martyrdom. Specifically, Paul's words are understood as referring to the process of the perfection of the martyr and to the martyr's witness to fellow believers and to the world. Within this framework the function of suffering is to bring the martyr to perfection and to witness to the martyr's perfection in the arena in which martyrdom takes place, namely, the battle between God and evil.

In the third case, however, interpretations of Philippians began to make the suffering passages more universally applicable as martyrdom began to recede into the historical past. With the peace of the church, suffering in Philippians began to be understood as that which effects union with Christ via death to the world and the flesh. This is not to say that suffering ceased to be the means to perfection, for the martyrological-based approach to perfection via suffering remained the foundation for the interpretation of Philippians. What changed was the *arena* within which suffering takes place—from imperial *stadia* to the daily life and activity of Christians faced with the evils of the flesh.

So suffering on earth begins to be seen as a means of preparation for eternal, resurrection glory as the sufferer dies with Christ to the world. The function of suffering becomes the mortification of the flesh with a view to inheriting the perfection of resurrection glory, and it becomes the experience of all Christian believers. The philosophical basis of this third view, evidenced in the writings of Victorinus, Jerome, Augustine and Chrysostom, and developed throughout the medieval period and into the critical period of New Testament studies, is spelled out most clearly in terms of Augustine's notion of the ethical *intentio*: the goal of the sufferer is the purification of the inner man so as to be one with Christ in intention, ultimately with a view to the inheritance of eternal life.

Chapter 2

FROM THE ORIGINS OF CHRIST-MYSTICISM TO SCHWEITZER

Changes in Pauline studies during the late nineteenth century brought about new approaches to the question of suffering in Philippians. Most twentieth-century commentaries on Philippians are based on a Christ-mysticism approach, which is itself a further reformulation of the martyrological approach. In what follows, therefore, I will examine the Christ-mysticism approach as to its origins, exponents and developments, turning finally to the great synthesis produced by Albert Schweitzer.

1. *Christ-Mysticism*

Origins

The revolution in Pauline studies that began with the Enlightenment came to fullest expression in the late nineteenth century.[1] During this latter period the grounds were laid for an important reformulation of the view of suffering in Philippians, as originally set forth by Ignatius.

In the 1870s, Carl Holsten,[2] Hermann Lüdemann,[3] Otto Pfleiderer[4] and others began to understand Paul's soteriology in physical, rather than intentional, terms.[5] So in 1903 Wilhelm Heitmüller, for example,

1. See S. Neill, *The Interpretation of the New Testament 1861–1961* (London: Oxford University Press, 1966), pp. 137-90.
2. C. Holsten, *Das Evangelium des Paulus* (2 vols.; Berlin: Reimer, 1880, 1898).
3. H. Lüdemann, *Die Anthropologie des Apostels Paulus und ihre Stellung innerhalb seiner Heilslehre* (Kiel: Universitäts, 1872).
4. O. Pfleiderer, *The Influence of the Apostle Paul on the Development of Christianity* (trans. J.F. Smith; New York: Charles Scribner's Sons, 1885). For an overview of these authors, see A. Schweitzer, *Paul and his Interpreters* (trans. W. Montgomery; London: Black, 1911), pp. 28-32, 237-49.
5. E.g. Pfleiderer, *Influence*, p. 58.

wrote that Paul conceived of the Christian's participation in Christ's death and resurrection in terms of a real 'physico-hyperphysical' union, not a juridical or intentional union, between the believer and Christ.[6] Also, at the end of the nineteenth century Paul's theology came to be understood in terms of the Hellenistic mystery religions.[7] In 1897 Heinrich Julius Holtzmann, for example, argued that Romans 6 signifies 'den Untergang des alten Fleischesmenschen, das Auftauchen aus dem Wasser den Hervorgang eines neuen, eines Geistesmenschen' after the fashion of the mystery religions.[8] In this way the ground was being laid for viewing suffering as bringing about not a new state of mind (or intention) but a new physical and spiritual state of the person.

Clearly, the ethical interpretation of Paul that arose in the early post-Nicene period was rejected. Nevertheless, these nineteenth-century authors had in one sense underscored the earliest martyrological interpretation in which transformation was precisely what was expected. However, they transposed the *locus* of the expected transformation from that of heavenly perfection after death to that of transformation in the present life via incorporation in Christ.

This dramatic shift in the *locus* of perfection dominates the writings of three important turn-of-the-century authors: Adolf Deissmann,[9] Marvin R. Vincent[10] and Martin Dibelius,[11] each of whom recasts

6. W. Heitmüller, *Taufe und Abendmahl im Urchristentum* (Tübingen: Mohr, 1911); cf. Schweitzer, *Paul*, pp. 165, 225.
7. So R. Reitzenstein, *Hellenistic Mystery-Religions* (trans. J.E. Steely; Pittsburgh: Pickwick, 1978), pp. 84-89; W. Bousset, *Kyrios Christos* (trans. J.E. Steely; Nashville: Abingdon, 1970), pp. 164-72, on which see O. Schmitz, *Die Christusgemeinschaft des Paulus im Licht seines Genitivgebrauchs* (Gütersloh: Bertelsmann, 1924), pp. 32, 35; R. Bultmann, *Theology of the New Testament* (trans. K. Grobel; New York: Charles Scribner's Sons, 1951), I, p. 298. Cf. Schweitzer, *Paul*, pp. 63-83.
8. H.J. Holtzmann, *Lehrbuch der neutestamentlichen Theologie* (Tübingen: Mohr, 2nd edn, 1911), II, p. 197; cf. Schweitzer, *Paul*, p. 163.
9. A. Deismann, *Paul* (trans. W.E. Wilson; New York: Harper & Row, 1957); *idem*, *Die neutestamentliche Formel 'in Christo Jesu'* (Marburg: Elwert, 1892); cf. Schweitzer, *Paul*, p. 60 n. 1.
10. M.R. Vincent, *A Critical and Exegetical Commentary on the Epistles to the Philippians and to Philemon* (Edinburgh: T. & T. Clark, repr. 1961 [1897]).
11. M. Dibelius, *Die Briefe des Apostels Paulus. II. Die Neun Kleinen Briefe* (Tübingen: Mohr, 1913); 'Glaube und Mystik bei Paulus', in *Botschaft und Geschichte: Gesammelte Aufsätze* (Tübingen: Mohr, 1956 [1931]), pp. 94-116; 'Paulus und die Mystik', in *Botschaft und Geschichte: Gesammelte Aufsätze*

2. From the Origins of Christ-Mysticism to Schweitzer 37

Paul's soteriology in terms of physical transformation and the Hellenistic mystery religions. These authors held that for Paul the believer is no longer in the flesh, understood by Vincent as

> the human nature without the divine Spirit; the state of man before or in contrast with his reception of the divine element whereby he becomes a new creature; the whole being of man as it exists and acts apart from the influence of the Spirit.

Thus, unlike writers throughout the Middle Ages and the Reformation,[12] these authors held that Christians have actually been freed from the flesh, have entered into the sphere of Christ, and so share in Christ's risen power![13] Thus Deissmann argues that for Paul, Christ is not a model of the past but a very real, present reality:

> an 'energy', whose life-giving powers are daily expressing themselves in him, and to whom, since that day at Damascus, he has felt a personal-cult dependence... the living Christ is the Pneuma... not far off, above clouds and stars, but near, present on our poor earth he dwells and rules in His own.[14]

Similarly, Vincent writes that for Paul, Christ is the very sphere in which the Christian lives, 'the normal life-element of the believer... as a bird in the air, a fish in the water, or the roots of a tree in the soil'.[15]

If, then, the believer lives Christ's life, the sufferings of the believer must also really be those of Christ. In this way Vincent can say that the believer lives Christ's life: 'Christ loves, obeys, suffers, sympathises, toils and hopes in him'.[16] 'In Christ' the believer experiences everything in 'fellowship with Christ at all points: his obedient life, his spirit, his sufferings, his death, and his glory'.[17] Or, as Deissmann might have put it,

---

(Tübingen: Mohr, 1956 [1941]), pp. 134-59.

12. The shift from intention to ontology is readily visible in Vincent, who rigorously opposes forensic or external righteousness (*Philippians*, pp. 127-28).
13. *Philippians*, p. 94, on Phil. 3.3.
14. Deissmann, *Paul*, pp. 136, 138; cf. Schweitzer, *Mysticism*, pp. 34-35.
15. Vincent, *Philippians*, p. 4, following Deissmann.
16. *Philippians*, pp. xxxv-xxxvi.
17. *Philippians*, p. 105; cf. Deissmann, *Paul*, pp. 181-82.

because of union with Christ, the Christian shares Christ's fate, that is, the cross, but not only the experience of Christ's death in the sacramental way, that is, in baptism; the Christian also shares in the on-going mystical communion in Christ's life.[18]

No longer was Paul's experience of sharing the sufferings of Christ (Phil. 3.10; cf. 2 Cor. 1.5) seen as a testing ground for his exercise of virtue. His sufferings have become a proof of 'the mystical-spiritual fellowship with Christ'[19] that continues the mystical dying and rising with Christ,[20] and a means (or *the* means) of direct communion with the crucified and risen Christ.[21] This was not for Paul alone but also for the Philippians, on whom God bestows faith *and* suffering (1.29), because

> faith implies oneness with Christ, and therefore fellowship with his sufferings (Rom. 8.17; 2 Tim. 2.12; Phil. 3.10). That you suffer with Christ proves your union with him, and your union with Christ insures your salvation.[22]

Developments

Radically new interpretations of Paul on suffering soon followed the advent of Christ-mysticism. Representative of these developments were Otto Schmitz's study of Paul's use of the genitive (1924),[23] Ethelbert Stauffer's work on Paul's martyrology (1933 and 1941),[24]

---

18. Paraphrase of Deissmann, in J. Kremer, *Was an den Leiden Christi noch mangelt* (Bonn: Hanstein, 1956), p. 131.
19. Vincent, *Philippians*, p. 35; cf. Deissmann, *Paul*, pp. 163-64; Dibelius, *Briefe*, pp. 46-47, citing 2 Cor. 12.10d.
20. Vincent, *Philippians*, p. 105; cf. Dibelius, *Briefe*, p. 47; *idem*, 'Glaube und Mystik', pp. 94-116; *idem*, 'Paulus und die Mystik', pp. 134-59; A. Wikenhauser, *Die Christusmystik des Apostels Paulus* (Freiburg: Herder, 2nd edn, 1956), pp. 17-18.
21. J. Schneider, *Die Passionsmystik des Paulus: Ihr Wesen, ihr Hintergrund und ihr Nachwirkungen* (Leipzig: Hinrichs, 1929), pp. 14, 31, 48, 339; cf. E. Güttgemanns, *Die leidende Apostel und sein Herr* (Göttingen: Vandenhoeck & Ruprecht, 1966), pp. 19, 102-103.
22. Vincent, *Philippians*, p. 35, on 1.29; cf. pp. 119-21.
23. See above n. 7.
24. E. Stauffer, 'Märtyrertheologie und Täuferbewegung', *ZKG* 52 (1933), pp. 545-609; *New Testament Theology* (trans. J. Marsh; London: SCM Press, 1955 [1941]).

2. From the Origins of Christ-Mysticism to Schweitzer 39

and Hans Windisch's study of Paul and Jesus (1934).[25] Schmitz was perhaps the most extreme representative of these developments. According to Schmitz, Phil. 3.10 not only speaks of a comparison of Paul's sufferings with those of Christ but of Paul's consciousness of immediate union with the crucified one.[26] Paul's sufferings and those of Christ are undifferentiated; in fact, any separation between Christ and Paul is eliminated![27]

Although less extreme, Stauffer's analysis of Paul was no less radical. Stauffer argued that Paul depicts himself as a Second Temple Jewish martyr who takes on the burden of suffering in history and thereby becomes the atonement for the sins of the world:[28]

> The martyr, who has given his innocent life, becomes the sacrifice for the sins of his people and the forebear of a new age.[29]

As the last martyr, Paul feels that at his death the requisite amount of blood will be spilled and the day of reckoning dawn—martyrs will be glorified, persecutors will be struck down,[30] and the new eon will be ushered in. In this way, Stauffer can say that Paul, like Christ, suffers for those who 'gain consolation from his afflictions, and day by day receive new life from his dying daily'.[31] Such a view commands a certain following even today, as is clear from the words of one author:

> In Paul's patient enduring of the Messianic woes he is helping to bring nearer the time when Christ will be manifested... Paul is encouraged to bear his hardships with fortitude because he knows that they have a purpose in God's plan and are bringing nearer the final day of salvation.[32]

---

25. H. Windisch, *Paulus und Christus* (Leipzig: Hinrichs, 1934); cf. G. Sass, *Apostelamt und Kirche* (Munich: Kaiser, 1939), p. 81.
26. Schmitz, *Christusgemeinschaft*, pp. 185-87; cf. Güttgemanns, *Leidende Apostel*, pp. 185, 187.
27. Schmitz, *Christusgemeinschaft*, pp. 187-88, citing Phil. 3.10; Col. 1.24; 2 Cor. 4.10-11; Rom. 8.17; and 2 Tim. 2.11.
28. Stauffer, 'Märtyrertheologie', p. 595 citing Isa. 53.12; 2 Macc. 15.11; and *T. Benj.* 3.5.
29. Stauffer, 'Märtyrertheologie', p. 545.
30. Stauffer, *Theology*, p. 188, citing 2 Thess. 1.6; Gal. 6.2; Phil. 1.28-29; 2.30; Col. 1.24; cf. 1 Pet. 4.17-18; Mk 10.43; *idem*, 'Märtyrertheologie', pp. 545-46.
31. Stauffer, *Theology*, p. 188, citing 2 Cor. 1.4-5; 4.12; cf. Eph. 3.1, 13.
32. G.H.P. Thompson, 'Eph. 3.13 and 2 Tim. 2.10', *ExpTim* 71 (1959–60), pp. 187-89; cf. W.H.C. Frend, *Martyrdom and Persecution in the Early Church* (Oxford: Basil Blackwell, 1965), p. 86; O. Michel, 'Leiden III: NT', *RGG*, IV,

Windisch also argues that Paul's sufferings continue Jesus' sufferings, which were incomplete until filled up by Paul.[33] Windisch, however, was more cautious than either Schmitz or Stauffer, for he sought to show how Paul mirrors Jesus' career. Jesus and Paul, for Windisch, are types of the 'Christus-Menschen' or 'divine men' (θεῖοι ἄνδρες),[34] who become saviours in the extension of the kingdom:[35] both are called and sent (implied in the δοῦλοι of Phil. 1.1);[36] both are 'servants of God' in service of the gospel of salvation and fulfil the work of the servant of Yahweh of Isaiah 53;[37] both are Spirit-filled bearers of a divine power in word and wonder-working; both are Spirit-enlightened, reform-minded Scripture teachers and Gnostics; both are Initiates and Mystagogues; and both are creators of Christian community and martyrs.[38]

As we shall see, Windisch intuits an important hermeneutical key for the understanding of the suffering passages in Philippians, namely, the mimetic nature of suffering in the followers of Jesus. He seriously jeopardizes his case, however, by adding that though the suffering of Paul mirrors that of his master, Paul's suffering was even greater than Jesus', since Paul's apostolic ministry was designed to continue that of Jesus. Thus Paul's ministry was characterized by suffering in a way that even Jesus' ministry was not![39]

---

p. 297. J.N.D. Kelly finds the same notion at work in the Pastorals: 'the more Paul himself... suffers now, the less his brethren who are also "in Christ" will have to suffer themselves, and so he will hasten the coming of the End' (*The Pastoral Epistles: I and II Timothy, Titus* [BNTC; London: A. & C. Black, 1963], p. 178, on 2 Tim. 2.10).

33. Windisch, *Paulus und Christus*, p. 40; cf. J. Schmid, 'Kol. 1.24', *BZ* 21 (1933), p. 342.

34. Windisch, *Paulus und Christus*, pp. 229-52; cf. Güttgemanns, *Leidende Apostel*, p. 14.

35. Windisch drew his parallels from the Greco-Roman world (*Paulus und Christus*, pp. 24-89), from the Old Testament (pp. 89-101), and from Hellenistic Judaism (pp. 101-14).

36. *Paulus und Christus*, p. 162.

37. *Paulus und Christus*, p. 163; cf. idem, *Der zweite Korintherbrief* (Göttingen: Vandenhoeck & Ruprecht, 9th edn, 1924), p. 145; Sass, *Apostelamt*, p. 81; T. Holtz, 'Zum Selbstverständnis des Apostels Paulus', *TLZ* 91 (1966), pp. 328-29, citing Col. 1.24; Phil. 2.17; 3.10; 1 Cor. 15.31; 2 Cor. 1.5-6; 4.10-11; Gal. 6.17 and others.

38. Windisch, *Paulus und Christus*, pp. 287-88.

39. *Paulus und Christus*, p. 235; cf. E. Kamlah, 'Was beurteilt Paulus sein

2. From the Origins of Christ-Mysticism to Schweitzer 41

Not surprisingly, the view that Jesus' sufferings and those of his disciples are to be seen as indistinguishable—or, at most, distinguishable only in degree—has come under severe criticism. First, it has been noted that though such authors as Schmitz and Windisch drew from literature contemporary with Paul, they omitted from their consideration the presence of a futuristic eschatological expectation in Paul by overemphasizing realized eschatology.[40] Accordingly, they failed to take into consideration the clear, futuristic indices that appear in Paul's discussions of his own suffering.

Secondly, it is suggested that the view of authors such as Windisch and Schmitz violates the theology of Paul's authentic letters by overlooking

> the christological distance between the redeemer and the redeemed, a distance that Paul presents with great emphasis in 1 Corinthians 15 over against a Gnostic Christology of identity.[41]

Accordingly, critics suggest that Paul stresses a difference between his experience and that of Christ rather than the identity of the two.

Thirdly, and most decisively, these views ignore the absence of New Testament references to the power of atoning suffering attributed to the sufferings or death of Christians, whether Paul or anyone else. The only atoning death spoken of in the entire New Testament, it is held, is that of Jesus.[42] Only when Paul is read in the light of later writings attributed to him but not written by him—for example, Colossians or Ephesians, in which a view of Paul's sufferings as atoning does, in fact, appear, perhaps as a direct result of his martyrdom (cf. Col. 1.24 and Eph. 3.1, 13)—is it possible to explain the enigmatic expressions of participation in Christ's sufferings found in, say, Phil. 3.10, in terms of atonement or *Passionsmystik*.[43]

Leiden?', *ZNW* 54 (1963), p. 227 on Phil. 3.10; R. Pesch, 'Zur Theologie des Todes', *BibLeb* 10 (1969), pp. 9-16.

40. Güttgemanns, *Leidende Apostel*, pp. 195-96.
41. Güttgemanns, *Leidende Apostel*, p. 102.
42. E. Lohse, *Märtyrer und Gottesknecht: Untersuchungen zur urchristlichen Verkündigung vom Sühntod Jesu Christi* (Göttingen: Vandenhoeck & Ruprecht, 2nd edn, 1963), p. 199; cf. P. Stuhlmacher, 'Achtzehn Thesen zur paulinischen Kreuzestheologie', in *Rechtfertigung* (ed. J. Friedrich, W. Pohlmann and P. Stuhlmacher; Tübingen: Mohr; Göttingen: Vandenhoeck & Ruprecht, 1976), p. 516.
43. Stuhlmacher, 'Achtzehn', p. 515; cf. M. de Boer, 'Images of Paul in the Post-Apostolic Period', *CBQ* 42 (1980), p. 368, following E. Lohse; B. Sanders, 'Imitating Paul', *HTR* 74 (1981), p. 359.

2. Schweitzer and his Followers

Albert Schweitzer

Albert Schweitzer is perhaps the single most influential author of the contemporary critical period for the study of suffering in Paul's letters.[44] Schweitzer's indebtedness to Christ-mysticism is clear:

> Every manifestation of the life of the baptized man is conditioned by his being in Christ. Grafted into the corporeity of Christ, he loses his creatively individual existence and his natural personality. Henceforth, he is only a form or manifestation of the personality of Jesus Christ, which dominates that corporeity.[45]

Schweitzer, however, found Christ-mysticism by itself inadequate, for (as we have seen) it does not take into account futuristic eschatology and because (as we have yet to see) it is individualistic.

Accordingly, Schweitzer turned to the work of Richard Kabisch, where he found the importance of Second Temple Jewish apocalypticism for the understanding Paul stressed.[46] In the light of Kabisch's work, Schweitzer argued that Paul not only envisioned an actual, physical transformation of Christians, as in Christ-mysticism, but also expected 'the immediate return of Jesus, of the Judgment, and of the Messianic glory'.[47]

But Schweitzer also turned to the work of Wilhelm Wrede,[48] for there he discovered that, contrary to Christ-mysticism's individualistic emphasis, redemption is cosmic. Accordingly, Schweitzer proposed that Paul awaited an eschaton that was 'the deliverance of mankind from the dominion of the powers'[49] and the transfer of the whole perishable world, including humanity, to the imperishable world.[50]

---

44. Cf. W.D. Davies, *Paul and Rabbinic Judaism* (New York: Harper & Row, repr. 1968 [1955]), p. xiii.
45. Schweitzer, *Mysticism*, p. 125; cf. p. 141.
46. R. Kabisch, *Die Eschatologie des Paulus in ihren Zusammenhängen mit dem Gesamtbegriff des Paulinismus* (Göttingen, 1893); cf. Schweitzer, *Paul*, pp. 58-63; W.G. Kümmel, *The New Testament: The History of the Investigation of its Problems* (trans. S.M. Gilmour and H.C. Kee; Nashville: Abingdon, 1972), pp. 232-35.
47. Schweitzer, *Paul*, pp. 52-53.
48. W. Wrede, *Paulus* (Tübingen: Mohr, 1907 [1905]); cf. Schweitzer, *Paul*, p. 167.
49. Schweitzer, *Paul*, p. 167.
50. Schweitzer, *Paul*, p. 54.

2. From the Origins of Christ-Mysticism to Schweitzer 43

The significance of Schweitzer's synthesis is apparent in his discussion of *how* this process of transformation of the perishable cosmos into the imperishable is verifiable. For Schweitzer, the invisible realities of Christ's cosmic death to the natural world and of his life to the supernatural world are verified through Christians' own sufferings and deaths.[51] Thus Paul's experiences of suffering—as enumerated in his 'lists of sufferings' (1 Cor. 4.9-13; 2 Cor. 6.4-5; 11.25-30), his mention of his sicknesses (Gal. 4.13-14; 6.17), his reference to his Ephesian battle with beasts (1 Cor. 15.32), and his sufferings at the hands of Jews and those connected with the Jerusalem apostles[52]—reveal to him that he and other believers are not suffering premessianic tribulations,[53] but rather death *with* Christ. Suffering and death evidence the withering away of the flesh and the growth of the life of the spirit within, by means of which the cosmic consequences of Christ's death and life are realized.

It is not individual suffering that verifies a believer's union with Christ, Schweitzer argued (*contra* Deissmann, Vincent and others), but the union of the body with Christ. Individuals are transformed into a real *corporate* identity (citing Phil. 1.20, 29; 2.17; 2 Cor. 4.10-12; Col. 1.24), namely, the church. The body of Christ in its sufferings and new life is the visible *locus* of the cosmic and eschatological transformation, the *locus* of God's work of creating the new order.

It is impossible to overestimate the magnitude of Schweitzer's contribution to the study of suffering in Paul. Still, it is striking that

---

51. Schweitzer, *Mysticism*, p. 141.
52. *Mysticism*, pp. 148-59. Schweitzer even invokes Acts here!
53. See *Mysticism*, pp. 142, 147; cf. K. Schelkle, *Die Petrusbriefe* (HTKNT, 13.2; Freiburg im Breisgau: Herder, 1961), p. 123; N. Brox, *Der erste Petrusbrief* (EKKNT, 21; Zurich: Benzinger; Neukirchen–Vluyn: Neukirchener Verlag, 1979), p. 215; B.M. Ahern, 'The Fellowship of his Sufferings (Phil. 3.10)', *CBQ* 22 (1960), p. 32 n. 90. Contrary to Schweitzer, E. Best maintains that the sufferings Paul speaks of are the apocalyptic–eschatological woes of the messiah spoken of in Second Temple literature and elsewhere in the New Testament, e.g., 1 Cor. 7.26-28 and 2 Thess. 2.3-10 (*One Body in Christ* [London: SPCK, 1955], pp. 131-34, citing 2 Cor. 1.4-5); cf. T. Baumeister, *Die Anfänge der Theologie des Martyriums* (Münster: Aschendorff, 1979), pp. 156, 187, 190-91; C.M. Proudfoot, 'Imitation or Realistic Participation?', *Int* 17 (1963), p. 151; J. Huby, *Saint Paul: Les épîtres de la captivité* (Paris: Beauchesne, 1947), p. 349; J.M. Court, 'Paul and the Apocalyptic Pattern', in *Paul and Paulinism* (ed. M.D. Hooker and S.G. Wilson; London: SPCK, 1982), pp. 63-64.

Schweitzer made such sparing use of Philippians in his discussion of Paul's theology. Thus, as a result of the paucity of his references to Philippians, one must deduce from Schweitzer's wider study of Paul what he would have said in terms of Philippians. This is, however, exactly what followers of Schweitzer have gone on to do.

Developments of Schweitzer's Model

Schweitzer's synthesis has become the dominant interpretative approach for understanding the suffering passages of Philippians (if not Paul generally): that believers' sufferings are the result of their real union with Christ and of participation in the sufferings of other believers.[54] In this 'physical solidarity', which is for many 'the most literal interpretation of Pauline mysticism',[55] 'a deepened bond of fellowship' between Christ and the believer makes 'our sufferings become his sufferings'.[56] As well, believers' sufferings are shared in an equally real union.[57] Consequently, Rudolf Bultmann can write that Ignatius's understanding of suffering as something external to be imitated represents a major post-Pauline regression from Paul's own doctrine of salvation.[58]

It is commonly held today, in line with Schweitzer's views, that spiritual union with Christ comes about by means of baptism, through which believers recapitulate sacramentally the soteriological experiences of Christ's death and resurrection and experience his sufferings.[59]

---

54. Ahern, 'Fellowship', pp. 31-32; 'In Phil. 3.10-11', *VD* 37 (1959), p. 28.

55. Proudfoot, 'Imitation?', pp. 140-41, 158; cf. Davies, *Paul*, p. xii; Ahern, 'Fellowship', p. 30; X. Léon-Dufour, *Resurrección de Jesús y mensaje pascual* (trans. R.S. Cosoyas; Salamanca: Sigueme, 1973), p. 102, citing Phil. 3.8, 10.

56. Beare, *Philippians*, pp. 123-24; cf. G. Bornkamm, *Paul* (San Francisco: Harper & Row, 1971), pp. 171-72; J.H. Schutz, *Paul and the Anatomy of Apostolic Authority* (Cambridge: Cambridge University Press, 1975), p. 221.

57. Ahern, 'Fellowship', pp. 31-32; Bornkamm, 'Der Philipperbrief als paulinische Briefsammlung', in *Neotestamentica et Patristica* (Leiden: Brill, 1962), p. 198; Bultmann, *Theology*, pp. 298-99, citing Phil. 3.10-11.

58. R. Bultmann, 'Ignatius und Paulus', in *Studia Paulina in honorem Johannes de Zwaan* (ed. J.N. Sevenster and W.C. van Unnik; Haarlem: Bohn, 1953), p. 40.

59. C.M. Proudfoot, 'The Apostle Paul's Understanding of Christian Suffering' (PhD dissertation, Yale University, 1956), ch. 4; *idem*, 'Imitation', pp. 150-52; Ahern, 'Fellowship', p. 31; Davies, *Paul*, p. xii; S. Kim, *The Origin of Paul's Gospel* (WUNT, 2.4; Tübingen: Mohr, 1981), p. 326; J.B. Polhill, 'Twin Obstacles in the Christian Faith: Philippians 3', *RevExp* 77 (1980), pp. 359-72.

2. From the Origins of Christ-Mysticism to Schweitzer 45

In baptism, through which one knows Christ (cf. 2 Cor. 3.18; 1 Cor. 15.45, 49; Phil. 3.21), a Christian dies with Christ—to the flesh (cf. Gal. 5.24), to righteousness from the law (cf. Rom. 7.4; Gal. 2.19), to the whole world (cf. Gal. 6.14), and to what is 'mine' or the self (cf. 2 Cor. 5.14-15). As a result, lordship that is not Christ's is broken,[60] and Christ becomes Lord.[61]

Yet real union with Christ at present is not fully realized. There remains a coming eschatological and cosmic glory,[62] a point recently emphasized by J. Christiaan Beker. According to Beker, 'the central Pauline claim' or 'the apocalyptic dawn of God's triumph in Christ' points, via Schweitzer's eschatological and cosmological emphases, to 'the reality of the cosmic victory of the creator over his created world'.[63] The reign of God 'will bring the created order to its glorious destiny according to God's promises'.[64]

Thus suffering is still very much a present reality because death with Christ is taking place with a view to eschatological fulfilment. The tension between present suffering and future fulfilment is well expressed by M. de Boer:

> Paul understands his suffering as a product of the fact that he finds himself, in testifying to the gospel of the crucified Messiah, at the juncture of the two ages. He stands at the point at which the old aeon is victoriously breaking in upon it. Paul's suffering, therefore, lies completely within an eschatological tension and dynamic which looks forward in hope to imminent deliverance and the unambiguous establishment of the new creation.[65]

In the 1960s a new and potentially revolutionary factor emerged in

---

60. Cf. E.P. Sanders, *Paul and Palestinian Judaism* (London: SCM Press, 1977), pp. 500, 554-55; J.C. Beker, *Paul's Apocalyptic Gospel* (Philadelphia: Fortress Press, 1982), p. 41.

61. R.H. Tannehill, *Dying and Rising with Christ* (Berlin: Töpelmann, 1967), pp. 115-22, 131; cf. G. Panikulam, *Koinōnia in the New Testament* (Rome: Biblical Institute Press, 1979), pp. 93, 103, 105; Sanders, *Paul*, p. 523; *idem, Paul, the Law, and the Jewish People* (Philadelphia: Fortress Press, 1983), p. 209.

62. Cf. Forestell, 'Christian Perfection', pp. 124-25; Beare, *Philippians*, pp. 123, 141 (on 3.21); Tannehill, *Dying and Rising*, p. 108; Panikulam, *Koinōnia*, pp. 96-97; Kim, *Origin*, pp. 324-25.

63. Beker, *Apocalyptic Gospel*, pp. 88-89, 118.

64. *Apocalyptic Gospel*, p. 29; cf. *idem, Paul the Apostle* (Philadelphia: Fortress Press, 1980), p. 137.

65. De Boer, 'Images of Paul', p. 368, citing 1 Cor. 4.9-13; 2 Cor. 4.7-12; Gal. 6.14-17; cf. Schütz, *Paul*, pp. 207-208.

the explication of this basically Schweitzerian approach to suffering in Paul's thought. It was then that attention began to be focused on how Paul's theological reflection arose as a result of conflict with his opponents. Prior to this, of course, the question of Paul's opponents in Philippians had been raised.[66] But with studies such as those of Walther Schmithals,[67] Helmut Koester,[68] Joachim Gnilka[69] and Robert Jewett,[70] Paul's words on suffering came to be seen as a polemical response to opponents who denied the place of suffering in the Christian life and presupposed a realized eschatology in which the present, resurrection bodies of believers cannot suffer.[71]

Thus in contrast to Hans Windisch, who understood Paul as viewing himself as a θεῖος ἀνηρ after the model of Jesus, these studies see Paul's *opponents* as those who believed themselves to be θεῖοι ἄνδρες! Gnilka, for example, following the lead given by Schmithals and Koester,[72] argues that Paul in Philippians is responding to Jewish Christian θεῖος ἀνηρ missionaries who were pretenders to the legacy of Moses and of all the other heroes of antiquity in whom the Spirit worked gloriously.[73] These latter-day pneumatic missionaries believed

---

66. See the survey in J.J. Gunther, *St Paul's Opponents and their Background* (Leiden: Brill, 1973).

67. W. Schmithals, *Paul and the Gnostics* (trans. J.E. Steely; Nashville: Abingdon, 1972).

68. H. Koester, 'The Purpose of the Polemic of a Pauline Fragment (Philippians 3)', *NTS* (1962), pp. 317-32.

69. J. Gnilka, *Der Philipperbrief* (Freiburg: Herder, 1968); 'Die antipaulinische Mission in Philippi', *BZ* 9 (1965), pp. 258-76.

70. R. Jewett, 'The Epistolary Thanksgiving and the Integrity of Philippians', *NovT* 12 (1970), pp. 40-53; 'Conflicting Movements in the Early Church as Reflected in Philippians', *NovT* 12 (1970), pp. 362-90; *Paul's Anthropological Terms* (Leiden: Brill, 1971).

71. Cf. Schmithals, *Paul*, pp. 83, 92-93, 321-22, 324; Koester, 'Purpose', pp. 322-24, 331; cf. A. Lincoln, *Paradise Now and Not Yet* (Cambridge: Cambridge University Press, 1981), pp. 92, 95.

72. See also D. Georgi, *The Opponents of Paul in Second Corinthians* (Philadelphia: Fortress Press, 1986).

73. Gnilka, *Philipperbrief*, p. 10; idem, 'Antipaulinische Mission', pp. 258-76; cf. J.J. Müller, *The Epistles of Paul to the Philippians and to Philemon* (Grand Rapids: Eerdmans, 1955), p. 75; C.R. Holladay, 'Paul's Opponents in Philippians 3', *ResQ* 12 (1969), pp. 80-83; J.F. Collange, *L'épître de saint Paul aux Philippiens* (Neuchâtel: Delachaux & Niestlé, 1973), pp. 29-30; Jewett, 'Conflicting Movements', pp. 365-71; idem, *Anthropological Terms*, p. 22; Lincoln, *Paradise*, p. 95.

2. From the Origins of Christ-Mysticism to Schweitzer 47

that they had overcome the earthly form of death by being transformed spiritually, intellectually and physically (evidenced by circumcision) by Christ.[74] The result was that suffering and pain no longer have a place in believer's lives.[75] That they questioned the validity of Paul's apostolate by pointing to his physical weakness is clear from Paul's defence in Phil. 3.10.[76]

Jewett, though he argues that three different groups of opponents were at work in the Philippian congregation and are addressed by Paul in Philippians (namely, libertines, divine-man missionaries and Judaizers), also argues that divine-man missionaries, as well as another group of outsiders, viz. Judaizers, succeeded at Philippi because libertine Philippian Christians had corrupted the Philippian congregation through their pride and sense of self-perfection (3.12-15).[77] By succumbing to 'the religious quest for perfection and transcendence and union with the divine',[78] the Philippians allowed themselves to become captivated by the Judaizers, who sought to lead them to circumcision as a means of perfection, and by the divine-man missionaries, who tried to lead them to an enthusiastic, non-suffering Christianity that, as Gnilka puts it, looked on Paul's cross-centred theology with ridicule.[79]

There are, of course, differences among the various scholars mentioned above. Yet all of them reconstruct Paul's response to the projected opponents at Philippi in terms of Schweitzer's synthesis. Accordingly, they first argue that Paul responds to his opponents by emphasizing the necessity of suffering and dying with Christ.[80] Against

74. Gnilka, 'Antipaulinische', pp. 262, 276. According to Gnilka, Koester is wrong to see the heretics as preaching a moral perfection based on keeping the law; their perfection was a spiritual one that allowed them direct insight into the Scriptures (pp. 273-76, following Lütgert [see E.E. Ellis, 'Paul and his Opponents', in *Christianity, Judaism and Other Greco-Roman Cults* (ed. J. Neusner; Leiden: Brill, 1975), I, p. 278]).
75. Gnilka, 'Antipaulinische', p. 276.
76. Gnilka, 'Antipaulinische', p. 268; *idem, Philipper*, p. 196; cf. Jewett, 'Conflicting', pp. 367-68; R.A. Culpepper, 'Co-Workers in Suffering', *RevExp* 77 (1980), pp. 349-58. Against W.G. Kümmel, 'Urchristentum', in *RGG*, VI, pp. 1187-1193.
77. Jewett, 'Conflicting', pp. 371-75.
78. Jewett, *Anthropological Terms*, p. 17.
79. Jewett, 'Conflicting', pp. 387-88.
80. W. Schmithals, *The Office of Apostle in the Early Church* (trans. J.E. Steely;

the opponents' supposedly realized eschatology, Paul argues that 'the resurrection in the future' (3.11) can only be reached through death.[81] Echoing the words of de Boer, Jewett writes that the believer stands 'between the two ages and between promise and fulfilment'[82] and so 'waits for a future exaltation which only God can provide'.[83] Standing clearly in the tradition of Schweitzer, Jewett points to Paul's stress on apocalyptic suffering that advances the gospel (1.12-26), on the coming of the parousia (cf. Rom. 11.25-26; 15.19; 2 Thess. 3.1), and on suffering within the Philippian congregation, which is not only a sign of divine grace but also of impending judgment (1.27-30).[84]

3. Conclusion

A major reformulation of the martyrological understanding of suffering occurs at the end of the nineteenth century when suffering understood in terms of commonality of intention—and usually this meant 'ethical intention'—is rejected in favour of suffering understood as the means or process whereby the ontological union of believers with Christ is verified or even realized. In the light of this ontological union, believers' sufferings—whether those of Paul or of others—really *are* the sufferings of Christ.

Such a union is most clearly seen in early Christ-mysticism, where suffering evidences union with Christ, and in Schweitzer, where suffering is the means whereby the death and life of Christ become real in the world.

Various criticisms can be levelled at the early formulation of Christ-mysticism and its immediate followers. I have already noted three: (1) the tendency to downplay the future-oriented nature of Paul's words, (2) the dangerous conflation of Christ and Paul, and (3) the insufficient attention given to Pauline soteriology that differs from

Nashville: Abingdon, 1969), p. 47; Koester, 'Purpose', p. 323; Gnilka, 'Antipaulinische', p. 266; *idem, Philipper*, p. 195. Cf. G. Friedrich, *Der Brief an die Philipper* (Göttingen: Vandenhoeck & Ruprecht, 1968), p. 119; Collange, *Philippiens*, p. 115 on 3.8, 118 on 3.13, and 70 on 1.29; Lincoln, *Paradise*, p. 95.

81. Koester, 'Purpose', p. 323; cf. pp. 325, 331, citing 1 Cor. 1.18; Schmithals, *Paul and the Gnostics*, pp. 91-93; Gnilka, 'Antipaulinische', p. 267; Jewett, 'Conflicting', p. 367; Lincoln, *Paradise*, p. 103.

82. Jewett, 'Conflicting', pp. 387-88.

83. 'Conflicting', p. 389.

84. Jewett, 'Epistolary Thanksgiving', p. 51.

2. From the Origins of Christ-Mysticism to Schweitzer 49

soteriologies found elsewhere in the New Testament or even in Second Temple Judaism.

Clearly, Schweitzer's approach was a significant advance in the study of suffering in Paul. It is a compelling approach that has created a consensus. Furthermore it has opened interesting and fruitful avenues of investigation in Paul's letters. For example, the view of some of Schweitzer's followers that in Philippians Paul is in conflict with opponents is a very significant step in the direction of understanding the function of suffering in Philippians.

Yet it is not universally accepted, as will become clear when we examine alternatives that have been proposed. Suffice it to say here that the question seems to be, did Schweitzer go far enough in his understanding of Paul? Schweitzer's almost total neglect of Philippians, in fact, is a clear indication that his picture of Paul's thought is incomplete. Even the view of his followers seems suspect. For example, the agonistic quality of Paul's letters may be due as much or more to his rhetorical approach to questions than to any actual attacks by opponents.

Thus we may ask, to what extent are the sufferings of Christ those of believers, as Schweitzer and his followers maintain? How can one account for the absence of reference to dying and rising with Christ in baptism in Philippians? One may appeal to Phil. 3.10 but, then, what does Paul mean there by 'to know'? Does he mean to imitate or to share by union in such a way that the sufferings of the one are the same as the sufferings of the other? These questions still demand answers.

Chapter 3

ALTERNATIVE APPROACHES

1. *Ernst Lohmeyer and Martyrology*

Lohmeyer's Approach

Although Schweitzer's approach to suffering in Paul's thought has gained a great following among New Testament scholars, it is not the only one to have developed the implications found in Christ-mysticism. Ernst Lohmeyer's 1930 commentary on Philippians suggests a different approach.[1] Firmly rooted in the history-of-religions approach to Paul, Lohmeyer begins with the thesis that Paul expected a corporeal transformation through baptism into death and resurrection.[2] Yet while Schweitzer developed a parallel notion in terms of the suffering of believers in the body of Christ as the *locus* of cosmological transformation, Lohmeyer contends that transformation takes place at martyrdom.

Philippians, as Lohmeyer sees it, is a treatise on martyrdom. Accordingly, he divides it into five sections: 1.12-26, the martyrdom of Paul; 1.27–2.16, the martyrdom of the community; 2.17-30, help in martyrdom; 3.1-21, dangers in martyrdom; and 4.1-9, final exhortations with respect to martyrdom.[3] Furthermore, martyrological terminology is to be found scattered throughout the letter—for example, ταπεινός and περισσευεῖν (4.12),[4] δοῦλοι (1.1),[5] and σωτηρία (2.13).[6]

Lohmeyer conceives of Paul's thought about martyrdom in terms of

1. E. Lohmeyer, *Die Briefe an die Philipper, an die Kolosser und an Philemon* (Göttingen: Vandenhoeck & Ruprecht, 1964 [1930]).
2. *Philipper*, pp. 140, 159.
3. *Philipper*, pp. 5-6, 36.
4. *Philipper*, p. 181.
5. *Philipper*, pp. 9-10.
6. *Philipper*, p. 103.

3. Alternative Approaches

Second Temple Judaism and the earliest Christian martyrological texts[7]—viz., that those who are suffered *for* share *in* the grace of the one who suffers, and so suffer *with* him.[8] Paul shares with the Philippians not by virtue of an ontological union, but because he shares with them in the grace of martyrdom (cf. 1.7).[9] Thus he gives thanks for the community and suffers on their behalf.[10]

It is because of his concern with Second Temple texts that Lohmeyer, like both Stauffer and Schweitzer, is careful to account for futurity in Philippians. For this reason, Lohmeyer concludes that the martyr, as the *locus* of suffering that leads to perfection, does not embody present resurrection power but rather points to the future triumph of Christ and the fulfilment of the martyr.[11] According to Lohmeyer, the clear meaning of τοῦ γνῶναι αὐτόν (3.10) has to do with a vision of the Lord in the world-to-come and of the final goal of 'being with Christ'.[12]

In fact, suggests Lohmeyer, Paul's expectation of the martyr's future in the world-to-come is tantamount to *creatio ex nihilo*. Thus the participle συμμορφιζόμενος (3.10) does not mean simply 'to change form' but 'to give form to that which has no form', or as he expresses it, 'that out of the formless and limitless chaos of earthly life comes a completed *Dasein* through the form-giving power of death'.[13]

Lohmeyer's advance on a Christ-mysticism perspective is also evident in his view that the martyr is a special bearer of God's revelation before public authorities. As a result of his union with God the martyr makes God known in the world.[14] The martyr, in effect, becomes an instrument of the spirit of Jesus Christ so as to bear witness, for the martyr has been given a greater fullness of the Spirit.[15]

Lohmeyer's suggestions concerning the function of suffering in Philippians are important, particularly those having to do with (1) futurity in the martyrological references, and (2) the revelatory nature

7. *Philipper*, pp. 53-54, 142, citing Ps. 25.3; 69.7; 119.36, 80, 116; Sir. 24.22; 51.18; *Odes* 29.2.
8. *Philipper*, pp. 80, 183 on 4.14 and 1.7.
9. *Philipper*, pp. 65, 139, 184, on 4.10-20.
10. *Philipper*, pp. 26, 46, on 1.17.
11. *Philipper*, pp. 5, 51.
12. *Philipper*, pp. 138-39, 51 on 1.19.
13. *Philipper*, p. 140.
14. *Philipper*, pp. 40, 78.
15. *Philipper*, pp. 52 (on ἐπιχορηγία τοῦ πνεύματος, 1.19) and 58.

of suffering. One can, however, dispute Lohmeyer's claim that Philippians can *only* be interpreted in martyrological terms—though Cerfaux's dismissal of such a thesis is extreme in the opposite direction.[16] Robert Jewett is more helpful in his assessment: although Lohmeyer overstates his case for martyrdom, he is correct 'in discerning a continuity in the letter at the point of the references to suffering'.[17]

Developments of Lohmeyer's Approach
It is difficult to cite scholars who have adopted Lohmeyer's insights in the same way that others have taken over Schweitzer's. Yet it is fair to see in certain authors an assumption of the problem as laid down by Lohmeyer. This is especially true of two authors, the value of whose assessments differs greatly.

The martyrological problem has recently been addressed by John S. Pobee.[18] In spite of the fact that his work reflects primarily the state of the question in the early 1960s (with only minor updating) and does not tackle the question in the same depth as Lohmeyer,[19] Pobee's work is of importance in that it draws attention to the testimonial nature of suffering in Paul: convinced that God is in control, not only in a general way but also specifically, Paul's suffering led him to strategic places as a witness.[20] Pobee also notes the perfecting nature of suffering when he says that Phil. 1.20 witnesses to Paul's conviction that Christ will be glorified in his own martyrdom,[21] for Paul will be 'raised at the last, following the example of Christ who died and was raised by God'.

---

16. L. Cerfaux, 'Las epístolas de la cautividad', in *Introducción a la Bíblia. II. Nuevo Testamento* (ed. A. Robert and A. Feuillet; trans. A. Ros; Barcelona: Herder, 1965), p. 442.

17. Jewett, 'Epistolary Thanksgiving', p. 51.

18. J.S. Pobee, *Persecution and Martyrdom in the Theology of Paul* (JSNTSup, 6; Sheffield: JSOT Press, 1985).

19. For example, on the question of influences on Paul, Pobee merely says, 'Paul, who himself had his full share of persecution and suffering for the sake of the gospel and preached Christ crucified for others, may have been influenced by the martyrological ideas of the world in which he travelled and taught and suffered' (*Persecution*, p. 16).

20. *Persecution*, p. 103 citing Phil. 1.29; 3.10; Col. 1.24; *4 Macc.* 1.18-23; 10.20-21; *3 Macc.* 4.1; Jos. *Ant.* 2.299; 1 Thess. 1.6; 2 Cor. 1.5-7; 6.10; 7.4; 13.9; 1 Pet. 4.13; Acts 5.41.

21. *Persecution*, p. 98, citing a parallel in 1QH 2.24-25.

3. Alternative Approaches 53

Significantly absent from Pobee's work, however, is any real concern to elucidate the problem raised by the Christ-mysticism approach and its followers, namely the relationship between the martyr apostle and the apostolic community. Concern for the community as such in Pobee's writing is absent, except for his words that 'it was in the destiny of followers of Christ to meet with persecution'[22] and that 'whatever persecution was to come upon the Philippian Christians was part of the wrestling match between the forces of Christ and the forces of Satan for the mastery of the souls of men'.[23]

Contrasting with Pobee's overly general work is Geoffrey Lampe's posthumous essay in which he deals seriously with the implications of a martyrological reading of Paul.[24] Following Lohse, Lampe rejects the contention that Paul's sufferings were viewed by him as atoning— what Lampe calls a 'soteriology' of martyrdom.[25] Rather, he argues, as does Lohmeyer, that Paul is a martyr or confessor. In Paul's bold witness to Christ, through which the gospel is brought to the attention of the whole praetorium, the Spirit is poured out on Paul. So Paul becomes a Spirit-filled, prophet-like recipient of divine inspiration, who consequently suffers for Christ's sake, thereby becoming a sign of perdition to his persecutors and of salvation to other suffering believers.[26] Lampe believes that for Paul

> the essence of martyrdom was not death, but the witness before hostile authorities. Accordingly, the role of the Spirit was not to give comfort and strength but to inspire confessors to proclaim the Lordship of Christ with uninhibited freedom (*parrhesia*).[27]

Accordingly, in opposition to a view of martyrdom in which grace is given to the martyr's followers as a result of the martyr's *death*, Lampe argues that in Philippians grace comes to Paul's churches as

---

22. *Persecution*, p. 108, citing 1 Thess. 3.14; Phil. 1.29-30.
23. *Persecution*, p. 109, citing *4 Macc.* 6.10; 9.23; 11.20; 13.15; 17.12; Wis. 10.2; 2 Tim. 2.5; 4.7; Ign. *Pol.* 6.1.
24. G.W. Lampe, 'Martyrdom and Inspiration', in *Suffering and Martyrdom in the New Testament* (ed. W. Horbury and B. McNeil; Cambridge: Cambridge University Press, 1981), pp. 118-35.
25. The only possible exception Lampe sees is the sacrificial imagery found in Phil. 2.17 and 2 Tim. 4.6 (cf. *Mart. Pol.* 14.1-2), where Paul's life is said to be poured out like a libation offering ('Martyrdom', p. 121).
26. 'Martyrdom', p. 132, citing Phil. 1.12-14, 19-20, 27-29.
27. 'Martyrdom', pp. 122-23.

they join with him in the *proclamation* of Christ's Lordship, because they see the Spirit of God operative in him.[28] Lampe builds on the problem of martyrdom as discussed by Lohmeyer. Lampe's essay, however, is also indebted to the work of a younger contemporary of Lohmeyer's, Ernst Käsemann, to whose work I now turn.

2. *Ernst Käsemann and the Epiphanic Role of Suffering*

Käsemann's Model

In the area of suffering in Paul (as, of course, elsewhere in New Testament study), Ernst Käsemann's influence has been very significant. Käsemann's unique contribution to the study of suffering in Paul is the way he develops the revelatory nature of those sufferings, specifically in drawing attention to Paul's apostolic consciousness as manifested in 2 Corinthians.[29] This contribution has been picked up by others and developed specifically in terms of Philippians.

Noting Paul's confession of his weakness through which God's power works,[30] Käsemann lays emphasis on Paul's statement that Christ is manifested in Paul's sufferings and not in his power. Käsemann deduces from this confession that it is in weakness and suffering that the risen Christ is revealed as the crucified one. For this reason, says Käsemann, Paul speaks of his weakness as 'the condition of his activity',[31] or as 'the pledge of the presence of Christ's power'.[32] In suffering Paul understands himself as the *locus* of the revelation of Christ, and so he becomes a *Christus incarnatus*.[33] Suffering is the proper 'Erscheninungsform des apostolischen Christusdienstes',[34]

---

28. 'Martyrdom', p. 132.
29. E. Käsemann, 'Die Legitimität des Apostels: Eine Untersuchung zu II Korinther 10–13', *ZNW* 41 (1942), pp. 33-71.
30. 'Legitimität', pp. 53-54, following G. Stählin, "Ασθενής κτλ.', *TDNT*, I, p. 491.
31. Käsemann, 'Legitimität', pp. 53-54, following A. Schlatter, *Paulus, der Bote Jesu* (Stuttgart: Calwer, repr. 1962 [1934]), p. 668, on 2 Cor. 12.9.
32. Käsemann, 'Legitimität', pp. 53-54, following W. Grundmann, *Der Begriff der Kraft in der neutestamentlichen Gedankenkraft* (Stuttgart: Kohlhammer, 1932), p. 104.
33. Käsemann, 'Legitimität', pp. 53-54.
34. H.D. Wendland, *Der zweite Korintherbrief* (Göttingen: Vandenhoeck & Ruprecht, 1933), p. 138.

3. Alternative Approaches

a grace in which the Philippians participate.[35]
Clearly Käsemann here allies himself with the position advanced by Windisch, according to whom,

> God's power becomes effective precisely in the apostolate, where that power reaches its *Telos* and also achieves completion, where the ἐπισκηνῶσαι of Christ's power, the earthly manifestation of Christ himself, is realized.[36]

Development of Käsemann's Model

Käsemann's stress on the epiphanic role of suffering in 2 Corinthians has been picked up by Dieter Lührmann[37] and Erhardt Güttgemanns,[38] with the latter presenting the more seminal thought on suffering. Güttgemanns's intention, as noted above,[39] is to undo a key error in Christ-mysticism, namely the view that believers' sufferings have atoning value[40] or continue Jesus' sufferings.[41] He follows Käsemann and Lührmann in stressing that participation in Christ's sufferings does not stem from participation in the glorified Christ, but rather that the risen Lord of glory, who called Paul to be his apostle, makes himself known in the apostle's weakness and suffering, and so mirrors himself to the world through Paul as the crucified Jesus.[42] Thus σῶμα is not, as with Schweitzer, a metaphysical corporeality that repeatedly experiences anew Christ's death and resurrection; nor is it, as with J. Schneider, a functional indication that Christ suffers when the church suffers. For Güttgemanns, as for Käsemann, the body of the one who suffers is a christological correlative to κύριος, the agent of

---

35. Cf. Dibelius, *Briefe*, pp. 46-47, citing 2 Cor. 12.10d; 'Paulus und die Mystik', pp. 144-45.
36. Windisch, *Paulus und Christus*, p. 232; Käsemann, 'Legitimität', p. 53.
37. D. Lührmann, *Das Offenbarungsverständnis bei Paulus und in paulinischen Gemeinden* (Neukirchen–Vluyn: Neukirchener Verlag, 1965).
38. E. Güttgemanns, *Der leidende Apostel und sein Herr: Studien zur paulinischen Christologie* (FRLANT, 90; Göttingen: Vandenhoeck & Ruprecht, 1966).
39. *Supra*, chapter 2, nn. 40-41.
40. As, for example, in Kamlah, 'Was beurteilt', p. 227; cf. Güttgemanns, *Leidende Apostel*, p. 27.
41. As in Holtz, 'Selbstverständnis', pp. 328-29, citing 2 Cor. 1.5-6; 4.10-11; Phil. 2.17; Col. 1.24.
42. Güttgemanns, *Leidende Apostel*, pp. 29-30, 102, 118-19, *passim*.

obedience whereby the Lord accomplishes his purposes.[43]

Güttgemanns, however, takes Käsemann's epiphanic approach to suffering a step further when he discusses the difference between the suffering of believers and the suffering of Paul. He argues that when believers suffer because of their acceptance of the gospel, there is no formal difference between their sufferings and those of Paul, for both suffer rejection by the world. When, however, Paul's suffering is intended as a means to proclaim Christ (i.e. when it is apostolic and as such christologically epiphanic), then that suffering is uniquely his and cannot be shared by the community (Phil. 1.29; 3.10; 4.14).[44] Here the apostle is not a type for the community to imitate; rather, his function is to reveal Christ.[45] He does so as the founder of the community (1 Cor. 3.6, 10), the father of the Christians (1 Cor. 4.14-15; 2 Cor. 6.13), and the nurturer of the Christians by means of the gospel (Gal. 4.19 and 1 Thess. 2.7).[46]

By means of a functional understanding of suffering, therefore, Güttgemanns seeks to correct an overly ontological approach that sees Paul's sufferings as somehow those of Christ. Building on Käsemann and (to some extent) Windisch, Güttgemanns develops the view that Paul's suffering mirrors to his Philippian congregation the sufferings of the Lord, and so becomes part of his apostolic proclamation to them.

Following Käsemann and Güttgemanns, William Weinrich also maintains that in Paul's apostolic suffering the crucified one is made visible.[47] It is as a result of Paul's suffering that believers recognize the crucified Lord himself and so are emboldened to preach the gospel.[48] Weinrich finds this situation paralleled in the early Christian belief that in the martyrdom of Blandina, Christ crucified was portrayed.[49]

Weinrich also picks up an important lead from Windisch when he writes that the one revealed in Paul's suffering is, in fact, the 'suffering servant' of Isaiah, who as 'God's messenger of salvation to

---

43. *Leidende Apostel*, pp. 108-109.
44. *Leidende Apostel*, p. 323; cf. Collange, *Philippiens*, p. 60, following Percy.
45. Güttgemanns, *Leidende Apostel*, p. 325.
46. *Leidende Apostel*, pp. 326-27; cf. pp. 28 nn. 30-31, 323.
47. W. Weinrich, *Spirit and Martyrdom* (Washington, DC: University Press of America, 1981), pp. 47, 50 and 53.
48. *Spirit*, p. 53. Weinrich takes πεποιθότας (1.14) with τοῖς δεσμοῖς μου, not with ἐν κυρίῳ.
49. *Spirit*, pp. 53-54 (cf. Eusebius, *Hist. Eccl.* 5.1.41).

3. Alternative Approaches 57

the nations (Isa. 42.1; 49.6) is brought into suffering (Isa. 50.4-6)'.[50] For Weinrich, then, Paul is not ontologically the *locus* of the revelation of God but rather functionally the revelational *locus* of the crucified Lord, who is mirrored in Paul as the suffering servant.[51]

3. *Karl Barth and Suffering as an Apostle*

Barth's Theological Stance

The authors I have examined up to this point have operated within a history-of-religions approach. However, in Karl Barth's commentary on Philippians[52] we find a rejection of such an approach in favour of interpreting texts theologically. Barth's approach, of course, has never governed New Testament exegesis in the way Schweitzer's reformulation of Christ-mysticism has. Nevertheless, Barth's treatment of the suffering passages of Philippians points up another side of Paul's perception of suffering, namely, the way suffering communicates what it means for Paul to be an apostle.

Not surprisingly, Barth's discussion of suffering in Philippians is, like much of his work, couched in a polemical context.[53] Specifically, his Philippians commentary represents a vigorous response to theologians who, in Barth's eyes, had minimized God's work and exalted human works. The vigour of Barth's polemic is due largely to his perception that these two errors were leading German Christianity to forsake the Pauline teaching on the relationship of God and the world. In a speech on 31 January 1931, entitled 'The Need of the Evangelical Church', Barth denounced the tendency of Bishop Otto Dibelius and his followers to see in the German Church 'the continuation or representation or embodiment of the revelation and reconciliation of Christ'.[54] Likewise, in his study of prayer in the catechisms of the

50. *Spirit*, p. 47.
51. Cf. F. Froitzheim, *Christologie und Eschatologie bei Paulus* (Würzburg: Echter, 1979), pp. 162, 164.
52. K. Barth, *The Epistle to the Philippians* (trans. J.W. Leitch; London: SCM Press, 1962 [1928]).
53. Cf. Barth's earlier Romans commentary and the prefaces to its six successive editions from 1918 to 1928; *Epistle to the Romans* (trans. E.C. Hoskyns; London: Oxford University Press, 1972), pp. 1-26.
54. Cited in H.M. Rumscheidt, 'The Need of the Evangelical Church: An Illustration of Transition in Karl Barth's Theology', *JTSA* 51 (December, 1986), p. 11. I am indebted to Professor Rumscheidt for making me aware of this important

Protestant Reformation, Barth clearly rejects the teaching that the world could become 'in a philosophical sense... the bearer of God's name'.[55]

Burghard Krause sees Barth's opposition as being directed against two diverse interpretations of the relationship between God and the world: (1) that God identifies with suffering in such a way that God and the world become indistinguishable, or (2) that God and suffering are to be seen as absolutely polarized, so that God has nothing to do with the world ('God should be understood as so radically opposed to suffering that he cannot be God for us so long as suffering remains').[56] Consequently, when we turn to his Philippians commentary—finished only a few months after his speech in January, 1931—we are not surprised to find Barth emphasizing strenuously his rejection of the teaching that Christians are a continuation of the work of Christ.

In his Philippians commentary Barth appears to have returned to the teachings of Calvin and Luther. Echoing Luther, Barth concludes that Paul's primary concern in Philippians was the advance of the gospel. To this advance, says Barth, Paul subordinates his own welfare. It is not because of *Passionsmystik*, says Barth, that Paul writes nothing about his own situation in abstraction from the gospel,[57] but because as an apostle of Christ Paul has 'sacrificed [to the gospel] his objectivity and therewith also all objective interest in his person'. Barth does not equivocate: 'To the question how it is with *him* an apostle *must* react with information as to how it is with the *Gospel*'.[58]

Barth echoes Calvin when he writes of how Paul conceived of his own Christian service. According to Barth, Paul becomes subordinate to the gospel precisely as suffering leads him to embrace and serve

---

speech and of his own study of it. See, also, a related matter discussed by T. Sheehan, 'Heidegger and Hitler', in *New York Review of Books*, 16 June 1988, pp. 38-47.

55. K. Barth, *Prayer according to the Catechisms of the Reformation: Stenographic Records of Three Seminars* (adapted by A. Roulin; trans. S.F. Terrien; Philadelphia: Westminster Press, 1952), p. 42.

56. B. Krause, *Leiden Gottes—Leiden des Menschen* (Stuttgart: Calwer, 1980); cf. W. Krötke, Review of Krause, *TLZ* 107 (1982), pp. 615-17, from which all quotes are taken.

57. Barth, *Philippians*, pp. 26, 45, citing Calvin on Phil. 1.27: 'quidquid de me agatur, vos nihilo minus pergite in recto cursu'.

58. *Philippians*, p. 26, on 1.12 (emphases his).

3. Alternative Approaches 59

Christ, and him only, as Lord. Barth's lengthy comment on 3.7-8 expresses graphically this view:

> But what was gain to me I later saw as indifferent, as unimportant—no: as *loss*. To repent—one surely turns here involuntarily to this concept—does not mean to be liberalized, to become indifferent to what we formerly were, to the former objects of our devotion and the former conduct of our lives, but—to be horrified by it all. Not realizing that it means *nothing*, but it means evil. Spinoza does not become a reformer, but Luther does. The Pharisee Gamaliel does not become an apostle, but the Pharisee Saul does. *Zemian hegemai* means: I perceived *loss*, detriment, *damnum* precisely in what was dearest and most precious to me. . . . The heights on which I stood are *abysmal*. The assurance in which I lived is *lostness*; the light I had *darkness*. It is not that nil takes the place of the plus, but the plus itself changes to a minus. Recognition not of some imperfection but precisely of the guiltiness, perversity and reprobateness of his glorious Pharisaism, irreproachable and upright as it was *en sarki* (in the flesh), recognition of the indictment not on his wickedness but on his *goodness*—that is what came upon him *dia ton Christon* (for the sake of Christ), that was the meaning which Christ's work had for his attitude to these things.[59]

Through his own suffering (παθήματα Χριστοῦ and θάνατος Χριστοῦ, 3.10), therefore, Paul realized that only when he is poor and destitute in himself, in his κέρδη (3.5-6), in δικαιοσύνη ἐμή (3.9), and in 'everything in which it is possible to put fleshly confidence', can he secure the riches of Christ.[60]

In this way, Barth revives medieval and Reformation martyrological views. Yet Barth is no slave to his Reformation predecessors in responding to the excesses of Christ-mysticism. In fact, he transforms Luther and Calvin in order to avoid tendencies in them similar to the ones he rejects among his contemporaries! Accordingly, he avoids the view that suffering is a route to perfection, noting, for example, that Paul is not 'like the people of Kierkegaard's Copenhagen, making *progressus infinitus*' towards the goal of perfection. Barth perceives that, were this Paul's view, it would seriously undermine his attack in Galatians against the Judaizers, who

---

59. *Philippians*, p. 97 (emphases his).
60. *Philippians*, pp. 64, 103-104.

too could have spoken of 'striving ever to high endeavour' and Paul for his part could then quite well have conceded that a touch of Jewish legalism in the way it is done is also permissible on occasion.[61]

No, says Barth! Only where *every* boasting and *every* reliance upon the flesh are removed, where the apostle is clothed with the shame of the cross and where everything is counted as dung, can Paul receive resurrection hope.[62] Barth maintains that Paul's death is not simply 'a painful preliminary, a catharsis, a *via negativa*, a mystical emptying, which would afterwards the more surely be followed by an uplift, a replenishment, a beatific vision and enjoyment';[63] rather, Paul's death is nothing more and nothing less than the death of the apostle.

Developments of Barth's Understanding
Barth's perspective on Philippians has been developed most noticeably in the French world by Pierre Bonnard,[64] Michel Bouttier[65] and, in a unique way, Jean François Collange.[66] Barth's influence is also to be noted in German commentaries on Philippians, most notably in Gerhard Friedrich's commentary[67] and his comparison of Philippians with letters from prisoners in antiquity.[68]

Bonnard, like Barth, stresses Paul's consciousness of being a servant in the advance of the gospel and for the glory of Christ.[69] For example, Phil. 1.20 describes 'une attente ardente de ce qui doit arriver bientôt, une attente la tête haute'. Here Paul expresses his assurance that Christ will be glorified in his service, whether in life or in death (to be preferred to a life that does not glorify Christ).[70] So it is not suffering

---

61. *Philippians*, p. 107.
62. *Philippians*, p. 105, citing Rom. 6.8. Cf. Bultmann, *Theology*, pp. 300-302, 351.
63. *Philippians*, pp. 103-104.
64. P. Bonnard, *L'épître de saint Paul aux Philippiens* (Neuchâtel: Delachaux & Niestlé, 1950).
65. M. Bouttier, *Christianity according to Paul* (trans. F. Clarke; London: SCM Press, 1966).
66. J.F. Collange, *L'épître de saint Paul aux Philippiens* (Neuchâtel: Delachaux & Niestlé, 1973); *De Jésus à Paul* (Geneva: Labor et Fides, 1980).
67. G. Friedrich, *Philipper* (Göttingen: Vandenhoeck & Ruprecht, 1968).
68. G. Friedrich, 'Der Brief eines Gefangenen', in *Auf das Wort kommt es an* (ed. J.H. Friedrich; Göttingen: Vandenhoeck & Ruprecht, 1978), pp. 224-35.
69. Bonnard, *Philippiens*, p. 9.
70. *Philippiens*, pp. 27-29.

3. Alternative Approaches 61

that Paul emphasizes in Philippians but the glorification of Christ.[71]

In suffering, Paul's example is Christ himself, who was always the obedient servant of God—even when that obedience meant death (cf. Phil. 4.12; 2 Cor. 11.7; 12.21).[72] Christ is also the example for the Philippian Christians (3.17-21), who were called to withstand the rejection of the world, to serve their brothers without a desire for results, to be concerned only with how God views their actions, and to ignore those who refuse to be 'stripped' by Christ of all their righteousness.[73] Their calling is not first of all to continue firm in faith in the midst of persecution (as often suggested),[74] but (1) to be constant in propagating the faith,[75] and (2) to be firm when facing false teaching, in order to assure the progress of the gospel.[76]

That such a Barthian approach conflicts at crucial points with the interpretations of suffering influenced by Christ-mysticism is clear from André Feuillet's fierce criticism of Bonnard. According to Feuillet, Bonnard's view is 'a systematic and extreme simplification of the Apostle's eschatological doctrine',[77] since, for Paul, death is the fulfilment of the process that begins with baptism—a process that leads the apostle constantly towards death, which is the more perfect gaining of Christ that 'permits the Christian to share in the life-giving death of Jesus even more perfectly than he or she had ever to that point been able to share'.[78]

The questions raised by Feuillet are important. Are the sufferings Paul speaks of instrumental or consequential? Is death with Christ entirely a future reality or is there a present participation that becomes more real in the death of the believer? How else, Feuillet would say, can resurrection be operative in the life of Paul unless Paul actually died and was raised with Christ?

The answer to many of these questions is provided by Bouttier, who develops further the notion, implicit in Barth, of Paul's relationship

---

71. P. Bonnard, 'Faiblesse et puissance du chrétien chez saint Paul', *ETR* 30 (1958), pp. 62-63.
72. Bonnard, *Philippiens*, pp. 44-45.
73. *Philippiens*, p. 66.
74. *Philippiens*, p. 76, citing 1.12, 25-26; 4.12, 14, 19.
75. *Philippiens*, p. 36 on 1.30; also p. 53 on 2.17.
76. *Philippiens*, p. 21 on 1.12.
77. A. Feuillet, 'Mort du Christ et mort du chrétien d'après les épîtres pauliniennes', *RB* 66 (1959), p. 503 n. 1.
78. 'Mort du Christ', pp. 506, 509.

with the Philippian community. For as Bouttier sees it, though in baptism all of Christ's sufferings become Paul's, Paul's pursuit of Jesus' example, his '"straining forward to what lies ahead"',[79] is not characterized by religion—that is, by a 'withdrawal, individualization, and inwardness',[80] a 'process of spiritualization' in which the body is transformed by contact with the πνεῦμα or a 'gradual ascent towards the eternal peaks'[81]—but by proclamation, by which Bouttier understands the living of a life oriented 'towards outward things, towards other people, towards communication'.[82] So, according to Bouttier, Paul knows Christ in his present life most fully in the form of the community.[83] This is so not because the body is the *locus* of the manifestation of Christ, but because Paul stands with the Philippian community 'as a landmark at the crossroads...a rallying-point on the way to the cross', along with others who 'are there with him, showing in their lives, too, what it means to be a disciple of the crucified one'.[84] Paul is no preacher of a proleptic resurrection experience; rather, he recognizes the long road that lies ahead of him and his communities until the parousia.

Bouttier's use of Barth to read Philippians is very important in that it underscores the way in which in Philippians the apostle and his converts live in a situation of longing (cf. 3.21). Paul's desire (cf. 1.23) is 'to overcome the resistance that time and bodily existence still offer to complete communion with his Lord, whose presence is revealed at the heart of an absence that the apostle at times feels poignantly'.[85] Suffering for Paul is a grace not because it brings believers into a more perfect ontological *union* with Christ but because it convinces believers in a decisive way that they remain infinitely *separated* from Christ and from the fullness of resurrection.[86] Suffering is not evidence of a proleptic *fullness* but of a *longing* for fullness, a longing that is itself a sign of grace.

79. Bouttier, *Christianity*, p. 77.
80. *Christianity*, p. 24.
81. *Christianity*, pp. 22-24.
82. *Christianity*, p. 24.
83. Bouttier quotes favourably Bonhoeffer's 'Christus als Gemeinde existierend' (*Christianity*, p. 60).
84. *Christianity*, p. 55.
85. Bouttier, *Christianity*, p. 36.
86. Cf. Rumscheidt, 'Need', p. 7.

3. Alternative Approaches 63

Collange also lays stress on the community as a hermeneutical key for understanding Philippians, and so reveals his indebtedness to Barth. He is also, however, clearly informed by contemporary critical treatments of Philippians. So Collange, following Gnilka, views Philippians as a redactional composition of two letters—the second of which particularly interests us—and argues that the occasion for the second letter (1.1–3.1a; 4.2-7; 4.21-23) was different from that of the first: the uproar that Paul's revelation of his Roman citizenship to the Roman authorities caused not at Rome but at Philippi. Paul is joyful at the surprise and wonder that this revelation caused among those around him.[87] The Philippian Christians' reaction to this news, however, was not so unambiguous. Some at Philippi received the news of Paul's imminent release with excitement and preached Christ boldly (1.14), while others, whom Collange (unlike Schmithals, Koester, Gnilka and Jewett) believes to have held to an orthodox cross-centered theology, opposed Paul's action. They saw in it a sign of cowardice in the face of a martyrdom, a martyrdom in which Christ would have been made even better known.[88] Thus in 'second' Philippians, Paul seeks to correct the state of affairs at Philippi—that is, inner rivalries, dissensions and jealousies—that resulted from his decision to declare his Roman citizenship.[89]

Collange understands Paul as responding to the affair by stressing his communion with the Philippians. Paul, says Collange, makes it absolutely transparent that his entire apostolic ministry is a participation with the Philippian believers.[90] Paul counters the reaction of those who begrudge him his freedom by stating that, in making known his Roman citizenship, his desire was to be spared for service in order to be able to strengthen the Philippian believers. At this juncture in history Paul feels that the gospel demands his life more than his death.[91] So in Philippians Paul fights to convince his readers that, in not fleeing to some artificial paradise, he follows his Lord who, having thrown himself into the fray, has turned the history of humanity upside down, 'la transformant de fond en comble, mais pour y établir son Règne',[92]

87. Collange, *Philippiens*, p. 53.
88. *Philippiens*, p. 54.
89. *Philippiens*, p. 27.
90. *Philippiens*, p. 131.
91. *Philippiens*, p. 51.
92. *Philippiens*, p. 34.

and, by so doing, has established the prime eschatological fact within history.[93]

Contrary to Christ-mysticism, Collange does not believe that Paul's joy is found in mystical martyrdom but in the community's delight at the advance of the gospel.[94] Life 'in Christ' does not so much express mystical participation as it does 'the life of the community of those who place themselves under the lordship of the one who strips himself of all lordship, as Phil. 2.1-11 shows so well'.[95] The advance of the gospel is not automatic, certainly not according to any *ex opere operato* quality of mystical martyrdom.

Barth's influence is also to be seen in Gerhard Friedrich's work on Philippians. Echoing Barth, Friedrich observes that in Philippians Paul does not show himself to be primarily concerned about his own fate. His words indicate, rather, selfless interest in the well-being of the community.[96] In fact, says Friedrich, Paul evidences none of the neuroses of prisoners in antiquity[97]—for example, their self-centredness, feelings of guilt, righteousness, sufferings, desires for freedom and feelings of isolation.[98] The extant letters of prisoners in antiquity are filled with concerns for release and evidence clear reversion to primitive, survival instincts. Philippians, however, reflects Paul's other-centred joy and concern not for his own release but for the good report from the community.[99]

Thus Friedrich highlights the striking fact that, in spite of dreadful prison life, the dominant note in Philippians is one of joy.[100] The tone is not

> one of a passing emotional surge, not a momentary mood; it does not arise from an unrealistic, optimistic view of life; rather, although Paul sees, knows, and experiences the vicissitudes of prison life, they do not bother him, for Christians, he says, should always be joyful (1.4; 4.4).[101]

93. *Philippiens*, p. 38.
94. *Philippiens*, p. 101 on 2.17.
95. Collange, *Jésus à Paul*, p. 201.
96. Friedrich, 'Brief', pp. 226-27; *Philipper*, p. 99 on 1.7, 101 on 1.12.
97. Friedrich, 'Brief', pp. 224-35; *Philipper*, p. 102 on 1.18.
98. Friedrich, 'Brief', p. 225, citing W. Michaelis, 'Die Gefangenschaftsbriefe des Paulus', *NKZ* 36 (1925), p. 587.
99. Friedrich, 'Brief', pp. 230-34, citing Phil. 1.24; 2.2, 19, 24; *Philipper*, p. 102 on 1.18.
100. Friedrich, 'Brief', pp. 224-25.
101. 'Brief', p. 233; cf. *idem*, *Philipper*, p. 103: 'die Freude des Apostels ist so

3. Alternative Approaches

It is this understanding of Philippians, suggests Friedrich, that allows us to resolve the meaning of 4.10-14, which must not be read as Paul's complaint about his situation—comparable to that of other prisoners who lacked food and feared starvation—but as an affirmation by Paul of the all-sufficiency of Christ.[102]

In fact, says Friedrich, suffering for Christ in the advancement of the gospel is a manifestation of the grace of God,[103] present also in the Philippian Christians who suffer for the gospel and so extend it.[104] Accordingly, in contrast to the experience of timelessness, aimlessness and resignation experienced by prisoners in antiquity, Paul's sufferings were understood by him as purposeful. His imprisonment was an opportunity for the further preaching of Christ and an indication that the parousia was closer.[105]

Barth's critique of previous views of Philippians provides us with a valuable corrective. It yields insights into the nature of Philippians, particularly those having to do with the stress on Paul's apostolate, the question of community, and the expected victory rather than perpetual suffering. In its stress on Paul's longing the Barthian approach clearly taps a vein that needs much more attention than it has as yet received.

4. Daniel Patte and Structural Semiotics

The study of New Testament texts has in recent years begun to shift away from both historical-critical approaches and theological approaches.[106] Of those interpretative approaches that have appeared today, two figure prominently: the structuralist approach[107] and that

---

gross und mächtig, dass sie durch nichts gemindert werden kann, was die Zukunft auch bringen mag'.

102. Friedrich, 'Brief', pp. 231-34; cf. *idem, Philipper*, p. 203 on 1.18-19.
103. Friedrich, *Philipper*, pp. 100 on 1.7, 106 on 1.29.
104. *Philipper*, pp. 105-106 on 1.27.
105. Friedrich, 'Brief', pp. 228-30.
106. On the demise of historical-critical and theological approaches to the New Testament, see P. Stuhlmacher, *Historical Criticism and Theological Interpretation: Toward a Hermeneutics of Consent* (trans. R.A. Harrisville; Philadelphia: Fortress Press, 1977), esp. pp. 66-71; *Vom Verstehen des Neuen Testaments: Eine Hermeneutik* (NTD, 6; Göttingen: Vandenhoeck & Ruprecht, 1979), esp. pp. 205-25.
107. Cf. D. Patte, *What is Structural Exegesis?* (GBSNTS; Philadelphia: Fortress Press, 1976); T. Hawkes, *Structuralism and Semiotics* (Berkeley: University of California Press, 1977).

of semiotics.[108] In his book on Paul Daniel Patte combines both.[109] In so doing Patte provides a significant advance over the interpretations examined above.

Unlike previous interpretations, Patte's arguments do not rest on a comparison of Paul with contemporary texts or on an appeal to preexisting interpretations. Patte breaks with interpretations that remain at the 'dialogic level' of the text, where Christ and Paul are simply figures whom believers are to imitate.[110] Patte discerns that at the 'warranting level' of Paul's discourse[111] there is a system of convictions operative in the letters that is expressed by means of descriptions of situations in which God manifests himself. These descriptions are what Patte calls 'types':[112] individuals or situations in which what the believers presently experience was first experienced.[113]

Patte divorces Paul's discourse from the prescriptive way it has been traditionally understood and shows how the discourse functions more in the realm of description. For example, in 1 Thessalonians, Patte notes, Paul points to God's manifestation of himself in the experience of believers at Thessalonica, an experience comparable to those of Paul and of Jesus because it is of the same 'type' as Paul's and Jesus'.

Patte argues that this same system of convictions is operative in Philippians.[114] He outlines five areas in which this system is worked out in Philippians and accordingly how it governs the meaning of the particular elements of the letter, including that of suffering.

First, in Philippians Paul views his life as a fulfilment of the Jesus-type. Patte carefully avoids the main pitfall of Christ-mysticism by showing how Paul can say that his life 'is Christ' (1.21) without confusing his identity ontologically with that of Christ. Patte does not point to a revelational or functional identity but to the way in which Paul's life is Christ-like, that is, how in his life there are Christ-like

---

108. In addition to Hawkes, see also an important series of essays showing the value of semiotics for biblical studies, *De Jésus et des femmes: Lectures sémiotiques, suivies d'une entrevue avec A.J. Greimas* (Recherches, 14; Montreal: Bellarmin; Paris: Cerf, 1987).

109. *Paul's Faith and the Power of the Gospel* (Philadelphia: Fortress Press, 1983). For Patte's definition of structural, see pp. xiv-xviii

110. For the meaning of 'dialogic level', see *Paul's Faith*, p. 127.

111. For the meaning of 'warranting level', see *Paul's Faith*, pp. 127-28.

112. *Paul's Faith*, p. 80.

113. *Paul's Faith*, p. 171.

114. *Paul's Faith*, p. 136.

3. Alternative Approaches 67

experiences. Patte is thus able to explain how knowing Christ (3.10) implies neither commonality of intention nor ontological union but rather

> finding in one's experience both resurrection-like events (manifestations of the power of the resurrection) and Christ-like sufferings (i.e. situations which are like Christ's death).[115]

So Paul's sufferings reproduce Christ's sufferings descriptively not ontologically.

Secondly, Patte discerns that as Jesus as type is fulfilled in Paul, Paul himself becomes a type for the believers at Philippi because they see Paul as the 'fulfillment of the type "Christ"'. Here again Patte carefully avoids an error of Christ-mysticism that even Käsemann and his followers did not avoid, for, though Käsemann and his followers see that Paul's sufferings are kerygmatic to the Philippian congregation, they hold that Paul actually becomes an incarnate Christ. Patte, however, notes that Paul's sufferings descriptively mirror the Christ reality, yet without actually making Christ present.[116]

Thirdly, Patte notes that believers at Philippi (as at Thessalonica) also becomes types when they fulfil the 'Christ' type and the 'Paul' type. Patte correctly stresses that this is literally the case of believers addressed in 1 Thessalonians who are called 'types' for other believers throughout Achaia. This was also, Patte insists, true of believers addressed in Philippians, who, though they are not referred to as types, can indeed be seen to have been so. Thus it is not that these believers have become apostles or new Christs; rather, they fulfilled the 'promises contained in Jesus' experience' in that they, like Paul, mirrored the Christ type.[117]

Fourthly, and as a result of the third point, Patte suggests that in Philippians types are teleological. Here Patte evidences clear indebtedness to the Barthian approach, although he succeeds in incorporating it into his own structuralism. In Patte's system the parousia is for Paul a consummation of all the experiences that are types,[118] which themselves point to 'the deliverance that Christ will effect at his parousia'

---

115. *Paul's Faith*, p. 173.
116. Cf. D. Stanley, '"Become Imitators of Me"', *Bib* 40 (1959), p. 865.
117. Patte, *Paul's Faith*, p. 177.
118. *Paul's Faith*, pp. 178-80.

(e.g. Paul's deliverance from imprisonment prefigures the parousia fulfilment).[119] Accordingly,

> Christ-like events in [Paul's] present experience... are not an end in themselves, but promises, prefigurations, or preliminary manifestations of what he will receive at the Parousia, the prize... At the Parousia the type, Jesus' death and resurrection and the promises contained in the Christ-like events of their experience, will be totally fulfilled.[120]

Thus, in Patte, eschatological expectation does not rest on ontological transformation or on the present experience of resurrection power, but on the confidence that Jesus' experience will be that of those who fulfil his type in their lives. Echoing Barth and his followers, Patte shows how resurrection is the dynamic feature of the letter and, accordingly, one of the key features in Paul's presentation of suffering.

Perhaps the one feature, however, that Patte has neglected is related to his fifth area. If Patte had stressed this feature more, his argument would have been complete. Patte notes that Jesus and Paul are themselves fulfilments of the type of Old Testament prophets—as evidenced, for example, by Paul's appeal to the figure of Moses and his final charge to the people of Israel.[121] Much more, however, could be said in terms of other Old Testament types, as, for example, that of the suffering servant. As Windisch and Weinrich suggested, Christ, Paul, the apostolic team and the Philippians themselves all seem to be fulfilments of the type of the suffering servant, whatever traditio-historical trajectory that figure followed from its origins to Paul's day. This is a point stressed recently by Gerd Theissen, who argues that Paul presents himself in various roles: in Gal. 1.15-16 in the role of the servant of Isa. 49.1; in Phil. 3.12-16 in the role of an athlete straining to leave behind and stretching forward; and in 1 Cor. 9.19-23 in the role of Christ who became all things to all men.[122] Combining Theissen's and Patte's suggestions, we might say that in each of these roles, Paul is fulfilling the Christ type.

Despite, however, this minor emendation of his work, the insights Patte presents us with are valuable for understanding Philippians.

---

119. *Paul's Faith*, p. 180.
120. *Paul's Faith*, p. 174 on 3.11.
121. *Paul's Faith*, p. 187.
122. Cf. G. Theissen, *Psychologische Aspekte paulinischer Theologie* (Göttingen: Vandenhoeck & Ruprecht, 1983), pp. 181-268, esp. 235, 254-55. Theissen acknowledges his indebtedness to Y. Watanabe and H. Sundén (p. 45).

3. Alternative Approaches

Patte's structural semiotics provides us with another alternative to approaches dominated by twentieth-century Western metaphysics of ontology.

5. Conclusion

In the first chapter we saw how interpretation of Philippians moved from interpretation governed by the experience of the persecuted church of that day to interpretation carried out under the aegis of philosophically significant categories, such as *intentio*. In the second chapter we saw how interpretation of suffering in Philippians shifted away from the traditional view as appeal was made to history-of-religions parallels. In this third chapter we have seen how suffering in Philippians continues to be interpreted in the light of history-of-religions parallels (Lohmeyer, Weinrich), but also how it begins to be interpreted in new, theological categories (Käsemann, Güttgemanns) or old ones (Barth, Collange).

To some extent Daniel Patte's work falls into this latter, theological category. Yet Patte's study also represents an attempt to break new methodological ground in the study of Paul by using structural semiotics to discover the underlying structure of Paul's thought, his system.

Here Patte has set before us the task of uncovering the material that still lies buried within Philippians, for Patte's work presupposes that the individual components of Paul's letters function to communicate a deeper meaning than the one immediately apparent to the reader today. For this reason Patte seeks (1) to understand what Paul is communicating to his readers but also (2) how Paul's statements communicate that message.[123] In this way Patte is able to suggest, for example, that Paul's concern is *not* how suffering unites him with Christ, for the fulfilment of Paul's life remains in the future for him (as Barth and his followers have stressed); rather, Paul's deeper concern is the mimetic function of suffering, that is, how suffering serves to describe Christian experience that is otherwise intangible.

Such a shift from apparent theological argumentation to structural analysis is an important one, for it has opened anew Paul's letters to

---

123. For a recent overview of the implications of the methodological shift at work here, see S. Brown, 'Reader Response: Demythologizing the Text', *NTS* 34 (1988), pp. 232-37.

scholarly study. The structuralist approach as used by Patte, however, is limited by its essential inability to go beyond the structures of Paul's *thought*—a secondary issue, with which commentators have occupied themselves from earliest times until our own day—to the structures of Paul's *letter*—a primary issue, since it is in the letter that Paul says what he thinks.

Thus more can and needs to be said regarding Paul's letters. The question is not primarily what the structures of Paul's thought are but first of all what the structures of Paul's letter are, and how the individual components within those structures play a role. So in discussing how suffering functions in Paul's message, one needs first to ask how suffering functions in the communication of that message and how the epistolary structure and rhetorical conventions of a particular letter carry that communication. Here, then, is clearly an area that has not been dealt with seriously enough—certainly not in the case of Philippians.

PART II

EPISTOLARY STRUCTURE AND RHETORICAL FUNCTIONS

Chapter 4

LETTER-WRITING AND RHETORIC IN ANTIQUITY

1. *Letter-Writing in Antiquity*

Epistolography and Non-Literary Letters

One of the most important contributions to the study of the Pauline *corpus* in recent years has been in the area of the form and function of Paul's letters. Although we have long been apprised of the uniqueness of Paul's letters, greater precision has now made it possible and necessary to say more than that in a broad way the letters of Paul are *sui generis*.[1] Such precision has come about through the examination of ancient Hellenistic letters.[2]

In 1907–1908, Adolf Deissmann challenged the scholarly world to a reassessment of Paul's writings in terms of non-literary letters as preserved on the papyri.[3] Deissmann's contention was that Paul's writings ought not to be considered epistolary literature but rather 'true' letters.

Deissmann assigned the name 'epistolary literature' to the letters of Dionysius of Halicarnassus, Plutarch, Seneca, Pliny the younger *et al.*, as well as to the pseudonymous letters of Aristotle and Cicero. He contended that these letters are essentially public, artistically created epistles intended for publication and preservation.[4] According to Deissmann, these writings are letters only in so far as they contain epistolary touches and are addressed.[5]

Paul's letters, however, he argued, are not epistolary but 'true'

---

1. H. Chadwick, *The Enigma of St Paul* (London: Athlone Press, 1969), p. 19.
2. See the history of this examination in J.L. White, 'The Ancient Epistolography Group in Retrospect', *Semeia* 22 (1982), pp. 1-14.
3. A. Deissmann, *Light from the Ancient East* (trans. L.R.M. Strachan; Grand Rapids: Baker, repr. 1965 [1927]).
4. Deissmann, *Light*, pp. 148, 229-33.
5. Deissmann, *Light*, p. 232.

letters. In the light of his examination of 26 non-literary papyri from the fourth century BCE to the seventh century CE, Deissmann concluded that Paul's letters, though 'less stereotyped' and containing different 'favorite epistolary phrases',[6] share with the non-literary papyri the form of 'true' letters, that is, letters intended simply as a means of communication between two individuals and intended to be read only by them.[7] There is no set form or content.[8]

This is not to say that Deissmann was right in claiming that non-literary letters had no set form. Deissmann himself admitted that over the course of centuries 'a number of formal peculiarities were developed, and we not infrequently find the same forms becoming stereotyped into formulae'.[9]

Indeed, since Deissmann, scholars have begun to note in these letters clearly defined structures and clearly defined epistolary formulae that determine the epistolary structure of a letter and keep it moving.[10] These conventions are not neatly defined and strictly delimited phenomena but rather conventions that 'punctuate a break in the writer's thought'.[11] Such breaks may be major structural ones or ones that are more comparable to contemporary punctuation.[12] I proceed therefore to an examination of the conventions and the structure to which they point.

Conventions and Structures in the Papyri and Paul
The opening. In the non-literary Greek papyri there are specific

---

6. For the first point, see J.L. White, *The Form and Function of the Body in the Greek Letter: A Study of the Letter-Body in the Non-Literary Papyri and in Paul the Apostle* (SBLDS, 2; Missoula, MT: Scholars Press, 2nd edn, 1972), p. 68, and W.G. Doty, *Letters in Primitive Christianity* (GBS; Philadelphia: Fortress Press, 1973), p. 27; for the second, Doty, *Letters*, p. 42.
7. Deissmann, *Light*, p. 228.
8. *Light*, pp. 228-29.
9. *Light*, p. 228.
10. See esp. F.X.J. Exler, *The Form of the Ancient Greek Letter* (Washington, DC: Catholic University of America, 1923); H. Koskenniemmi, *Studien zur Idee und Phraseologie des griechischen Briefes bis 400 n. Chr.* (Helsinki: Suomalaien Tiedeakatemie, 1956); J.L. White, *Light from Ancient Letters* (Philadelphia: Fortress Press, 1986).
11. T.Y. Mullins, 'Formulas in New Testament Epistles', *JBL* 91 (1972), p. 387.
12. Mullins, 'Formulas', p. 388: 'Except for the Pauline thanksgiving and perhaps the opening, it is not the nature of these forms to introduce, but to punctuate'.

opening formulae. These opening formulae—together with closing formulae—are directed specifically to the epistolary function of keeping the sender and recipient in touch. The letter opening, together with the letter closing, 'reveals the general character of the correspondents' relationship toward each other'.[13]

Normally the letter opening formula contains the following tripartite structure: (1) identification of sender(s) in the nominative case, (2) identification of addressee(s) in the dative case, and (3) a greeting such as χαίρειν.[14] For example, PHib 1.40 contains Πολέμων 'Α[ριμο]ύθηι χαίρειν, a clear example of the customary tripartite structure.[15] In fact, so stereotyped are these formulae that Exler has suggested four kinds of letters according to their opening formulae: familiar, business, petitionary or applications, and official.[16] Parts (1) and (2) are inverted in some business letters, in petitionary letters and in the later Roman adaptation of the Greek letter,[17] possibly in order to stress the sender's inferiority.[18] Expansion is made on the letter opening when familial relations are at stake[19] or when authority demands it.[20]

In Paul the opening formulae follow the same tripartite structure: 'A (nominative) to B (dative)' plus greetings. Usually one finds expansions both of the sender(s)—Paul (or a Pauline imitator) often

13. White, *Light*, p. 219.
14. Studies of the opening formulae in Greek letters are found in Exler, *Form*, pp. 23-132; J.L. White, 'Epistolary Formulas and Cliches in Greek Papyrus Letters', in *Society of Biblical Literature 1978 Seminary Papers* (ed. P.J. Achtemeier; Missoula, MT: Scholars Press, 1978); idem, *Light*, pp. 19 and 198, and the texts adduced therein, pp. 23-186.
15. White, *Light*, p. 24; for a list of papyri containing parallel opening formulae, see Exler, *Form*, pp. 24-25.
16. Exler, *Form*, p. 23.
17. White, 'Epistolary Formulas', pp. 291-93. See his summary of forms from the third century BCE to the fourth century CE ('Epistolary Formulas', p. 295); also Exler, *Form*, pp. 33-132.
18. White, *Light*, p. 19. E.g. PTebt 1.48: Μεγχεῖ κωμογραμματεῖ Κερκεοσίρεως παρὰ Ὤρου κωμάρχου καὶ τ[ῶν] πρεσβυτέρων (in White, *Light*, p. 86).
19. White, 'Epistolary Formulas', p. 291; idem, *Light*, pp. 19, 199. E.g. BGU 4.1207: Ἰσιδώραι Ἀσκληπιάδηι τῶι ἀδελφῶι χαίρειν (in White, *Light*, p. 105). See also Exler, *Form*, pp. 25-27.
20. E.g. PTebt 2.289: [Ἀ]πολλώνιος στρατηγὸς Ἀκοῦτι τοπάρχῃ Τεβτύνεως χαίρειν (in White, *Light*, p. 116).

4. Letter-Writing and Rhetoric in Antiquity 75

identifies himself by means of a distinctive appellative, such as ἀπόστολος (1 Cor. 1.1; 2 Cor. 1.1; Rom. 1.1; Gal. 1.1 [cf. Eph. 1.1; Col. 1.1])[21]—and of the addressee(s)—when making mention of the addressees Paul may invoke a theological theme (e.g. referring to the addressees as ἅγιοι, as in 1 Cor. 1.2) or note the readers' geographical region (as in 1 Cor. 1.2).[22] This might suggest a familial background or an appeal to authority, after the pattern of the papyri. Finally, Paul consistently expands on the greetings found in the papyri and in other New Testament letters by means of his own Christianized revision (χάρις) and by the addition of εἰρήνη, a 'conscious' continuation of the Hebrew שלום.[23]

The thanksgiving. In some papyrus letters, following the letter opening but preceding the information that the writer wished to communicate, a thanksgiving or formulaic health wish may be found.[24] This section of an ancient letter functions by way of maintaining the relationships between writer and addressee(s).[25] It takes the form of thanks to the god(s) for the addressees' health or well-being[26]—thus being often an intercession to the gods[27]—or of thanks to the addressee(s) for a favour.[28] It is generally followed by a statement of the sender's own health.[29] Consistency, however, is not the norm in these thanksgiving periods, for 'though the phraseology is generally similar within

---

21. White, *Light*.
22. Cf. White, *Light*, pp. 29-30. We find the former in PRyl 2.231: Ἀμμώνιος Ἀφροδισίωι τῷ φ[ι]λτ[άτῳ] χαίρειν (White, *Light*, p. 123); the latter in PBour 12: Πλάτων τοῖς ἐν Παθύρει ἱερεῦσι καὶ τοῖς ἄλλοις τοῖς κατοικοῦσι χαίρειν (White, *Light*, pp. 95-96). For the former, cf. the extensive list in Exler, *Form*, pp. 29-30.
23. Doty, *Letters*, p. 30. For double greetings in Greek letters, cf. Exler, *Form*, pp. 32-33; White, *Light*, p. 200.
24. White, 'Epistolary Formulas', pp. 295-98.
25. According to Mullins ('Formulas', p. 388) the thanksgiving is not a prerequisite until Paul's letters (though cf. Galatians and 2 Corinthians).
26. PCair Zen 1.59060: [εἰ ἔ]ρρωσαι, ἔχοι ἂν καλῶς (White, *Light*, p. 38).
27. PCair Zen 1.59076: εἰ σύ τε ἔρρωσαι καὶ τὰ σὰ πάντα καὶ τὰ λοιπά σο[ι κατὰ νοῦν ἐστίν, πο]λλὴ χάρις τοῖς θεοῖς (White, *Light*, p. 39).
28. PYale 40.24: εὐχαριστήσεις οὖν μοι ἐπιμελούμενος τοῦ σώματός σου ἵνα ὑγιαίνηις (White, 'Epistolary Formulas', p. 297).
29. White, *Light*, p. 200; e.g. UPZ 2.68: εἰ ἔρρωσαι, ἔρρωμαι δὲ καὐτός (White, *Light*, p. 74).

each century, the subtle variety of expression is almost bewildering'.[30] In Paul's letters—with the exception of Galatians (where it is absent)[31] and 2 Corinthians (where it is replaced by a blessing formula)[32]—the thanksgiving period takes two forms: (1) a brief, structurally simple four-part unit: εὐχαριστῶ + τῷ θεῷ + πάντοτε περὶ ὑμῶν + ὅτι (1 Cor. 1.4-9; Rom. 1.8-10; 2 Thess. 1.3-12); or (2) a slightly more complex four-part unit: εὐχαριστῶ + a temporal participial construction defining the action of the principal verb (e.g. μνείαν ποιούμενος) + a second, causal participial construction defining the action of the principal verb (e.g. ἀκούων) + a final clause, modifying the entire principal clause (e.g. ὅπως) (Phlm 4-6; 1 Thess. 1.2-10; Col. 1.3-8; Phil. 1.3-11; cf. Eph. 1.3-14).[33]

The body. The primary unit of the Greek private letter is the letter body. Here the writer seeks (1) to inform his addressee(s) of the information that has motivated the letter, or (2) to request something of the recipient.[34] The structure of the body is usually tripartite, divided into the body opening, body middle and body closing.

1. The body opening, marked by readily identifiable body opening devices, 'plays the role of "disclosing" a pressing matter of mutual concern',[35] that is, of introducing the information the writer will pass on or the request with which the body will deal. It is, thus, 'the point at which the principal occasion for the letter is usually indicated',[36] proceeding, as does spoken conversation, from a basis common to both parties. It lays the foundation from which the superstructure may grow.[37]

The body opening can usually be identified by an introductory

---

30. White, 'Epistolary Formulas', p. 295; cf. Mullins, 'Formulas', p. 382.
31. Though cf. POxy 2.291 (White, *Light*, p. 119), where the demand follows directly on the opening.
32. Doty, *Letters*, p. 33.
33. Schubert, 'Pauline Thanksgivings', pp. 3-4; cf. White, 'Epistolary Formulas', p. 296.
34. White, *Light*, p. 207.
35. White, *Body*, p. 59.
36. White, *Body*, pp. 18-19; cf. *idem*, 'Introductory Formulae in the Body of the Pauline Letter', *JBL* 90 (1971), p. 97.
37. White, *Body*, pp. 18-19; cf. *idem*, 'Introductory Formulae', p. 97; J.T. Sanders, 'The Transition from Opening Epistolary Thanksgiving to Body in the Letters of the Pauline Corpus', *JBL* 81 (1962), pp. 349-53.

4. Letter-Writing and Rhetoric in Antiquity 77

formula.³⁸ White discusses the following introductory formulae found in the papyri:

Informational formulae
1. Disclosure phrases (e.g. γινώσκειν δὲ θέλω ὅτι).
2. Notice of appended letter (e.g. ὑπογέγραφα σοι τῆς [τά] παρὰ... ἐλθούσης μοι).
3. Response to information received (e.g. ἐκομισάμην τὸ παρὰ σοῦ ἐπιστόλιον, ἐν ὧι γράφεις...).
4. Acknowledgment of or compliance with received information or questions (e.g. καθάπερ ἡμῖν ἔγραψας or περί + genitive).³⁹

Request formulae (plus instructions and background statements)
1. Expressions or dissatisfaction or disbelief (e.g. θαυμάζω ὅτι; ἐγὼ δὲ καὶ πρότερόν σοι ἐγεγράφειν περὶ τούτων).
2. Expressions indicating the need of urgent response (e.g. ὡς ἂν τάχιστα λάβῃς τὴν ἐπιστολήν, λαβέ...).
3. Presentation of circumstances or background (non-formulaic, though common usage employed the genitive absolute, other participial constructions, or ἐπεί) (e.g. παραγινουμένου μου ἐγ Βουβάστου...; ἐπεὶ διέγνωσται τὸν ἐπιμελητὴν παραγίνεσθαι...).
4. Simple requests introducing the material of the body (introduced by καλῶς ποιήσεις or by non-formulaic instructions).⁴⁰

Body opening disclosure formulae are well documented in Paul's letters as well.⁴¹ They may be classified as disclosure formulae (1 Thess. 2.1; Phil. 1.12; 2 Cor. 2.8; Gal. 1.11-12; Rom. 1.13), request formulae (Phlm 8-14; 1 Cor. 1.10), joy expressions (Phlm 7; cf. Phil. 4.10), expressions of astonishment (Gal. 1.6-7), statements of compliance (Gal. 1.9), formulaic uses of a verb of hearing or learning (Gal. 1.13-14).⁴²

2. The body middle is where the information to be passed on or the request to be made is related. Although the subjects dealt with in an

---

38. White, 'Introductory Formulae', p. 97.
39. White, *Light*, p. 207.
40. White, *Light*, p. 208.
41. Cf. 1 Thess. 2.1; 4.13; 1 Cor. 10.1; 12.3; 15.1; 2 Cor. 1.8; 8.1; Rom. 1.13; 7.1; 11.25; Gal. 1.11; Col. 2.1; 4.7-9; Eph. 6.21-22.
42. White, *Body*, pp. 48-52, 69-75.

ancient letter were as varied as the topics of daily life,[43] the categories of information dealt with in the body largely fall under certain discernible headings, viz., requests (or thanks) for favours, disclosure of information of interest to both parties in the correspondence, response to previous correspondence, communication, reception of parcel post, or mention of a visit on the part of the sender.[44] White discusses five different types of letters—introduction and recommendation, petition, family, memoranda and consolation—in terms of the content communicated in the body of the letter.[45]

Although non-literary papyri rarely contain a body middle of sufficient length to discuss fully,[46] two types of transitional formulae can be discerned. First, there are the major formulae, whose function is to introduce and, in some cases, to conclude the middle. White suggests two forms: 'formulaic references to writing and set verbs of saying and informing'.[47] These formulae are not limited to the body middle,[48] so that the use of one form early in the letter (e.g. a disclosure formula) will lead to its recurrence throughout the letter[49]— including its appearance in the body middle.

Secondly, there are lesser transitional formulae, whose function is to keep the argument moving.[50] Such formulaic conventions may be simple conjunctions (οὖν, διό, ὅθεν), more elaborate conjunctions (ἔτι οὖν καὶ νῦν, δὲ καί,[51] ὁμοιῶς δὲ καί, ἀλλὰ μήν or καὶ μήν[52]), περί plus genitive,[53] conditional clauses,[54] a disclosure formula,[55]

---

43. J. Sykutris, 'Epistolographie', RE Supp., V, pp. 199-200.
44. White, 'Epistolary Formulas', pp. 302-305.
45. Cf. White, Light, pp. 193-97, 203.
46. White, Light, p. 211.
47. White, Body, p. 33; cf. pp. 33-36.
48. Mullins, 'Formulas', pp. 386-87.
49. As happens in PMich 203; so Mullins, 'Formulas', p. 387: 'The use of one form tends to precipitate the use of others with it'.
50. White, Light, p. 211.
51. White, Body, pp. 36-37.
52. Epicurus, Letter to Herodotus, in C. Bailey, Epicurus (Oxford: Clarendon Press, 1926), passim.
53. White, Body, pp. 16-17.
54. Body, pp. 13-15.
55. Body, pp. 2-5. Cf. POxy 745.6: οὐχ οἶδας γὰρ πῶς μοι ἐχρήσατο..., or POxy 1219.11: ἀλλὰ οἶδα ὅτι καὶ ταῦτα μου γράμματα, from the first and third centuries CE, respectively (White, Body, p. 5).

4. Letter-Writing and Rhetoric in Antiquity 79

expressions or reassurance,[56] responsibility statements,[57] grief or anxiety statements,[58] as well as non-formulaic transitional statements, such as receipt or writing statements.[59] Also significant are epistolary 'clichés', whose role is not essential to the argument but which 'provide nuance, tone or mood to an epistolary convention'.[60] These clichés may take the form of softening a request by using the ethical dative, conditional verbs and adverbial expressions with verbs of writing, speaking and making, or by intensifying an imperative by adverbial expressions or the use of the vocative.[61]

A variety of transitional devices are found throughout the Pauline body middles. For example, one finds disclosure formulae,[62] temporal clauses with ὅτε δέ,[63] the use of the vocative,[64] οὐ γάρ,[65] etc.

3. The body closing is the section in which the sender reiterates his good wishes for the health of the addressee(s) and/or his desire to visit or to have news about them.[66] Underlying these functions is the function of acting as a bridge to future contact.[67] Not surprisingly, then the body closes with reiteration of the reason for writing (e.g. γέγραφα οὖν ὅπως εἰδῆς), with requests for information (e.g. γράψον ἡμῖν ἵνα εἰδῶμεν), or with urgings to responsible action (e.g. μὴ οὖν ἀμελήσῃς..., or φρόντισον οὖν ἵνα...).[68] Sometimes the addressee(s) is (are) encouraged by the sender's word of confidence that the action will be taken (e.g. οἶδα γὰρ ὅτι);[69] sometimes the

---

56. White, *Body*, pp. 5-7.
57. *Body*, pp. 7-9.
58. *Body*, pp. 9-10.
59. *Body*, pp. 10-13.
60. White, *Light*, pp. 211-12, following the work of H.A. Steen, 'Les clichés épistolaires dans les lettres sur papyrus grecques', *Classica et Medievalia* 1 (1938), pp. 119-76.
61. Cf. White, *Body*, pp. 15-16.
62. 1 Thess. 2.1; 4.13; 1 Cor. 10.1; 12.3; 15.1; 2 Cor. 1.8; 8.1; Rom. 1.13; 7.1; 11.25; Gal. 1.11; Col. 2.1; 4.7-9; Eph. 6.21-22.
63. Gal. 1.15; 2.11.
64. Gal. 3.1.
65. Rom. 1.15; 2.13; 3.22.
66. White, *Light*, p. 204.
67. White, *Body*, p. 59; *Light*, p. 205.
68. White, *Light*, pp. 204-205.
69. White, *Light*, p. 205; 'Epistolary Formulas', p. 306.

sender(s) make(s) threats so that action will be taken.[70] Finally, in the body closing we often find a recommendation to the addressee(s) of the letter carrier or emissary.[71]

The Pauline body closings have been closely analysed by R.W. Funk.[72] As in the body closing of the Greek private letter, in Paul we also find a reiteration of the reason for writing and of the responsibility incumbent upon the reader(s) to comply with the motivation.[73] It is also in the body closing, however, that we find a formula by means of which Paul expresses confidence in the obedience of his reader(s),[74] an expression which, according to White, represents 'the greatest formal difference between the body closing in Paul and the corresponding section in the papyri'.[75] For it is in his body closings that Paul alleges confidence that the claims that he, as an apostle, has set forth in the preceding motivation section will be heeded. In fact, so strong is the note of apostolic authority in the body closings of Paul's letters that Funk has suggested that the Pauline body closings may be the strategic centre of his various letters, a centre that sets out a statement of apostolic authority and presence through the apostle's own personal presence, the letter, or the emissary carrying the letter.[76]

It is this function that has led Funk, who once called this section a 'travelog', to give the name 'apostolic parousia' to the whole of the Pauline body closing.[77] Given the epistolographic understanding of a

---

70. White, *Light*, p. 205.
71. Contrast this with the earlier letters of recommendation where this function is found immediately after the letter opening (White, 'Epistolary Formulas', pp. 300-301; *Light*, p. 204).
72. R.W. Funk, 'The Apostolic Parousia', in *Christian History and Interpretation* (ed. W.R. Farmer, C.F.D. Moule and R.R. Niebuhr; Cambridge: Cambridge University Press, 1967), pp. 249-68; *idem, Language, Hermeneutic, and Word of God* (New York: Harper & Row, 1966), *idem, Parables and Presence* (Philadelphia: Fortress Press, 1982).
73. Phlm 19; Gal. 5.2; Rom. 15.14-15; 1 Thess. 2.17-19; Phil. 2.19-23; 1 Cor. 4.14-15. Here one often finds a 'formulaic statement of authorship', such as ἐγὼ Παῦλος; cf. White, *Body*, p. 63.
74. Phlm 21; Gal. 5.10; Rom. 15.14-15; 1 Thess. 2.19-20; Phil. 2.24; 1 Cor. 4.16; cf. White, *Body*, p. 99.
75. White, *Body*, p. 99.
76. Phlm 21-22; Gal. 4.12-20; Rom. 15.14-33; 1.8-13; 1 Thess. 2.17–3.13; Phil. 2.19-24; 1 Cor. 4.14-21; cf. White, *Body*, pp. 60-61; Doty, *Letters*, p. 37.
77. Funk, 'Apostolic Parousia', pp. 249-68; White, *Body*, p. 60.

4. Letter-Writing and Rhetoric in Antiquity 81

letter as a substitute for one's physical presence, Funk argues that the Pauline letter is itself an apostolic presence to the community wherein Paul particularly stresses the confidence he has in the recipients to fulfil and complete what he had written. This confidence is due, in part, to their faithfulness. It is also due, however, to the apostolic nature of the words: the message itself requires fulfilment.

Beyond the letter itself, Funk has drawn attention to the role played by the apostolic emissary. On the basis of Romans 15, Funk argues that 'the apostolic emissary... substitutes for the apostle himself, while the letter is at best written authority for what the emissary has to say'.[78] He spells out the following scenario: although Paul desired to visit his addressees, he suffered a delay which forced him to send an envoy in his place; the envoy, in effect, substituted for the apostle.[79] By means of the body closing, not only did Paul indicate to the addressees his trust in these carriers, who were also his co-workers; Paul also used the letter-carriers as bearers of oral information or interpretation of the letter. Paul 'did not think of his written letters as exhausting what he wished to communicate. He thought of his associates, especially those commissioned to carry his letters, as able to extend his own teachings.'[80]

Despite, however, the importance of the letter-carrier, Funk's findings are inadequate grounds for his statement that

> since Paul gives precedence to the oral word, the written word will not function as a primary medium of his apostleship. It is for this reason that [an expression of writing in the body closing] does not loom so large in the Pauline letters as it does in the non-literary papyri.[81]

Funk contradicts himself when he notes that Paul emphasized the physical letter when mention of an apostolic emissary was lacking but left the letter unstressed when the emissary was mentioned.[82] The point is that Paul saw his letters as having apostolic character, but expressed that character differently depending on the concrete situation. The

---

78. White, *Body*, p. 260.
79. According to Doty, the trusted carrier of a letter had great importance in antiquity because of political intrigue and an insecure postal system. In fact, Doty goes so far as to suggest that the importance of all letter-carriers in antiquity derives from the importance given to Paul's letter-carriers (*Letters*, pp. 45-46).
80. Doty, *Letters*, pp. 45-46.
81. Funk, 'Apostolic Parousia', p. 260.
82. 'Apostolic Parousia', p. 261.

Pauline letters were, as Doty describes them, 'the essential part of the messages Paul had to convey, pressed into brief compass as a basis for elaboration by the carrier'.[83]

The closing. Epistolary conventions also appear in the closing of non-literary letters. Such conventions include not only a word of farewell (ἔρρωσο / ἔρρωσθε) but also formulae that recall the opening and the thanksgiving, for example, a wish for good health for the recipient(s) of the letter[84] or other assurances of goodwill and greetings.[85] In addition, the closing provides 'a convenient clustering place for matters of minor importance which the writer wants to add before breaking off'.[86]

All Paul's letters, with the exception of Galatians, conclude with greetings. A closing blessing is also frequently found (1 Thess. 5.23-24, 28; 2 Thess. 3.16, 18; Phil. 4.23; Rom. 16.20; 15.13; 2 Cor. 13.11, 13). Paul's letters also show other concluding elements: a signature in Paul's own hand (2 Thess. 3.17; 1 Cor. 16.21; Gal. 6.11; Col. 4.18a; Phlm 19), mention of an amanuensis (Rom. 16.22), specific paraeneses from Paul himself that are probably in his own handwriting (1 Thess. 5.25; 1 Cor. 16.22; Col. 4.17-18b; Gal. 6.12-17; Rom. 16.1-2, 17-19), instructions about the reading of the letter (1 Thess. 5.27; Col. 4.16), an order to greet believers with a holy kiss (1 Thess. 5.26; 1 Cor. 16.20; 2 Cor. 13.20; Rom. 16.16), and a doxology (Rom. 16.25-27).

Paul's Letters: Literary, Non-Literary, or Mixed?

Deissmann enabled us to take seriously the form and function of non-literary papyri. The fruits of his revolutionary stance are clear and are daily more appreciated. Nevertheless, the question needs to be asked: are Paul's letters non-literary in the way the papyri examined by Deissmann and others are? Deissmann insists that they are indeed, 'real letters, not epistles... written by Paul not for the public and posterity, but for the persons to whom they are addressed'.[87] Or, are Paul's letters more like the examples of literary letters adduced by

83. Doty, *Letters*, pp. 45-46.
84. Exler, *Form*, pp. 69ff.
85. E.g. PMich 8.476: ἀσπαζεταί σε Ἐπιτυγχάνων. ἄσπασαι πάντες τοὺς φιλοῦντες [ἡμᾶς] κατ' ὄνομα (White, *Light*, p. 175); cf. White, *Light*, p. 202.
86. Mullins, 'Formulas', p. 387.
87. Deissmann, *Light*, p. 234; cf. p. 240.

4. Letter-Writing and Rhetoric in Antiquity 83

Klaus Thraede.[88] In actual fact it is not clear whether Paul's letters are non-literary in the same fashion as the non-literary papyri or are literary letters.

More cautiously, and writing less than 30 years after Deissmann, J. Sykutris criticized Deissmann's radical distinction between literary and non-literary: 'Die Grenzen zwischen dem literarischen und dem Privatbrief nicht scharf gezogen werden'.[89] Sykutris himself notes the diverse *Gattungen* available to letter-writers in antiquity, including 'der publizistische Brief', 'der Lehrbrief', magical and poetical letters, etc.[90] Recently, A. Malherbe has noted some 40 letter types that the epistolary theorist Ps. Libanius had classified.[91]

Thus while it appears that Paul's letters share with the non-literary papyri close formulaic and structural parallels, Paul's letters are not reducible to the merely personal and inconsequential nature of non-literary communications. On the other hand, however, it does not appear that Paul's letters were intended to be the literary monuments envisioned for many epistolary essays. It might perhaps be more accurate to view Paul's letters as examples of a mixing of letter styles and types. In part Paul's letters come close to the 'mixed form' of the letter so disparaged by Deissmann as examples of 'what a real letter should not be'.[92] For while Paul's letters share formulaic and structural elements of the non-literary papyri, they are also 'more than half-intended for publication'.[93] In fact, in terms of content, Paul's letters resemble more Sykutris's *Lehrbrief*, associated with the letters of Epicurus and Seneca, than they do the papyri examined by Deissmann.

Whether this means that they also evidence 'frigidity, affectation, and vain insincerity', Deissmann's words of invective for the mixed letter,[94] remains to be seen. Deissmann's words, however, raise an important question for us: if Paul's letters are more than mere communication of information, then they are more than Deissmann's

---

88. K. Thraede, *Grundzüge griechisch-römischer Brieftopik* (Munich: Beck, 1970).
89. Sykutris, 'Epistolographie', p. 187.
90. 'Epistolographie', pp. 200-208.
91. A.J. Malherbe, 'Ancient Epistolary Theorists', *Ohio Journal of Religious Studies* 5 (1977), pp. 3-77.
92. Deissmann, *Light*, p. 230.
93. *Pace* Deissmann, *Light*.
94. Deissmann, *Light*.

'true' letter; but if they are indeed more than that, then how, in fact, do they function? The answer to this question must come through a closer examination of Paul's letters in the context of ancient rhetoric.

2. Rhetoric in Antiquity

Rhetoric and Letters

A key presupposition underlying epistolography is that a letter is a substitute for the personal presence of its author.[95] The letter is a tool 'for communication between a writer and a specific reader or group of readers' and shows 'the writer's attitude toward the *audience* to which he is writing'.[96] As White points out, 'the letter is, after all, only a substitute for the actual presence'.[97] Letter style and its component elements were modelled for ancient scribes in epistolary handbooks, such as those of Ps. Demetrius and Ps. Libanius.[98] According to the epistolary theorist who wrote under the name of Demetrius in *On Style*, the letter ought to be a 'worthy substitute for one's conversation'[99] and so ought consequently to proceed like conversation.[100]

As the author of *On Style* goes on to note, however, this is not the whole story, since neither posturing not dramatic discourse have a place in the letter (4.226), nor does mere dialogue (4.224). Although a letter, like conversation, will convey 'the writer's personality and reflect his mood',[101] providing glimpses of character (4.227), it will also be 'un produit artificiel qui demande le travail d'un homme formé par les livres et qui se rend compte des différences de style'.[102] This balance is to be achieved, writes Ps. Demetrius, by using what Aristotle defined as 'periods' loosely (4.229), simply (4.231), and gracefully (4.235)—qualities that accord with Ps. Demetrius's discussion of

---

95. So Doty, *Letters*, pp. 11-12.
96. Mullins, 'Formulas', p. 388 (emphasis his). As we shall see, a letter does indeed also show a writer's 'attitude toward the *material* he is presenting' (*pace* Mullins).
97. White, 'Epistolary Formulas', p. 307.
98. Cf. Malherbe, 'Ancient Epistolary Theorists'; White, *Light*, pp. 189-90.
99. White, *Light*, p. 191.
100. Ps. Demetrius, *On Style* 4.223: δεῖ ἐν τῷ αὐτῷ τρόπῳ διαλογόν τε γράφειν καὶ ἐπιστολὰς εἶναι γὰρ τὴν ἐπιστολὴν οἷον τῷ ἕτερον μέρος τοῦ διαλόγου.
101. White, *Light*, p. 191.
102. Steen, 'Clichés', p. 122.

4. Letter-Writing and Rhetoric in Antiquity 85

epistolary theory under the general heading of simple style.[103] Furthermore, a letter is motivated by a situation that a sender seeks to address, and so to convey what he would have said orally were he to have been present. Occasionality is very evident in the letters of the non-literary papyri, for all deal with a specific matter that necessitated in the sender's mind the letter at hand. Occasionality, in fact, is for ancient epistolary theorists at the very root of all letters. Cicero noted that letters are occasioned by necessity, that is, in order 'that we might inform those at a distance if there were anything which it was important for them or for ourselves that they should know'.[104]

The three basic principles that underlie epistolography—substitute for personal presence, occasionality and a desire to persuade—suggest that while a letter's *structure* may be determined by epistolary analysis, the *function* of the structural components must be examined not only in terms of epistolary analysis but also in terms of ancient rhetoric.

Rhetoric in Antiquity

Discussion of epistolary structure, then, obliges us to discuss rhetorical presuppositions and structure. The reason is that the science of letter-writing was governed by the general canons of rhetoric. Rhetoric was divided, according to Aristotle, into three γένη:[105] τὸ δικανικόν, τὸ συμβουλευτικόν, τὸ ἐπιδεικτικόν, or, respectively, *genus iudiciale*, *genus deliberativum*, *genus demonstrativum*.[106] Each of the three *genera* has a specific function. Forensic rhetoric is used when something is controverted, when there is an accusation or petition with a defence.[107] Deliberative rhetoric is used when persuasion or dissuasion in the course of deliberation is involved.[108] Epideictic rhetoric or rhetoric of praise is used when praise or blame is assigned to someone.[109] In each of these *genera*, particular or multiple *quaestiones* or *causae* are involved, 'because there the *causa* is first brought or because

---

103. See G.M.A. Grube, *A Greek Critic: Demetrius on Style* (Toronto: University of Toronto, 1961), pp. 104-14.
104. Cicero, *Letters* 2.4.1, cited in White, *Light*, p. 190.
105. *Rhet.* 1.3 (1358b7-8).
106. *Rhet. Her.* 1.2.2.
107. *Rhet. Her.* 1.2.2.
108. *Rhet. Her.* 1.2.2.
109. *Rhet. Her.* 1.2.2.

the *causa* consists in that'.¹¹⁰ Furthermore, each rhetorical *genus* will develop the *quaestiones* in its own terms.¹¹¹

The process of discovering the *quaestio* (*intellectio*) is followed by the formulation of the process of argumentation (*inventio*) through which the rhetor will seek to convince his listeners of the truth of his position.¹¹² This argumentation will proceed through *oratio* in parts, about which, however, there appears to have been no consensus of specifics.¹¹³ Thus *Rhet.* 3.13 states that the necessary parts of a rhetorical address are two, πρόθεσις and πίστις. Later authors, however, find as many as seven parts to an *oratio*: *exordium, narratio, digressio, propositio, partitio, argumentatio, epilogus*.¹¹⁴ Lausberg has conveniently divided the necessary parts of a rhetorical *oratio* into four: *exordium, narratio, argumentatio* and *peroratio*.¹¹⁵

The Parts of a Rhetorical Address

Exordium. A rhetorical *oratio* commences with a προοίμιον¹¹⁶ or *exordium*.¹¹⁷ Stated most simply, the *exordium* 'is all that can be said before the judge prior to his being informed of the matter itself'.¹¹⁸ It appears, however, to have two specific functions. First, according to Cicero, 'the beginning is a clear oration, primarily making the audience well-disposed, or docile, or attentive'.¹¹⁹

The shape of the *exordium* will depend on the kind of the *causa*.¹²⁰

---

110. *Inst.* 3.6.4. According to Lausberg, though the *quaestio* is proper to forensic and deliberative rhetoric, which are close in their form of argumentation, it is also found in epideictic rhetoric (H. Lausberg, *Handbuch der literarischen Rhetorik*, I [Munich: Hueber, 1960], pp. 123, 61).
111. Cf. Lausberg, *Handbuch*, pp. 85-138 for examples.
112. *Rhet. Her.* 1.2.3: 'inventio est excogitatis rerum verarum aut veri similium, quae causam probabilem reddant'.
113. Lausberg, *Handbuch*, p. 147.
114. *Handbuch*, pp. 148-49.
115. *Handbuch*, pp. 150ff.
116. *Rhet.* 3.14 (1414b19).
117. *Inv.* 1.15.20–18.26; *Inst.* 4.1; Lausberg, *Handbuch*, p. 150; J. Martin, *Antike Rhetorik: Technik und Methode* (Handbuch der Altertumswissenschaft; Munich: Beck, 1974), pp. 60-75; D.F. Watson, 'A Rhetorical Analysis of Philippians and its Implications for the Unity Question', *NovT* 39 (1988), pp. 61-63.
118. R. Volkmann, *Die Rhetorik der Griechen und Römer in systematischer Übersicht* (Hildesheim: Olms, 1963 [1885]), p. 128.
119. *Inv.* 1.15.20; Volkmann, Rhetorik, p. 128; Lausberg, Handbuch, pp. 150-60.
120. Martin, *Antike Rhetorik*, p. 70.

4. Letter-Writing and Rhetoric in Antiquity 87

In the *genus causae honestum* (or εὔδοξον) 'either we defend what appears to be defended by all, or we oppose what it seems ought to be rejected by all'.[121] In this case, since the audience is already sympathetically inclined and need not be won over,[122] the *exordium* may be omitted and appeal is made to narrative, law, strong reason, or to goodwill that already exists.[123] In the *genus causae dubium* or *anceps* (or ἀμφίδοξον), 'the *causa* has within it both an element of honesty and of deceit'.[124] That is, the person may be respectable but the action be in doubt, or vice versa.[125] Here the *exordium* opens with an appeal made on the basis of that which is perceived to be not in doubt 'so that the *causa* should appear to fall within the domain of the *genus honestum*'.[126] In the *genus causae admirabile* (or παράδοξον) both the action and the person are looked on with disfavour by the audience.[127] In this case the *causa* needs to be proven and justified against all expectations, either by winning the goodwill of the audience or by *insinuatio* ('an oration that covertly makes suggestions to the mind of the audience by means of dissimulation and circumvention').[128] In the *genus causae humile* (or ἄδοξον), the speaker dismisses the *causa* as unimportant (*Bagatellsache*), thus removing the audience's upset at the *causa* and, hopefully, at the person involved.[129] Finally, in the *genus causae obscurum* (or δυσπαρακαλούθητον) the audience is slow or the subject is extremely complex.[130] An introduction is an absolute necessity in order to prepare the audience for what follows.[131]

A second function, according to Anaximenes, is that the *exordium*

---

121. *Rhet. Her.* 1.3.5; cf. Lausberg, *Handbuch*, p. 57; Martin, *Antike Rhetorik*, p. 70.
122. *Inv.* 1.15.20.
123. *Inv.* 1.15.21.
124. *Rhet. Her.* 1.3.5.
125. *Inv.* 1.15.20; cf. Lausberg, *Handbuch*, pp. 57-58; Martin, *Antike Rhetorik*, pp. 70-71.
126. *Inv.* 1.15.21.
127. *Inv.* 1.15.20; cf. Lausberg, *Handbuch*, p. 58; Martin, *Antike Rhetorik*, p. 71.
128. *Inv.* 1.15.20-21; cf. Lausberg, *Handbuch*, pp. 160-61.
129. *Inv.* 1.15.20; Lausberg, *Handbuch*, pp. 58-59; Martin, *Antike Rhetorik*, p. 70.
130. *Inv.* 1.15.20; cf. Lausberg, *Handbuch*, p. 59; Martin, *Antike Rhetorik*, p. 71.
131. *Inv.* 1.16.21.

88   *The Function of Suffering in Philippians*

summarizes the pertinent matters.[132] It does so by establishing the point of view of the addressor,[133] or by preparing the readers for what is to come.[134]

Narratio. The *exordium* is followed by a *narratio*, a statement of past events, explanations of present events, or prediction of future events.[135] The purpose of the *narratio* is to establish the matter in dispute, as well as the persons involved[136] and to persuade concerning the particular presentation made[137]—a persuasion that will be completed in the *argumentatio* that follows.

The necessary qualities of the *narratio* are 'ut brevis, ut aperta, ut probabilis sit'.[138] Brevity implies that the *narratio* says only what needs to be said, does not include details that might distract from the substance of the story, and does not digress.[139] Quintilian, however, seems to allow for considerable embellishment,[140] even to the extent of a lengthy excursus.[141] Clarity or *perspicuitas* is gained by presenting the details of the *causa* in an ordered fashion and, in general, in such a way that accords with the simplicity and brevity just described.[142] Plausibility or credibility is gained if the story appears to accord with real life—that is, characters act as they are supposed to act; the reasons for their actions are clear and convincing; events could have happened as explained; etc.[143]

Argumentatio. Because of its centrality and importance to the rhetorical *oratio*, the *argumentatio* takes a variety of forms and is structured according to the needs of the *oratio*. Briefly stated, however, the

132. *Rhet. ad Alex.* 1436a34-39; *Inv.* 1.16.23.
133. Volkmann, *Rhetorik*, p. 142.
134. *Rhet. ad Alex.* 1436a33–1438a1; cf. *Rhet.* 3.14 (1415a23-24); Martin, *Antike Rhetorik*, p. 63.
135. *Rhet. ad Alex.* 1438a4-6; *Inst.* 4.2.3; *Inv.* 1.19.27 mentions only past and present events (cf. *Inst.* 4.2.31).
136. *Inv.* 1.19.27; *Inst.* 4.2.4.
137. *Inst.* 4.2.21; Lausberg, *Handbuch*, p. 167.
138. *Inv.* 1.20.28; cf. *Inst.* 4.2.31; *Rhet. Her.* 1.9.14.
139. *Inv.* 1.20.28; *Inst.* 4.2.40-51; *Rhet. ad Alex.* 1438a22.
140. *Inst.* 4.2.116-24.
141. *Inst.* 4.2.64.
142. *Inv.* 1.20.29.
143. *Inv.* 1.20-21.29; *Inst.* 4.2.36-39, 52-60.

4. Letter-Writing and Rhetoric in Antiquity 89

purpose of the *argumentatio* is to develop the material introduced in the *exordium* and *narratio*.[144]

Rhetoric is no simple, artless presentation of proofs,[145] but skilful *argumentatio*, developed using the forms of *signa, argumenta* and *exempla*.[146] *Signa* consist of 'anything by which something else is understood',[147] that is, something which represents or stands for something other than what it is immediately (e.g. a blood-stained rag from which a crime may be inferred). *Signa* are used by the rhetor to bring his audience to the necessary inference that something has happened that accords with his *causa*.[148]

If *signa* are things by which something is inferred, *argumenta* are 'the means by which reason offers proof, whereby something is gathered by means of something else, and by which what is doubtful is confirmed by what is not doubtful'.[149] This is done by means of proofs or appeal to higher principles,[150] either through syllogistic inductive or deductive *ratiocinatio*,[151] or by drawing arguments from *loci*, that is, persons or actions,[152] viz., a person's *nomen, natura, victus, fortuna, habitus, affectio, studium, consilium, facta, casus,* or *orationes*,[153] or an action's coherence and performance.[154]

Exempla or παραδείγματα also form part of rhetorical induction.[155] In these cases, by appeals to *similia, dissimilia,* or *contraria*, one infers the conclusions of the *quaestio* on the basis of points already conceded.[156] Among *exempla*, Quintilian notes, the most powerful kind and which we properly call *exemplum* is 'the calling to mind of a

---

144. *Inst.* 5.Pr.4.
145. Lausberg, *Handbuch*, pp. 191-92.
146. *Inst.* 5.9.1; cf. Lausberg, *Handbuch*, p. 194.
147. *Inst.* 5.9.9; cf. 5.9.1 for examples.
148. *Inst.* 5.9.12.
149. *Inst.* 5.10.11.
150. *Inv.* 1.24.34-41.77; cf. *Rhet ad. Alex.* 1438b29-1439b2.
151. See below; cf. Lausberg, *Handbuch*, pp. 198-99, for a helpful overview of the inductive side.
152. *Inv.* 1.24.34; Lausberg, *Handbuch*, pp. 201-20.
153. *Inv.* 1.24.34-25.36; *Inst.* 5.10.23-31; cf. Lausberg, *Handbuch*, pp. 204-206.
154. *Inv.* 1.26.37-28.43; *Inst.* 5.10.32-52; cf. Lausberg, *Handbuch*, pp. 206-20.
155. *Inst.* 5.11.1-2.
156. *Inst.* 5.11.3, 6.

deed itself or of a deed that will be useful for persuading the audience of what you intend'.[157] The first half of the rhetorical argument is the *confirmatio*[158] or *probatio*.[159] In it the speaker provides a ground of credibility, authority and solidity in an attempt to confirm and prove the *narratio*.[160] The intention is thus to show *probabiliter* or demonstrate *necessarie* the truth of the *narratio*.[161] According to Quintilian, it opens with a *propositio*[162] or *partitio*,[163] although, according to Lausberg, the *propositio* 'is the intellectual core of the *narratio* itself'.[164]

The second half of the *argumentatio* is the rhetorical ἀνασκευή[165] or *reprehensio*,[166] sometimes also called the *refutatio*.[167] Its function is to introduce arguments against the speaker's opponents: 'in argumentation the *reprehensio* is the means whereby the *confirmatio* of the opponents is refuted, or weakened, or impaired'.[168] According to Cicero, it uses the same sources of invention as does the *confirmatio*, viz., inductive or deductive reasoning,[169] either (1) 'when, from those things that are mentioned, nothing at all be conceded', (2) 'if the assumptions are granted, it is appropriate to deny that a conclusion follows from them', (3) 'if the genus itself of the argumentation can be shown to be fallacious', or (4) 'if, against strong argumentation, other equally strong or even stronger points can be made'.[170] At times, those opponents may be real persons who engage in dialogue with the speaker; more often than not, however, they are negative foils for the speaker, that is, figures who hold a position that is con-

---

157. *Inst.* 5.11.6.
158. *Inv.* 1.24.34.
159. *Inst.* 5.
160. *Inv.* 1.24.34.
161. *Inv.* 1.29.44.
162. *Inst.* 4.4.1.
163. *Inst.* 4.5.1.
164. Lausberg, *Handbuch*, p. 189. It is not a separate rhetorical unit (*pace* H.D. Betz, *Galatians: A Commentary on Paul's Letter to the Church in Galatia* [Hermeneia; Philadelphia: Fortress Press, 1979], p. 114).
165. *Rhet. ad Alex.* 1439b4–1439b14.
166. *Inv.* 1.42.78.
167. Lausberg, *Handbuch*, p. 236.
168. *Inv.* 1.43.78.
169. *Inv.* 1.43.78.
170. *Inv.* 1.42.79.

4. *Letter-Writing and Rhetoric in Antiquity* 91

trary or opposed to that of the speaker. It is possible that Quintilian's words on *exemplum dissimile* and *exemplum contrarium* may have been invoked here.[171]

Peroratio. The *peroratio* or *conclusio* is the 'exitus et determinatio totius orationis'.[172] Its function is twofold. First, it summarizes the *oratio*, and thus functions as *enumeratio* or *recapitulatio*.[173] As a summary, 'the matters that have been dealt with at various, scattered points are collected in one place and are placed under one point of view in order to bring them to mind once more'.[174] Secondly, the *peroratio* contains the parting words of the *oratio* and the final attempt by the rhetor to persuade his audience by exciting ill-will against the opponent (*indignatio*)[175] and/or by arousing pity and sympathy for his own *causa* or person (*conquestio*).[176]

Exhortatio. As noted above, although the structure of the *oratio* in its constituent parts is clear, much scope is given in rhetorical treatises to the development of an argument in terms that suit the speaker, audience and matter discussed. Rhetorical texts, however, have been viewed by some as falling far short of a clear understanding of the place of exhortation.[177] There is no clear consensus concerning the place of exhortation in rhetorical argumentation.[178] In fact, it is striking that Betz's commentary on the extensive portion he assigns to the Galatian exhortation, viz. 5.1–6.10, does not attempt to integrate the passage 'into the general rhetorical scheme which he finds in the

171. *Inst.* 5.11.7.
172. *Inv.* 1.52.98.
173. *Inst.* 6.1.1.
174. *Inv.* 1.52.98. According to Quintilian the *enumeratio* should be brief and concise *(Inst.* 6.1.2).
175. *Inv.* 1.53.100: 'oratio per quam conficitur ut in aliquem hominum magnum odium aut in rem gravis offensio concitetur'.
176. *Inst.* 6.1.1; *Inv.* 1.53.106: the *conquestio* 'est oratio auditorum misericordiam captans', which the speaker does 'locis communibus... per quos fortunae vis in omnes et hominum infirmitas ostenditur'. *Inst.* 6.1.9-12 establishes the emotional *peroratio* as a separate form of *peroratio*, not simply different *loci*.
177. Betz, *Galatians*, pp. 253-54.
178. Cf. Betz, *Galatians*, p. 254 n. 13: A. Malherbe, *Moral Exhortation: A Greco-Roman Sourcebook* (Library of Early Christianity, 4; Philadelphia: Westminster Press, 1986), pp. 121-34.

letter'.[179] The reason is that a detailed exposition of exhortation as such is lacking in rhetorical manuals. Discussion of exhortation can nevertheless be found in the rhetorical treatises, though not under a specific heading. Quintilian, for example, treats ἦθος, together with πάθος or *adfectus*, in the context of the rhetorical *peroratio*,[180] although he does not seem to limit it to that part of the *oratio*.[181] According to Quintilian,

> since there is nothing that the orator does not deal with from an ethical angle, ἦθος is whatever is said about matters relating to honesty and usefulness, in short, what is to be done and not done.[182]

Quintilian is not, however, concerned so much with what may or may not be said but with what context is requisite for exhortation to obtain. Ethical injunction of this nature, he writes,

> is especially recommended among persons who are well-known to each other, who may act in ignorance, may make amends, and may admonish, but without anger and without hate.[183]

Furthermore, it requires that the speaker be a good and courteous man, rather than evil or vile, since 'he either ought to have or be believed to have those same virtues for which he commends the litigant'.[184]

A. Malherbe has classified at least three styles of moral exhortation in ancient rhetorical address: protreptic, paraenetic and diatribe.[185] Protreptic, according to Malherbe, is characterized by Aristotle's *Protrepticus* and Ps. Isocrates' *To Demonicus*, as well as by later works such as the *Epistle to Diognetus*. It is a form of moral exhortation 'designed to win someone over to a particular enterprise or way of life by demonstrating its superiority'.[186] Paraenetic, on the other hand, is found in Paul, as well as in authors such as Seneca. In paraenetic exhortation 'someone is advised to pursue or abstain from

---

179. D. Aune, Review of H.D. Betz, *Galatians*, *RelSRev* 7 (1981), pp. 324-25.
180. See below.
181. *Inst.* 6.2.8-17. The reason for the treatment here concerns the origin in the emotions of both.
182. *Inst.* 6.2.11.
183. *Inst.* 6.2.14.
184. *Inst.* 6.2.18.
185. Malherbe, *Exhortation*, pp. 121-34.
186. *Exhortation*, p. 122.

4. Letter-Writing and Rhetoric in Antiquity 93

something'.[187] Finally, Malherbe points to the most complex form of moral exhortation, the diatribe, a 'philosophical treatment of an ethical topic designed to move people to action rather than reflection'.[188] It is especially known for its dialogical framework, as has been clarified by S.K. Stowers:

> the diatribe is... discourses and discussions in the school when the teacher employed the 'Socratic' method of censure and protreptic [in order] to transform the students, to point out error and to cure it.[189]

As is clear, each of these three styles could be used in the three *genera* of rhetoric discussed above. Thus while one can discover cases where one genre of rhetoric is contrasted with a style of moral exhortation,[190] it seems more accurate to see moral exhortation or ἦθος as exhortation that functions differently within a particular rhetorical *genus* and within each of the four parts.[191]

Rhetoric and the Letters of Paul

Clearly, Paul's letters are themselves best understood as substitutes for Paul's personal presence and as occasionally motivated.[192] Each of Paul's letters is directed to a particular situation and is Paul's own 'immediate response to a concrete life-situation'.[193] Accordingly, each has an 'epistolary situation' which, in the words of Paul Schubert,

> denotes the entire historical background in which writer and addressee are united. In its strictest sense it denotes the specific problems existing between and uniting the sender and the recipient in a unique and exclusive relationship. The letter is then the specific means through which these specific problems are being dealt with.[194]

---

187. *Exhortation*, p. 124.
188. *Exhortation*, p. 129.
189. S.K. Stowers, *The Diatribe and Paul's Letter to the Romans* (Chico, CA: Scholars Press, 1981), p. 76 (emphasis his).
190. *Diss.* 3.23, cited in Stowers, *Diatribe*, p. 59.
191. In fact, *Diss.* 3.23, may be viewed as a debate, not between epideictic rhetoric and protreptic exhortation, but between the epideictic and deliberative *genera* of rhetoric; cf. Lausberg, *Handbuch*, pp. 54-55.
192. Funk, 'Apostolic Parousia', p. 264 (citing 1 Thess. 2.17; Phil. 1.27; 2.12; 1 Cor. 5.3; 2 Cor. 10.1-2, 10-11; 13.2, 10; Col. 2.5).
193. P. Schubert, 'Form and Function of the Pauline Letters', *JR* 19 (1939), p. 376.
194. Schubert, 'Letters', p. 376.

As noted throughout Part I, much of preceding commentary study of Paul's letters has erred in that it has forced the argumentation of his letters to resemble the logical flow of arguments in a *quodlibetal* or theological manual. Paul's letters, however, are much more a concrete pastoral response to a situation that demands his attention.[195] Paul is 'not so much forging religious dogma as he is conveying his understanding of how Christianity might be structured in the concrete situational contexts of the particular addressees'.[196] His letters, in other words, are structured in the light of pressing needs.[197] Yet Paul's letters also reflect the epistolary theorists' awareness that a letter is more than just a conversation. For Paul, as for the theorists, a letter is also an attempt to persuade and so to bring his addressee(s) into line with his own way of thinking.

As noted above, various epistolary conventions allow a letter-writer to suggest strongly that the addressee(s) pay heed to what he says. We find this same persuasive authority in Paul's letters. Now it may be possible to argue, as Funk does, that Paul was conscious, whether in person or by letter, of 'charismatic, one might even say, eschatological power' accruing to his words.[198] It seems more accurate, however, to view Paul's injunctions as falling under the heading of rhetorical persuasion, similar to what can be found in many of the non-literary papyri and literary letters, as well as in rhetorical addresses of antiquity.

The role of rhetoric in the letters of Paul has recently begun to be stressed. Not only do we now have the more programmatic studies of Kennedy and Wuellner,[199] but now also the in-depth studies of H.D. Betz on Galatians and 2 Corinthians 8–9,[200] S. Stowers and F. Siegert

---

195. L. Keck, *Paul and his Letters* (Philadelphia: Fortress Press, 1979), p. 17; Beker, *Paul*, p. 62; Doty, *Letters*, p. 79.
196. Doty, *Letters*, p. 44.
197. G. Johnston, 'The Life of Christians in the World (Phil. 1.1–2.4)', *CJT* 3 (1957), p. 249.
198. Funk, 'Apostolic Parousia', p. 265.
199. G.A. Kennedy, *The Art of Rhetoric in the Roman World: 300 BC–AD 300* (Princeton: Princeton University Press, 1972); *idem, New Testament Interpretation through Rhetorical Criticism* (Chapel Hill, NC: University of North Carolina Press, 1984); W. Wuellner, 'Where is Rhetorical Criticism Taking Us?', *CBQ* 49 (1987), pp. 448-63. See S.K. Stowers, *Letter Writing in Greco-Roman Antiquity* (Philadelphia: Westminster Press, 1987).
200. See now also the work of G.W. Hansen, *Abraham in Galatians: Epistolary*

on Romans, M. Bünker and K. Plank on 1 Corinthians, R. Jewett and B.C. Johanson on 1 Thessalonians, D. Watson on the rhetorical structure of Philippians, and G. Lyons on Pauline autobiography.[201] A presupposition of these studies is not that Paul engaged in formal study and imitation of rhetorical models but that he and other New Testament authors shared basic cultural insights into appropriate forms of communication and address.[202] David Aune is still correct, however, to caution those who engage in rhetorical criticism:

> Perhaps one of the chief perils of the enterprise is the tacit assumption that all ancient literary compositions worthy of the name were consciously or unconsciously patterned after generic models which, when recognized, can provide the necessary keys for unlocking some of the enigmatic features of such texts. Literary variation, however, was one of the hallmarks of the Greco-Roman period.[203]

In spite of the possibility of error, it is fair to say that the present situation is a productive one. It is, however, also a confusing one. As C.C. Black notes:

> Characteristic of recent studies is a high degree of variance, if not outright confusion, among definitions of biblical rhetoric.[204]

Furthermore, 'while rhetorical models may function as heuristic guides, particular texts often resist preset patterns'.[205] In the chapters that follow I will suggest that our investigation of Philippians may

and Rhetorical Contexts (JSNTSup, 29; Sheffield: JSOT Press, 1989); H.D. Betz, *2 Corinthians 8 and 9: A Commentary on Two Administrative Letters of the Apostle Paul* (Hermeneia; Philadelphia: Fortress Press, 1985).
  201. Stowers, *Diatribe*; F. Siegert, *Argumentation bei Paulus: Gezeigt an Rom 9–11* (WUNT, 34; Tübingen: Mohr, 1985); M. Bünker, *Briefformular und rhetorische Disposition im 1. Korintherbrief* (GTA, 28; Göttingen: Vandenhoeck & Ruprecht, 1984); K.A. Plank, *Paul and the Irony of Affliction* (SS, 17; Chico, CA: Scholars Press, 1987); R. Jewett, *The Thessalonian Correspondence: Pauline Rhetoric and Millenarian Piety* (FFNT; Philadelphia: Fortress Press, 1986); B.C. Johanson, *To All the Brethren* (ConBNT, 16; Uppsala: Almqvist & Wiksell, 1987); G. Lyons, *Pauline Autobiography* (SBLDS, 73; Chico, CA: Scholars Press, 1975). For a recent update on the literature, see C.C. Black II, 'Keeping Up with Recent Studies, 16: Rhetorical Criticism and Biblical Interpretation', *ExpTim* 100 (1989), pp. 252-58.
  202. Cf. Kennedy, *New Testament Interpretation*, pp. 3ff.
  203. Aune, Review of Betz, p. 324.
  204. Black, 'Rhetorical Criticism', p. 253.
  205. 'Rhetorical Criticism', p. 255.

help to clarify some of the confused issues and, as well, show how particular texts can be clarified by means of rhetorical analysis.

3. Conclusion

Epistolary analysis has adequately shown that letters in antiquity have a structure of their own. While this has always been known concerning the literary letter of antiquity, it has now been abundantly demonstrated with regard to the non-literary letter as well. Furthermore, the structure is able to be traced using the formulaic conventions known to ancient letter-writers. Such an analysis has begun to reveal the structure of Paul's letters.

The function of Paul's letters, however, lies largely within the domain of rhetoric. For while the non-literary letter has a simple, unadorned structure intended for a simple purpose, Paul's letters appear to follow non-literary structure without being limited to the non-literary genre. They may be, as suggested above, an example of the mixed letter. As such, their purpose transcends the purely petitionary or informative purpose of the mass of non-literary letters. These letters use rhetorical devices to persuade.

The rhetorical function of the letter has begun to be studied in New Testament studies. This has resulted in exciting advances in our understanding of letters we have long possessed. These studies have also, however, raised the need for a method that will ensure scientific guidelines for the use of rhetorical analysis, rather than it simply serving as a backdrop for already established opinions.

Chapter 5

THE INTEGRITY AND EPISTOLARY STRUCTURE OF PHILIPPIANS

Prior to any discussion concerning Philippians as a letter and a rhetorical address, it is necessary to discern whether canonical Philippians is, in fact, one letter or a composite of two or three letters. This is an important task, for if Philippians is a redactional composition, then we cannot interpret the letter as an integral whole without doing serious injustice to Paul's words and their intent in his writing to the Philippian church.

1. *The Integrity of Philippians*

Arguments against the Integrity of Philippians
Various factors have led scholars to conclude that canonical Philippians, rather than being one letter, is, in fact, a redactional composite of two or three letters.[1] External evidence suggests that more than one letter to the Philippians existed. According to Polycarp *Phil.* 3.2, Paul wrote more than one letter to the Philippians:

> ὃς [Paul] γενόμενος ἐν ὑμῖν κατὰ πρόσωπον τῶν τότε ἄνθρωπον ἐδίδαξεν ἀκριβῶς καὶ βεβαίως τὸν περὶ ἀληθείας λόγον, ὃς καὶ ἀπὼν ὑμῖν ἔγραψεν ἐπιστολάς. . .[2]

In his chronicle of world events (*Chronographia*, c. 806–808 CE), Georgius Syncellus testifies to the existence of a first letter of Paul to the Philippians:

> τούτου καὶ ὁ ἀπόστολος ἐν τῇ πρὸς Φιλιππησίους μέμνηται πρώτῃ ἐπιστολῇ εἰπὼν κτλ.[3]

---

1. B.D. Rahtjen, 'The Three Letters of Paul to the Philippians', *NTS* 6 (1960), p. 167.
2. Lightfoot, *Apostolic Fathers*, II, p. 911.
3. G. Syncellus, *Chronographia* (Bonn, 1829), XII, p. 651.

Furthermore, the Syriac *Catalogus Sinaiticus* mentions a First Philippians and a Second Philippians.[4]

Internal evidence indicates literary seams, which have been taken by many to signal the juxtaposition of originally independent letters. So, for example, different topics seem to be conjoined within the letter without attention being paid to the unity of these themes. Thus in 1.12-26 Paul writes of his imprisonment; in 1.27–2.18 he exhorts the congregation; in 3.1-16 he deals with his opponents; in 3.17-4.7 he again exhorts the congregation; in 4.10-20 he adds a note of thanksgiving for a gift he received. Are all these seemingly disjoined sections telling us that Philippians as we now have it was originally in more diverse form?

Or, again, in Philippians the flow of Paul's logic from one topic to the next is unclear. For example, it has been argued that 1.1–3.1 is friendly while 3.2-11 is polemical. In chs. 1–2 a threat to the congregation is unclear, while in ch. 3 the threat is ominously clear.[5] As noted above, 4.10-20 seems to some to be an entirely separate letter of thanks,[6] for the end of a letter is hardly a proper place for a thank-you.[7] Henry Chadwick notes that the early fathers, too, were uneasy with Paul's hurried style, difficult intellectual arguments and sudden shifts in thought.[8] Such incongruities are, for some scholars, evidence that originally independent textual units were combined at some date after the actual writing of the units.

Thus, rather than one letter, Philippians is seen by many to be a redactional composition of two or more letters.[9] The consensus among those who advocate partition theories for Philippians is that 1.1–2.30 forms a single letter, that 3.2–4.1 forms another single letter, and that 4.10-20 forms a third single letter.[10]

In addition, it is proposed that these three letters were motivated by three entirely different occasions: (1) that 1.1–2.30 was originally a

---

4. Cf. Rahtjen, 'Three Letters', p. 168.
5. See Rahtjen, 'Three Letters', pp. 170-71.
6. Cf. Culpepper, 'Co-Workers', p. 349.
7. Rahtjen, 'Three Letters', pp. 172-73.
8. Chadwick, *Enigma*, pp. 4-5.
9. E.g. Bornkamm, 'Briefsammlung', p. 196.
10. Doubts concerning the actual parameters of these three letters are entertained only concerning the transitional verses 3.1 and 3.2, the paraenetic portion 4.2-9, and the closing 4.21-23.

5. The Integrity and Epistolary Structure of Philippians

letter of personal news and news about Timothy and Epaphroditus, (2) that 3.2–4.1 was a letter that sought to warn the Philippians concerning false teachers, and (3) that 4.10-20 was a thank-you note occasioned by the Philippians' financial gift. Only later were these three letters combined and redacted to form our present canonical letter.

Arguments for the Integrity of Philippians

Arguments against these partition theories have, of course, been suggested. First, the external evidence adduced can be explained in ways that do not negate the integrity of Philippians. The term ἐπιστολαί in Polycarp *Phil.* 3.2, for example, may refer to all of Paul's extant Macedonian correspondence, that is, 1–2 Thessalonians and Philippians;[11] may mean that Paul wrote more than one letter to the Philippians, of which Polycarp had knowledge, but of which only canonical Philippians remains extant;[12] may be an epistolary plural, in which case only one letter is in view;[13] or may refer to the collection of Paul's letters that was sent to all the churches, including Philippi.[14] With regard to George Syncellus's biblical history, it is possible that a copy error is involved.[15] Finally, the reference to a First and a Second Philippians in the *Catalogus Sinaiticus* is, according to Souter, 'an obvious case of dittography and παραβλεψία'.[16]

11. Lightfoot, *Philippians*, pp. 138-40, though cf. *idem*, *Apostolic Fathers*, II, p. 911.
12. Cf. Vincent, *Philippians*, p. 91 and B.S. Mackay, 'Further Thoughts on Philippians', *NTS* 7 (1961), p. 162.
13. Cf. Lightfoot, *The Apostolic Fathers*, II, p. 911; Vincent, *Philippians*, p. 91; R.P. Martin, *The Epistle of Paul to the Philippians* (Grand Rapids: Eerdmans, 1975 [1959]), p. 37, citing Eusebius.
14. So C.L. Mitton, cited in G.F. Hawthorne, *Philippians* (Waco, TX: Word Books, 1983), pp. xxx-xxxi.
15. J. Leipoldt, *Geschichte der Christentum*, cited in A. Wikenhauser and J. Schmid, *Introducción al Nuevo Testamento* (trans. C.R. Garrido; BHSE, 36; Barcelona: Herder, rev. edn, 1978), p. 751, and Mackay, 'Further Thoughts', p. 162, respectively. Cf. J. Moffatt, *An Introduction to the Literature of the New Testament* (New York: Charles Scribner's Sons, 3rd edn, 1918), p. 175. Rahtjen rejects Moffatt's arguments with no explanation ('Three Letters', p. 168).
16. A. Souter, *The Text and Canon of the New Testament* (London: Duckworth, 2nd edn, 1954), p. 209 n. 3, cited in Mackay, 'Further Thoughts', p. 161. See also Feine-Behm, cited in Martin, *Philippians*, p. 137; Moffatt, *Introduction*, pp. 174-75.

Furthermore, external evidence can be cited in which the integrity of Philippians is upheld. For throughout the second century, Philippians was referred to as being only one letter and assigned to Paul by such important and early witnesses as Irenaeus, Tertullian and Clement of Alexandria. Also, Polycarp *Phil.* 11 mentions only one letter to the Philippians.[17] Lightfoot is probably correct to argue that it is unlikely that more than one letter to the Philippians would have survived until the time of Polycarp, only to pass out of memory so shortly thereafter.[18]

Internal reasons for the problematic structure of the text can also be posited. For example, the abrupt transitions may be due to Philippians's style, a 'personal, almost conversational, letter written by a man accustomed to abrupt shifts in style'.[19] Murphy-O'Connor, for example, suggests that Paul's expression of overflowing love for this loyal community make all attempts at systematization useless.[20] Or it may be that the abrupt change in Paul's tone in 3.2 reflects his own psychological response to the issues at hand,[21] or that the material vicissitudes inherent to a prison setting obviate elegant composition,[22] or that Paul was interrupted (e.g. at 3.1) and returned to the letter with a different mind-set and perhaps new information (e.g. in 3.2).[23]

Some have simply taken refuge in a denial of any existing problems. Mackay argues that the break between chs. 1–2 and ch. 3 is merely

---

17. Lightfoot, *Apostolic Fathers*, II, p. 926. The text is noted by Lightfoot, *Philippians*, p. 141 n. 4, and by K. Aland, 'Die Entstehung des Corpus Paulinum', in his *Neutestamentliche Entwürfe* (Munich: Kaiser, 1979), p. 349, but F.F. Bruce ('St Paul in Macedonia', *BJRL* 63 [1981], p. 273 n. 2) reminds us that the Greek of this passage is no longer extant.

18. Lightfoot, *Philippians*, p. 142; cf. P. Benoit, *Les épîtres de saint Paul aux Philippiens, aux Colossiens, à Philémon, aux Ephesiens* (Paris: Cerf, 1959), p. 31, who argues that 3.1 refers to previous letters that are no longer extant.

19. Hawthorne, *Philippians*, p. xxxi, following E. Strange, 'Diktierpausen in den Paulus-Briefen', *ZNW* 18 (1918), pp. 115-16 (citing Rom. 16.16-19; 1 Thess. 2.13-16).

20. J. Murphy-O'Connor, 'Philippiens (Epître aux)', *DBSup*, VIII, pp. 1211-1212.

21. E.g. K. Staab, *Briefe des Apostels Paulus* (Würzburg: Echter, 1968), p. 29.

22. W.J. Dalton, 'The Integrity of Philippians', *Bib* 60 (1979), pp. 98-99.

23. H. Ewald, *Die Sendschreiben des Apostels Paulus* (Göttingen, 1857), p. 448; Lightfoot, *Philippians*, pp. 69-70; Staab, *Briefe*, p. 39; Dalton, 'Integrity', pp. 98-99.

5. The Integrity and Epistolary Structure of Philippians

perceived and may be accounted for by assuming that Paul had 'repeatedly warned the Philippians against the "judaizers", and that in 3.1 he is simply apologizing for giving this warning again'.[24] Lightfoot makes light of the problem posed by 4.10-20 by assuming that Paul had consciously or unconsciously left his words of thanks to the Philippians to the end:

> But [even after his parting words of 4.8-9] something still remains unsaid. He has not yet thanked them for their gift by Epaphroditus, though he has alluded to it in passing. With a graceful intermingling of manly independence and courteous delicacy he acknowledges this token of their love, explaining his own circumstances and feelings at some length.[25]

These apologies for the integrity of Philippians have, however, failed to convince. They do not, for example, do 'justice to the seriousness of the break and the complete lack of connection between [ch. 3] and the remainder of the letter'[26] or to that of the break between 4.10-20 and the rest of the letter. They ignore that certain themes of chs. 1 and 2 are picked up in ch. 4 (e.g. 4.4 picks up the note of rejoicing from 3.1), thus all but ignoring 3.2–4.3.

Lexical and Thematic Parallels

One of the most significant indexes of the mutual interdependency of allegedly independent units of Philippians, namely, 1.18b–2.18, 3.1–4.1 and 4.10-20, is the way in which these three units are related in terms of lexical and thematic parallels. According to Dalton, 'if a regular pattern of words and ideas is repeated in a way which reveals the inner movement and meaning of the text, then we have a new fact which the hypothesis of division will find hard to explain'.[27]

First, then, it is to be noted that among the epistolary units there are lexical parallels:

---

24. Mackay, 'Further Thoughts', pp. 163-64, citing 1.28, 29; 2.14-16; 3.18.
25. Lightfoot, *Philippians*, pp. 70-71.
26. Beare, *Philippians*, p. 100.
27. Dalton, 'Integrity', p. 99; cf. Vincent, *Philippians*, pp. xxix-xxx; M.D. Hooker, 'Interchange in Christ', *JTS* n.s. 22 (1971), p. 356.

Terms	1.18b–2.18	3.1-21	4.10-20
χαίρω	1.18; 2.2, 17, 18	3.1; 4.1	4.10
κέρδος[28]	1.21	3.7	
καρπός	1.22		4.17
περισσεύω	1.26		4.12, 18
πολιτευ-[29]	1.27 (-ομαι)	3.20 (-μα)	
ἀπώλεια[30]	1.28	3.19	
σωτηρία[31]	1.28	cf. 3.20	
κοινωνία	2.1	3.10	cf. 4.14, 15
φρονέω	2.2 (τό), 5 (τοῦτο)	3.15 (τοῦτο), 19	4.10 (τό)
σκοπέω[32]	2.4	3.17	
ἐν Χριστῷ Ἰησοῦ	2.5	3.13, 14	
μορφή[33]	2.6, 7	cf. 3.10 (συμμορφίζομαι), 20 (σύμμορφος)	
ἡγέομαι	2.6 (+ ἅρπαγμον)	3.7 (+ ζήμιαν)	
ὑπάρχω	2.6	3.20	
ἴσα[34]	2.6	cf. 2.20 (ἰσόψυχος)	
σχῆμα[35]	2.7	cf. 3.21 (μετασχηματίζω)	
εὑρίσκω	2.7 (ὡς ἄνθρωπος)	3.9 (ἐν αὐτῷ)	
θάνατος	2.8	3.10	
σταυρός[36]	2.8	3.10	

28. The only other New Testament use of κέρδος is Tit. 1.11.
29. The only other use of πολιτεύομαι is Acts 23.1; πολίτευμα is not used elsewhere in the New Testament.
30. Used elsewhere in Paul only at Rom. 9.22; 2 Thess. 2.3; cf. 1 Tim. 6.9.
31. The term σωτήρ is used elsewhere in the New Testament only in the Pastorals *passim* and Eph. 5.23.
32. The term σκοπέω is used elsewhere in Paul only at Rom. 16.17; 2 Cor. 4.18; Gal. 6.1.
33. The term μορφή is used elsewhere in the New Testament only at Mk 16.12.
34. This is the only occurrence of ἴσα in Paul and of ἰσόψυχος in the New Testament.
35. The term σχῆμα is found elsewhere in the New Testament only at 1 Cor. 7.31, and in the LXX only at Isa. 3.17; μετασχηματίζω is found elsewhere in the New Testament only at 1 Cor. 4.6 and 2 Cor. 11.13, 14, 15 and in the LXX only at 4 Macc. 9.22.
36. The term σταυρός is found elsewhere in Paul only at 1 Cor. 1.17, 18;

5. The Integrity and Epistolary Structure of Philippians 103

ταπεινόω[37]	cf. 2.3 (ταπεινοφροσύνην)	cf. 3.21 (ταπείνωσις)	4.12
ἐπουράνιοι	2.8	cf. 3.20 (ἐν οὐρανοῖς)	
ἐπίγειον[38]	2.18	3.19	
δόξα	2.11	3.19, 20	
κύριος Ἰησοῦς Χριστός	2.11	3.8, 20	
θυσία	2.17		4.18

Secondly, there are significant thematic parallels:

Call to unity	1.27-28 (cf. 2.2)	3.16
Adversaries	1.28; 2.1-4	3.2
Sufferings	1.29-30	3.10
Exhortation to imitate	1.30; 2.11	3.17
Humility	2.1-11	3.1-11
Emptying	2.5-11	3.10
Glorification	2.10-11	3.11
Progress in Christian life	2.12-18	3.12-13
Race motif	2.16	3.12-16

These lexical and thematic parallels found throughout Philippians must be considered significant indexes of the integrity of the letter if they are such as are not to be found in Paul's other letters. And, in fact, this is the case: the most striking parallels *within* Philippians are *unparalleled* in Paul's other letters.

When one adds to this the recurrence of specific, unique phrasing, one is left with the probability of intentional cross-referencing of vocabulary and themes within the same letter. Even Collange, a supporter of the partition theory, is forced to say that 'that the only solid argument in favour of integrity resides in the relationship of themes between chapter 3 and 1.27–2.18'.[39] So I believe we may proceed—if not with absolute certainty, at least with probability—to treat Philippians as one integral letter.

Gal. 5.11; 6.12, 14; Col. 1.20; 2.14; cf. Eph. 2.16.
37. The verb ταπεινόω is found elsewhere in Paul only at 2 Cor. 11.7; 12.21; ταπείνωσις here is the only occurrence in Paul.
38. The term ἐπίγειον is found elsewhere in Paul only at 1 Cor. 15.40; 2 Cor. 5.1.
39. Collange, *Philippiens*, p. 22.

2. The Epistolary Conventions in Philippians and the Structure of the Letter

Having established the probability of the integrity of Philippians, we need now to discover the epistolary structure of the letter itself. Once I have done that, I may then proceed to determine the rhetorical functions of its constituent parts.

We can determine the epistolary structure of the letter by following the epistolary conventions that Paul uses in Philippians. In order to do so, I will follow Mullins's suggestion that we first discern what forms Paul uses that were 'in common use around the first century' and then identify the differences between Paul's use and that of his contemporaries.[40] My goal, however, is much more restrained than that of Mullins, for I will not be seeking out a broad catalogue of characteristic New Testament formulae but rather identifiable epistolary conventions in order to establish the epistolary structure of Philippians.

The Opening

Phil. 1.1-2, as the letter opening of Philippians, contains the tripartite structure of the non-literary letter opening. We find the senders in the nominative (Παῦλος καὶ Τιμόθεος...) and the addressees in the dative (πᾶσιν τοῖς ἁγίοις...), thus recalling the 'A to B' formula common to the papyri collections. The greeting (χάρις ὑμῖν καὶ εἰρήνη...), using the ethical dative, is apparent, though different in form from other introductory greetings (cf. 1 Thess. 1.1; Col. 1.2; Gal. 1.3-4)[41].

The Thanksgiving

Once the tripartite letter opening is stated, the writer is free to move on to the thanksgiving. In Philippians the epistolary thanksgiving is easily discerned in 1.3-11. The opening of the thanksgiving (1.3-4) appears to be a conflation of the Pauline thanksgiving as examined by Schubert, comprised, on the one hand, of the formulaic expression ἐπὶ πάσῃ τῇ μνείᾳ ὑμῶν (1.3; cf. Rom. 1.9; 1 Thess. 1.2; Phlm 4), which would seem to modify the main verb, and of πάντοτε ἐν πάσῃ δεήσει μου ὑπὲρ πάντων ὑμῶν... ποιούμενος (1.4; cf. Rom. 1.9-

---

40. Mullins, 'Formulas', p. 390.
41. Steen, 'Clichés', pp. 125-26.

5. *The Integrity and Epistolary Structure of Philippians* 105

10; Col. 1.3; 1 Thess. 1.2; Phlm 4), in which the temporal participial clause defining the action of εὐχαριστῶ is coalesced with the clause πάντοτε from the first set of Pauline letters. The close relation, however, of both expressions in Philippians—as well as in Rom. 1.9-10; 1 Thess. 1.2; Phlm 4—would appear to indicate that they are to be taken together. Accordingly, as Lightfoot suggested, μετὰ χαρᾶς τὴν δέησιν does seem to be an explanatory clause.⁴² Viewing 1.3-4 as a structural whole resolves the often debated question of how 1.5 relates to the preceding verses. While nearly all contemporary exegetes have taken the expression as dependent on εὐχαριστῶ (1.3),⁴³ it would seem that 1.5 is dependent on the entire transitional device 1.3-4. Thus, sub-section 1.3-7 is concluded by the invocation of God: μάρτυς γάρ μου ὁ θεός.⁴⁴

Phil. 1.9-11 as a sub-section beginning with a prayer (καὶ τοῦτο προσεύχομαι) concludes the thanksgiving and fulfils the function of the Greek private letter's intercession on the part of the sender for the addressee(s). In fulfilling both roles it functions as an 'eschatological climax', which brings the thanksgiving to a close, as also in 1 Thess. 1.10 and 1 Cor. 1.8 (cf. 2 Thess. 1.3-12; 2 Cor. 1.7; Col. 1.13-20, 21-29; Eph. 1.20-23).⁴⁵ It not only marks the end of the thanksgiving period but also draws attention to Paul's eschatological hope.⁴⁶

The stereotypical nature of the thanksgiving period is apparent from a comparison of the thanksgivings of Philippians and 1 Corinthians:

Phil. 1.3-11		*1 Cor. 1.4-9*	
1.3	εὐχαριστῶ τῷ θεῷ μου	1.4	εὐχαριστῶ τῷ θεῷ μου
1.5	ἐπὶ πάσῃ τῇ μνείᾳ ὑμῶν πάντοτε ἐν πάσῃ δεήσει μου ὑπὲρ πάντων ὑμῶν	1.4	πάντοτε περὶ ὑμῶν ἐπὶ τῇ χάριτι τοῦ θεοῦ τῇ δωθείσῃ ὑμῖν ἐν Χριστῷ Ἰησοῦ

---

42. Lightfoot, *Philippians*, p. 82.
43. Cf. L.M. Dewailly, 'La part prise à l'Evangile', *RB* 80 (1973), p. 248; R.L. Omanson, 'A Note on the Translation of Philippians 1.3-5', *BT* 29 (1978), p. 244; Panikulam, *Koinonia*, pp. 81-82.
44. Cf. Rom. 1.9; Steen, 'Clichés', pp. 157-58.
45. Cf. Sanders, 'Transition', p. 357.
46. *Pace* Sanders, 'Transition', p. 357.

106   *The Function of Suffering in Philippians*

1.5	ἐπὶ τῇ κοινωνίᾳ ὑμῶν εἰς τὸ εὐαγγέλιον	1.9	(πιστὸς ὁ θεὸς δι' οὗ ἐκλήθητε) εἰς κοινωνίαν τοῦ υἱοῦ αὐτοῦ Ἰησοῦ Χριστοῦ τοῦ κυρίου ἡμῶν
1.6	... ἐπιτελέσει ἄχρι ἡμέρας Χριστοῦ Ἰησοῦ	1.8	... ἕως τέλους ἀνεγκλήτους ἐν τῇ ἡμέρᾳ τοῦ κυρίου ἡμῶν Ἰησοῦ
1.7	... βεβαιώσει...	1.6, 8	... ἐβεβαιώθη... βεβαιώσει
1.9	... ἵνα ἡ ἀγάπη ὑμῶν ἔτι μᾶλλον καὶ μᾶλλον περισσεύῃ ἐν ἐπιγνώσει καὶ πάσῃ αἰσθήσει	1.5	... ὅτι ἐν παντὶ ἐπλουτίσθητε ἐν αὐτῷ, ἐν παντὶ λόγῳ καὶ πάσῃ γνώσει

Such a comparison also enables us to discern elements that are proper to Philippians and to 1 Corinthians. For example, while both thanksgivings speak of κοινωνία, 1 Cor. 1.9 speaks of κοινωνία τοῦ Ἰησοῦ Χριστοῦ while Phil. 1.5 speaks of κοινωνία ὑμῶν. Again, 1 Cor. 1.5 speaks of the enrichment of the Corinthians while Phil. 1.9 speaks of the Philippians' ἀγάπη.

Such themes as can be discerned from the Philippian thanksgiving are important for understanding Paul's purpose in the letter. Fred O. Francis has, for example, discovered themes treated in the following Pauline thanksgiving passages that are then picked up in their respective letter bodies:[47]

Thanksgiving	Letter Body
1 Thess. 1.2-10	2.13; 3.19-20
2 Thess. 1.3	2.13
Phil. 1.3-11	4.10
2 Cor. 1.3-5	1.11
Eph. 1.3	1.15-17
Col. 1.3-4	1.9-12

While insightful, Francis's suggestions are too timid and general. While it is true that the thanksgiving periods of Paul's letters are developed throughout their respective bodies, more precision must be used in defining where, how and why. Robert Jewett's assessment is thus more to the point, when he boldly asserts that the thanksgiving period announces and introduces the topics of the letter in such a way that 'despite the abrupt transitions, the entire letter as it now stands is

47. F.O. Francis, 'The Form and Function of the Opening and Closing Paragraphs of James and 1 John', *ZNW* 61 (1970), pp. 112-13.

5. The Integrity and Epistolary Structure of Philippians 107

the product of the author's intention set forth in the epistolary thanksgiving'.[48]

The Body

As is clear from the above discussion concerning the integrity of Philippians, most confusion surrounds the epistolary structure of the letter body. In the light of my presentation of epistolary conventions in the letter, however, it seems possible to suggest a tentative structure to canonical Philippians. Accordingly I would suggest that the epistolary body of Philippians is 1.12–4.20. This body may further be divided into the following epistolary sections: 1.12-14; 1.15-18a; 1.18b–2.18; 2.19-30; 3.1–4.7; 4.8-20.

Philippians 1.12-14. Phil. 1.12-14 appears to be the epistolary body opening, in which Paul's concerns are expressed.[49] The opening disclosure formula (1.12: γινώσκειν δὲ ὑμᾶς βούλομαι), as we have seen, is well documented in both the papyri and in Paul.[50] Discussion really only surrounds the limits of the opening. I would suggest that the body opening concludes with a formulaic verb of speaking (1.14),[51] rather than with πλήν plus the rejoicing formula in 1.18a,[52] and so leads into the body middle (1.15-18), which is an expansion of that matter of concern.

Philippians 1.15–2.18. The chiasm of vv. 15-17 (τινὲς μὲν καὶ... τινὲς δὲ καὶ... οἱ μὲν... οἱ δὲ...) is a formulaic introduction to a section that develops the material introduced in the body opening (1.12-14).[53] Formally this section has the contours of a body middle

---

48. Jewett, 'Epistolary Thanksgiving', p. 53; cf. Funk, 'Apostolic Parousia', p. 261.
49. Cf. White, *Body*, pp. 96-97; P. Schubert, cited in Sanders, 'Transition', pp. 349-53.
50. Cf. 1 Thess. 2.1; Gal. 1.11; Rom. 1.13; 2 Cor. 1.8; POxy 295.2: γίνωσκε ὅτι Σελεῦκος ἐλθὼν ὧδε πέφευγε, from about 35 CE (White, *Body*, p. 3). The use of (1) infinitive, (2) accusative, (3) first person indicative, plus (4) ὅτι, appears to be later than the first century in the papyri.
51. The apparent choice of the editors of the United Bible Societies, *Greek New Testament* (3rd edn), p. 682.
52. The apparent choice of the editors of the 26th edn of the Nestlé–Aland *Novum Testamentum Graece*, p. 516.
53. White, *Body*, pp. 78-79.

that concludes with the 'eschatological conclusion' in 2.14-18 (introduced by the imperative of purpose in 2.14-15 [ποιεῖτε...ἵνα...] and concluded by ἀλλὰ εἰ, plus formulaic χαίρω in 2.17 and δὲ καί, plus the imperative of rejoicing in 2.18).[54] There are, however, three major subdivisions within this section. A first sub-section, 1.15-18a, commences with the chiasm as noted above (1.15-17) and concludes with interrogative τί (1.18a) and the first occurrence in the letter of the significant χαίρω–χαρά language, a word group that recurs at structurally significant transitional points throughout this letter (1.18a, 18b; 2.17-18, 28; 3.1; 4.10).

A second sub-section, 1.18b-26, opens with ἀλλὰ καί and picks up the rejoicing formula from 1.18a (χαρήσομαι), adding further a disclosure formula with οἶδα γὰρ ὅτι (1.19; cf. 4.15). It concludes with the tense changes, disclosure formula (οἶδα ὅτι) with καὶ τοῦτο (Phlm 18; Gal. 2.17; cf. Eph. 2.8), πείθω perfect, and purpose clause (1.25-26: ἵνα...).[55] Minor transitions within this sub-section are found in the use of the emphatic first person and a tense change (1.21: ἐμοὶ γὰρ τὸ ζῆν) and in the conditional clause and tense change (1.22: εἰ δὲ... καὶ τί αἱρήσομαι οὐ γνωρίζω). Accordingly we may divide this sub-section into 1.18b-20, 21, and 22-26, with 22-26 apparently a continuation of the material in 21.

A third sub-section (1.27–2.18) is introduced by a cliché of adverbial intensity (μόνον)[56] and the imperative of purpose (1.27: πολιτεύεσθε ἵνα...). It concludes with the closing formula of the body middle (2.18: δὲ καί, plus the rejoicing formula in the imperative). This section has been termed a practical follow-up in an epistolary body middle to a prior theological one (1.18b-26), which has been termed 'Paul's *apologia*'.[57]

This sub-section can also be further subdivided into three segments. (1) There is a first segment (1.27-30) that begins as noted. (2) A second segment is introduced by a conditional enumeration (2.1 εἰ... εἰ...εἰ...εἰ...), followed by the imperative of purpose (2.2:

---

54. Cf. PHib 54, where a final δὲ καί transition 'leads directly to the letter closing' (White, *Body*, p. 37).
55. White (*Body*, p. 79) speaks of 1.26 as an 'eschatological climax'; he does not, however, speak of 1.18b-26 as an 'inclusion' nor does he mention the formulaic πείθω in 1.25.
56. Steen, 'Clichés', p. 153.
57. White, *Body*.

5. The Integrity and Epistolary Structure of Philippians 109

πληρώσατέ μου...ἵνα and the formulaic rejoicing formula, expressed by χαρά). There is a minor—but important!—transition at 2.5, which picks up in φρονεῖτε the imperative φρονῆτε from 2.2. It is this minor transition that introduces the Philippian hymn (2.6-11). The hymn's doxological conclusion (2.9-11), introduced by a minor transition (διό) at 2.9, brings this segment to a close. (3) A third segment is introduced by ὥστε, plus the epistolary cliché of vocative and imperative (2.12: ἀγαπητοί μου, καθὼς... κατεργάζεσθε). The third segment concludes with two separate epistolary conventions in 2.17: ἀλλὰ καί + a conditional clause (εἰ καὶ...) + a rejoicing formula (χαίρω καὶ συγχαίρω) and in 2.18: δὲ καί + the rejoicing formula in the imperative (χαίρετε καὶ συγχαίρετε μοι). This segment, of course, also brings the entire section 1.12–2.18 to a close. Not insignificantly, the way in which that is done is through an inclusion using χαίρω, in which 1.18b and 2.18 are made the limits of a wider section.

Philippians 2.19-30. Phil. 2.19-30 is a characteristically Pauline body closing, which serves 'as the means of finalizing the motivation for writing (either by reiterating or accentuating what was stated earlier) and as the bridge to future correspondence'.[58] That 2.19-30 is a body closing is clear from the formulaic devices found here that are common to Hellenistic letters and to Paul's other letters.[59]

Three common epistolary conventions are to be found in this body closing. The first is in 2.19-23 and 2.25-30, in both of which there is not only a sending formula (2.19: ἐλπίζω... πέμψαι;[60] 2.25-26: ἀναγκαῖον δὲ ἡγησάμην[61]) but also a reiteration of the reason for the letter's existence.[62] ἐλπίζω + πέμπω in 2.19 and 23 is a substitute for the 'motivation for writing' phrase often found in the body closing using γράφω,[63] but absent when a comparable phrasing is found in the

---

58. White, *Body*, p. 59.
59. See *Body*, pp. 84-90.
60. 2 Cor. 8.18–9.3.
61. Note also the cliché of adverbial intensity (Steen, 'Clichés', p. 153). Cf. 2 Cor. 9.5.
62. Cf. Phlm 19; Gal. 5.2; Rom. 15.14-15; 1 Thess. 2.17-19; 1 Cor 4.14-15.
63. Cf. 1 Thess. 3.1-2; 1 Cor. 4.17; 16.11; 2 Cor. 8.22; 12.18; Col. 4.7-9 and Eph. 6.21-22. According to White (*Body*, pp. 87-88) 2.19-23 'functions structurally in a way comparable to the motivation for writing formula in the other letters'.

body opening.⁶⁴ There may also be a reiteration introduced by the minor transition at 2.28: πέμπω + χαίρω.

A second convention is the responsibility clause ἵνα κἀγὼ εὐψυχῶ (2.19),⁶⁵ which is further strengthened by the confidence formula of 2.24 (a self-designation [καὶ αὐτός], the perfect πείθω, and ὅτι + the object of confidence) and a necessity formula (ἀναγκαῖον ἡγέομαι + πέμπω).⁶⁶ In this latter formula, which White calls 'the greatest formal difference between the body closing in Paul and the corresponding section in the papyri',⁶⁷ Paul expresses his trust that the reader(s) will obey his apostolic words.

The third convention, found in 2.24, is Paul's 'apostolic parousia', which expresses his intention, hope, or desire to pay the reader(s) a personal visit.⁶⁸ It is interwoven with a confidence formula. The body closing concludes with the imperative of purpose and rejoicing formula (προσδέχεσθε...μετὰ πάσης χαρᾶς...ἵνα...) in 2.29-30.

The structure of the Philippian body closing resembles closely the body closings of 1 Corinthians (4.14-21) and 1 Thessalonians (2.17–3.8). In each of these closings one finds the following elements: (1) an introductory formula (1 Cor. 4.17a; 1 Thess. 3.2a; Phil. 2.25aα and c; cf. Phil. 2.19a), (2) a credentials clause (1 Cor. 4.17b; 1 Thess. 3.2b; Phil. 2.25aβ-b; cf. Phil. 2.20-22), and (3) a purpose clause (1 Cor. 4.17c-d; 1 Thess. 3.2c; Phil. 2.26; cf. Phil. 2.19b), with an introductory formula (1) and purpose clause (3) picked up in 1 Thess. 3.5 and Phil. 2.28.⁶⁹ Interestingly, in both 1 Thess. 3.2-5 and Phil. 2.25-30, the two parts of the formula for the sending of an emissary are separated by an expansion of the third element (1 Thess. 3.3b-4 and Phil. 2.27). In both cases the expansion concerns the suffering of the community or of the emissary. The expansion in Phil. 2.20-22 has to do mainly with Timothy's credentials (2); yet, as we shall see, this expansion has also to do with suffering.

64. White, *Light*, p. 207.
65. White, *Body*, pp. 87-88.
66. *Body*, p. 90. According to White, the confidence formula (found in Phlm 21; Gal. 5.10 and Rom. 15.14-15) is lacking only the emphatic pronoun for the complete formula; cf. Phlm 22; 1 Thess. 3.6; 1 Cor. 4.19; 16.5; 2 Cor. 9.3-5; 12.14; 13.1.
67. *Body*, p. 99.
68. Phlm 21, 22; Gal. 4.12-20; Rom. 15.14-33; 1.8-13; 1 Thess. 2.17–3.13; 1 Cor. 4.14-21; 16.5; 2 Cor. 12.14; 13.1; White, *Body*, pp. 29-31, 60-61; Doty, *Letters*, p. 37.
69. Funk, 'Apostolic Parousia', pp. 255-58; *Parables*, pp. 87-90.

5. The Integrity and Epistolary Structure of Philippians 111

Furthermore, a comparison of these three letters yields the discovery that in none of them is the body closing found where we might have been led to expect it, namely, at the end of the canonical letter. Funk, for example, notes that Paul did not always set the 'travelogue' or 'apostolic parousia' or 'body closing' at the end of his letters.[70] Paul speaks of his travel plans and his associates at various points throughout his other letters,[71] but in 2 Thessalonians (cf. also Ephesians) he writes nothing of either his travel plans or his associates. The variety of placement and content seems to imply that Paul 'speaks of his co-workers and travels in the body of a letter when these matters are relevant to the problems of the church or the agenda of the letter',[72] and that there is no *a priori* reason for arguing that the location of the body closing in Philippians is an indication that the letter is actually drawing to a close.

Accordingly, then, the body closing of Philippians may be divided into three parts: 2.19-23, 24, and 25-30.

Philippians 3.1–4.7. After the epistolary body closing (2.19-30), we find a further epistolary section that, in some respects, mirrors 1.15–2.18. This section opens in 3.1 with the epistolary cliché of vocative (ἀδελφοί μου) plus imperative (χαίρετε), in this case, an imperative of an already significant convention.[73] Furthermore, we find in 3.1 a τὸ λοιπόν formula that is common to the non-literary papyri where a conclusion is introduced.[74] The section concludes with the blessing of 4.7.[75]

As with 1.15b–2.18, so here, too, we may subdivide 3.1–4.7 into sub-sections, though here there are only two, 3.1-16 and 3.17–4.7. As in 1.18b–2.18, however, the two sub-sections are theological and practical. Phil. 3.1-16 is a theological sub-section that opens as just noted and is concluded by formulaic φρονέω (cf. 2.5) and πλήν (cf. 1.18a and 4.14). Phil. 3.17–4.7 is a practical sub-section that com-

---

70. Funk, *Language*, pp. 264-65.
71. Rom. 1.8-13; 15.14-33; 1 Cor. 4.14-21; 16.1-12; Phlm 17-22; cf. Col. 4.7-9.
72. Culpepper, 'Co-Workers', pp. 349-50.
73. 1.18a, 18b; 2.17, 18, 28; cf. 4.8; 2 Cor. 10.1-2; 13.11; 1 Thess. 4.1; 2 Thess. 3.1.
74. Cf., e.g., PCol. 3.6: τὰ δὲ λοιπὰ πυνθάνου τοῦ φέροντος σοὶ τὰ γράμματα, οὐ γὰρ ἀλλότριος ἡμῖν ἐστιν (White, *Light*, p. 34; cf. p. 206).
75. Cf. Rom. 15.33; 16.20.

mences with the epistolary cliché of vocative plus imperative (3.17: συμμιμηταί μου γίνεσθε ἀδελφοί),[76] is characterized by this formula throughout (4.1, 2-3) or by simple imperatives (4.4, 5, 6), and concludes at 4.7 with the blessing, as noted above.

Within the sub-sections, also, we again find sub-divisions primarily through the use of tense changes. Thus, here in 3.1-16, we have two segments, 3.1-11 and 3.12-16, with the remaining epistolary conventions representing minor transitions within these two segments: 3.3-7, beginning in 3.3-4a with the emphatic first person and formulaic πείθω (ἡμεῖς γὰρ... καίπερ ἐγὼ ἔχων πεποίθησιν) and in 4b by the conditional clause (εἰ...) and continuing in 3.4b with εἰ (conditional clause); 3.8-11, beginning in 3.8 with ἀλλὰ μενοῦνγε; 3.12, with the significant transition οὐχ ὅτι + tense changes; and 3.13-16, beginning in 3.13 with the vocative (ἀδελφοί) + emphatic first person (ἐγώ) + formulaic λογίζω,[77] and continuing on in 3.13c with ἕν δέ (formulaic enumeration),[78] 3.15 with ὅσοι οὖν,[79] τέλειοι, τοῦτο φρονῶμεν, and 3.16 with πλήν.

Phil. 3.17–4.7 can also be broken down into two segments, 3.17-21 and 4.1-7. Phil. 3.17-21 begins as noted above and is followed immediately in 3.18 by δὲ καί plus a verb of speaking: ἔλεγον ὑμῖν, νῦν δὲ καὶ κλαίων λέγω. It concludes with a hymnic portion (3.20-21).

Stylistically, it seems clear that in both 2.6-11 and 3.20-21 we are dealing with a hymn—or at least a hymnic portion—[80] as noted above and as can be seen diagrammatically in the case of 3.20-21:[81]

---

76. 1 Cor. 4.16; 11.1; Eph. 5.1; 1 Thess. 1.6; 2.14; cf. Heb. 6.12.
77. Cf. Phlm 20.
78. Cf. 2 Cor. 6.13.
79. Rom. 2.12; 8.14; 13.4; 2 Cor. 1.20; Col. 2.1; 3.10, 27; 6.12, 16; 1 Tim. 6.1.
80. J. Becker, 'Erwägungen zu Phil. 3.20-21', *TZ* 27 (1971), pp. 16-29; R.H. Gundry, *SOMA in Biblical Theology, with Emphasis on Pauline Anthropology* (SNTSMS, 29; Cambridge: Cambridge University Press, 1976), pp. 177-78, though cf. pp. 178-81 and Lincoln, *Paradise*, pp. 87-89 for arguments against.
81. Lohmeyer suggests a six-member hymn, paralleling that of 2.6-11; 2.6 / 3.20a; 2.7a / 3.20b; 2.7b (θανάτου δὲ σταυροῦ) / 3.21 (including ἡμῶν); 2.9 / 3.21 (σύμμορφον... αὐτοῦ); 2.10 / 3.21 (κατὰ... αὐτόν); 2.11–3.21 (καὶ ὑποτάξαι...). See Becker, 'Erwägungen', pp. 17-18.
    In all likelihood, we either have two originally independent hymns, possibly stemming from the same milieu and totally reworked by Paul for inclusion in this letter (Becker, 'Ewägungen', p. 25; Güttgemanns, *Leidende Apostel*, pp. 241-45,

5. *The Integrity and Epistolary Structure of Philippians* 113

ὃς μετασχηματίσει
  τὸ σῶμα
    τῆς ταπεινώσεως
      ἡμῶν
σύμμορφον
  τῷ σώματι
    τῆς δόξης
      αὐτοῦ

The hymnic portion alerts us to the lexical and thematic ties between 3.17–4.7 and 1.27–2.18:

3.17–4.1

a. συμμιμηταί μου γίνεσθε, ἀδελφοί (3.17)
b. καὶ σκοπεῖτε τοὺς οὕτω περιπατοῦντας καθὼς ἔχετε τύπον ἡμᾶς (3.17)
c. πολλοὶ γὰρ περιπατοῦσιν... τοὺς ἐχθροὺς (3.18)
d. τοῦ σταυροῦ τοῦ Χριστοῦ (3.18)
e. οἱ τὰ ἐπίγεια (3.19)
f. φρονοῦντες (3.19)

g. ἡμῶν γὰρ τὸ πολίτευμα (3.20)
h. ἐν οὐρανοῖς (3.20)
i. ὑπάρχει (3.20)

j. ἐξ οὗ καὶ σωτῆρα ἀπεκδεχόμεθα κύριον Ἰησοῦν Χριστόν (3.20)
k. ὃς μετασχηματίσει (3.21)

1.27–2.18

a. τὸν αὐτὸν ἀγῶνα ἔχοντες οἷον εἴδετε ἐν ἐμοὶ καὶ νῦν ἀκούετε ἐν ἐμοί (1.30)?
b. μὴ τὰ ἑαυτῶν ἕκαστος σκοποῦντες, ἀλλὰ [καὶ] τὰ ἑτέρων ἕκαστοι (2.4)
c. τῶν ἀντικειμένων (1.28)?

d. θανάτου δὲ σταυροῦ (2.8)

e. καὶ ἐπιγείων (2.10)
f. τὸ αὐτὸ φρονῆτε (2.2); τὸ ἓν φρονοῦντες (2.2); τοῦτο φρονεῖτε (2.5)
g. πολιτεύεσθε (1.27)
h. ἐπουρανίων (2.10)
i. ὃς ἐν μορφῇ θεοῦ ὑπάρχων (2.6)
j. κύριος Ἰησοῦς Χριστός (2.11)

k. καὶ σχήματι εὑρεθείς (2.7)

following Lohmeyer, E. Norden and G. Strecker), or two hymns that are the work of the apostle Paul himself (Dalton, 'Integrity', p. 100; Collange, *Philippiens*, p. 122; Friedrich, *Philipper*, p. 92). Even if the former be the case, however, the reworking has been so total as to mask the origins of the hymns and, consequently, in this case as in the case of 2.6-11, one may simply talk of Paul as the author of the hymns in their present epistolary context.

114   *The Function of Suffering in Philippians*

l. τὸ σῶμα τῆς ταπεινώσεως ἡμῶν (3.21)
m. σύμμορφον τῷ σώματι τῆς δόξης αὐτοῦ κατὰ τὴν ἐνέργειαν τοῦ δύνασθαι αὐτόν (3.21)
n. καὶ ὑποτάξαι αὐτῷ τὰ πάντα (3.21)

o. ὥστε ἀδελφοί μου ἀγαπητοὶ καὶ ἐπιπόθητοι (4.1)
p. χαρὰ καὶ στέφανός μου (4.1)

q. οὕτως στήκετε ἐν κυρίῳ, ἀγαπητοί (4.1)

l. ὡς ἄνθρωπος ἐταπείνωσεν ἑαυτὸν γενόμενος ὑπήκοος μέχρι θανάτου (2.7-8)
m. ὃς ἐν μορφῇ θεοῦ (2.6); μορφὴν δούλου (2.7)

n. ὑπερύψωσεν καὶ ἐχαρίσατο αὐτῷ τὸ ὄνομα τὸ ὑπὲρ πᾶν ὄνομα, ἵνα...πᾶν γόνυ... πᾶσα γλῶσσα (2.9-11)
o. ὥστε, ἀγαπητοί μου (2.12)
p. χαίρω καὶ συγχαίρω... καὶ...χαίρετε καὶ συγχαίρετε μοι (2.17-18)
q. στήκετε ἐν ἑνὶ πνεύματι (1.27)

Furthermore, the paraeneses that begin the three sections of 1.27–2.18 and the two of 3.17-21 are addressed to the community. The paraeneses in 2.12-18 and 4.1-7 are set forth in similar ways: a praise word followed by an imperative. The paraeneses of 2.1-11 and 3.17-21 are both justified by an appeal to a christological state of affairs. Furthermore, both sections do so by means of hymnic portions.

The transition from 3.17-21 and 4.1-7 is comparable to the one we have already examined above, namely, the transition from 2.1-11 to 2.12-18. For example, both 2.1-11 and 3.17-21 end with hymnic portions. Phil. 2.12 and 4.1 both employ ὥστε + ἀγαπητοί (μου) + imperative.[82] Strikingly, where 2.12 has καθώς and no apodosis, 4.1 has οὕτως and no protasis!

What follows the transition, however, is no mere repetition of 2.12-18. True, both are exhortations directed to the Philippian community. Yet, while the exhortation of 2.12-18 is still exhortation, it appears to be less specific than that of 4.1-7 which, at least in 4.1-3, is exceptionally so.

Thus, we have a series of short and terse exhortations, each separated from the other by transitional devices: 4.1 ὥστε + vocative + imperative + vocative + οὕτως (ὥστε, ἀδελφοί μου ἀγαπητοὶ καὶ ἐπιπόθητοι, χαρὰ καὶ στέφανός μου, οὕτως στήκετε ἐν κυρίῳ);

82. Cf. also 1 Cor. 11.33-34.

5. The Integrity and Epistolary Structure of Philippians 115

4.2 personal petition[83] (παρακαλῶ... παρακαλῶ τὸ αὐτὸ φρονεῖν ἐν κυρίῳ);[84] 4.3 familiar petition[85] (ναὶ ἐρωτῶ καὶ σὲ, γνήσιε σύζυγε, συλλαμβάνου...);[86] 4.4 formulaic joy expression + a verb of speaking (χαίρετε ἐν κυρίῳ πάντοτε,[87] πάλιν ἐρῶ, χαίρετε); 4.5 imperative (τὸ ἐπιεικὲς ὑμῶν γνωσθήτω); and 4.6 formulaic imperative (μηδὲν μεριμνᾶτε ἀλλ'... γνωριζέσθω...). For this reason it seems correct to term 4.2 an incorporated paraenesis, rather than a structurally separate unit characterized by short, ethical exhortations. In 4.2-3 we have a 'terse, gnomic style',[88] and we see a reliance by Paul 'upon his background and training to supplement and to support his contextualism'.[89] In 4.4-6, furthermore, we find more of the kind of exhortation we have been led to expect from Paul's paraeneses.

Accordingly, in the section 3.1–4.7, we have two major sub-sections, 3.1-16 and 3.17–4.7, with dependent segments, viz., 3.1-11 and 3.12-16, and 3.17-21 and 4.1-7, respectively.

Philippians 4.8-20. Finally, we discern a third section of this long epistolary body. Following the conclusion of 3.1–4.7 with the blessing in 4.7 (καὶ ἡ εἰρήνη τοῦ θεοῦ),[90] this section opens with introductory conventions (4.8-9), namely, a τὸ λοιπόν formula (cf. 3.1), as well as conditional enumeration (six ὅσα clauses and two εἰ

---

83. Mullins, 'Formulas', p. 380. This verse not only yields the cliché of παρακαλῶ, followed by an infinitive (Steen, 'Clichés', p. 136), but also of repetition (pp. 137-38).
84. 2 Cor. 3.8; 12.18; cf. 2 Cor. 6.1; Phlm 8-10; Col. 4.7-9; Eph. 4.1; 6.21-22; Rom. 12.1; 15.30; 16.17; 1 Thess. 3.7; 4.10; 5.14; 2 Thess. 3.12; 1 Cor. 1.10; 4.16; 16.15.
85. Mullins, 'Formulas', p. 380. The appearance of παρακαλῶ and ἐρωτῶ in such close proximity appears to be another example of a 'cliché', described by Steen ('Clichés', p. 138). Furthermore, here ἐρωτῶ is followed by the imperative ('Clichés', p. 148). The resulting combination of 4.2-3 (and perhaps the following imperatives 4.4-6) leads one to view this portion of Philippians in terms of the accumulation of urbane expressions that Steen documents in the papyri ('Clichés', pp. 150-51).
86. Cf. Phlm 20 for ναί + vocative + imperative.
87. Cf. 3.1.
88. Roetzel, *Letters*, pp. 35-36.
89. Doty, *Letters*, pp. 37-38.
90. Cf. Rom. 15.33; 16.20.

clauses, cf. 2.1), and the frequent vocative plus imperative (ἀδελφοὶ...
ταῦτα λογίζεσθε... ταῦτα πράσσετε) and blessing (καὶ ὁ θεὸς
τῆς εἰρήνης).[91] It concludes with the doxology in 4.19-20 (ὁ δὲ θεός
μου... ἀμήν).[92] As in the case of the thanksgiving period of Philippians (1.3-11), the first part of Philippians' letter closing (4.8-20) is also divided into two sub-sections, viz., 4.8-14 and 4.15-20. Following the introductory phrases of 4.8-9, 4.10-14 opens with the joy formula (ἐχάρην) plus ἐν κυρίῳ (4.10) and concludes with πλήν (4.14; cf. 1.18a; 3.16). Phil. 4.15-20 opens with a disclosure formula plus δὲ καί (οἴδατε δὲ καὶ ὑμεῖς... ὅτι... ὅτι)[93] and the vocative (Φιλιππήσιοι) and concludes with the doxology (4.20). Within each of the sub-sections, there are minor transitions. Thus we find in 4.8-14, the use of οὐχ ὅτι (cf. 3.12), plus a verb of speaking and tense change (cf. 3.12; 4.17) and in 4.12 a disclosure formula (οἶδα... οἶδα...). In 4.15-20 we again find οὐχ ὅτι and a tense change (4.17; cf. 3.12; 4.11).

The Closing
As we have seen in the non-literary papyri, the letter closing is closely related to the letter opening. Both have as their intended purpose the maintenance of contact between sender(s) and addressee(s). This is seen in Philippians' letter closing proper, namely 4.21-23, where greetings from οἱ σὺν ἐμοὶ ἀδελφοί and οἱ ἅγιοι are extended, as are instructions to the Philippians to greet πάντα ἅγιον. The entire letter comes to a conclusion with the blessing (ἡ χάρις τοῦ κυρίου...) in 4.23.[94]

3. *Conclusion*

Arguments for the composite character of canonical Philippians are perceptive. For example, Phil. 1.1–2.30 presents all of the component parts of a non-literary papyrus letter—a letter opening (1.1-2), a thanksgiving (1.3-11), plus a letter body divided into opening (1.12-14), middle (1.15–2.18) and closing (2.19-30)—with the exception of

91. Rom. 15.33; 16.20; 1 Thess. 5.32; 2 Thess. 3.16.
92. Eph. 3.20-21; Rom. 7.25; 11.33-36.
93. Cf. 1 Thess. 2.1.
94. Exler, *Form*, pp. 111-13. In the letters examined by Exler the blessing was probably transposed to the beginning.

5. The Integrity and Epistolary Structure of Philippians   117

a closing epistolary convention to bring the letter to completion. The arguments for the redactional nature of Philippians, however, are also inconclusive. Moreover, as I have indicated in this chapter, there are good reasons for believing that canonical Philippians is an integral letter.

Furthermore, my discovery of epistolary conventions, whereby Paul has indicated transition points in his argumentation, enables me to suggest a probable epistolary structure for the letter. This structure may be set out as follows:

```
1.1-2         Letter opening
1.3-11        Thanksgiving
1.12-4.20     Body
   1.12-14            Body opening
   1.15-2.18          Section (body middle)
      1.15-18a   Sub-section
      1.18b-26   Sub-section
         1.18b-20   Segment
         1.21-26    Segment
      1.27-2.18  Sub-section
         1.27-30    Segment
         2.1-11     Segment
         2.12-18    Segment
   2.19-30   Body closing
      2.19-23   Sub-section
      2.24      Sub-section
      2.25-30   Sub-section
   3.1-4.7    Section (body middle)
      3.1-16    Sub-section
         3.1-11     Segment
         3.12-16    Segment
      3.17-4.7  Sub-section
         3.17-21    Segment
         4.1-7      Segment
   4.8-20     Section (body middle)
      4.8-14    Sub-section
      4.15-20   Sub-section
4.21-23      Letter closing
```

This analysis of the epistolary structure of Philippians provides us with a scientifically ascertained foundation on which we may build our discussion of the letter. For in following the epistolary conventions the author himself has used we are able to chart the author's own intended flow in his communication.

Having discerned the epistolary structure of Philippians, however, we now have to ask how this structure and its component parts function and why the epistolary body of the letter is structured in this rather unconventional way. Furthermore, though it is probable, as we have seen, that Philippians has the essential structure of a letter—according to Deissmann Philippians, the 'most gracious of all St Paul's writings to the churches, is obviously letter-like'[95]—the question remains: what *kind* of a letter? In order to answer such questions we must consider the rhetorical functions of these structurally discerned parts.

---

95. Deissman, *Light*, p. 238.

Chapter 6

THE RHETORICAL FUNCTIONS OF PHILIPPIANS

Having provided a general overview of the epistolary structure of letters in antiquity (Chapter 4) and set out the epistolary structure of Philippians in particular (Chapter 5), I am now in a position to discuss how rhetorical address as understood in antiquity can enable us to understand the rhetorical functions of Philippians. For Philippians is clearly more than a mere rehearsal of events and a brief expansion of those events for a reader, as in many Hellenistic private letters. Rather, it is an extensive statement of the meaning of the situation with a view to action on the part of the addressees.[1] As such it must be understood in terms of the wider rhetorical canons available to Paul.

1. *The Rhetorical 'Genus' of the Letter*

As we have seen, 'Paul appears to combine some features of forensic rhetoric with others from deliberative and/or epideictic oratory... and [was] able to combine many traditions and approaches in achieving the results and effects he desired'.[2] One need not, however, deduce from this that the attempt to discern the *genus* of the rhetorical *oratio* 'is not a crucial factor in understanding how rhetoric actually works in units of the New Testament'.[3] Granting that New Testament authors have mixed genres and that literary conventions are not 'as sharply discriminated in the ancient world as in the modern', C.C. Black can also note:

---

1. Cf. *Inst.* 3.8.12.
2. Aune, Review of Betz, p. 326. Aune's conclusion, viz., 'that [Paul] was not schooled in one rhetorical tradition', is not a necessary one.
3. Kennedy, *New Testament Interpretation*, p. 33.

Cicero's first *Catlinarian* is a different creature from, say, the first book of Samuel; though both intend to persuade, they invite different approaches.[4]

Philippians appears to be primarily an example of the deliberative or persuasive *genus*.[5] Philippians is concerned with choosing *dignitate* or *honestum*, for again and again Paul presents his readers with choices. In 1.5-7 he refers to their choice of serving with him in the gospel ministry. In 1.12-26 he notes the choices of self-service or service of the community that lie before him as 'prudentissimus... et optimus',[6] characteristics that are a prerequisite of any speaker in a deliberative address. In 2.1-4 he sets clear choices before the Philippians, and follows this in 2.5-11 with the hymn that speaks of Christ's choice. In 1.27–2.18 he urges the Philippians to choose the better way. In 2.19-30 he sets before them two co-workers who have done so. In 3.1-6 and 18-19 he depicts those who have chosen the *via turpiditudinis* and contrasts their way with his own high, exalted way in 3.7-16. In 4.8-15 he again posits himself as an example of choosing what is honourable.

Nonetheless, Philippians may have more than one *genus*. Philippians may, as Black and others have noted, be an example of mixed rhetorical *genera*, a suggestion made by David Aune concerning Galatians. Aune's review, while not vitiating Betz's argument, has done Pauline studies a service by alerting us to the possibility of an admixture of rhetorical *genera*. Thus Galatians, as Betz argues, may be an example of the forensic *genus*, though deliberative and epideictic elements also enter in.[7] Likewise Philippians is probably an example of the deliberative *genus*. Yet forensic and epideictic elements can also be found in it as well.

2. *The Rhetorical Features of the Letter*

Between the epistolary prescript of 1.1-2 and the epistolary postscript of 4.21-23, Paul's letter to the Philippians should probably be seen

---

4. Black, 'Rhetorical Criticism', p. 257.
5. So Watson, 'Rhetorical Analysis', p. 59; cf. *Rhet. ad Alex.* 1421b10. It seems unlikely that Philippians is epideictic rhetoric (so Kennedy, *New Testament Interpretation*, p. 77; cf. *Rhet.* 1.3 [1358b 10-20]).
6. *Inst.* 3.8.13.
7. So Aune, Review of Betz, p. 326. Aune's statements that the forensic *genus* does not necessitate Betz's 'apologetic form' (p. 324) is acute but not directly relevant to our discussion.

rhetorically in terms of (1) an *exordium* (1.3-11), (2) a *narratio* (1.12-14), (3) a *partitio* (1.15-18a), (4) an *argumentatio* that is made up of a number of sub-units (1.18b–4.7), and (5) a *peroratio* (4.8-20). Each of these will be analysed separately in what follows.

Exordium (1.3-11)

While a deliberative *oratio* does not need an *exordium*,[8] there must nevertheless be a beginning to the *oratio*.[9] The thanksgiving period of Philippians (1.3-11) is this *exordium*. Much more than an opening salutation of 'unusual length',[10] it functions rhetorically as a proem intended for a well-disposed audience.[11]

The Philippian *exordium* differs radically from, say, the Galatian *exordium*. In the latter case, following an epistolary prescript (Gal. 1.1-5), Paul introduces the *oratio* with an *exordium* (1.6-10)[12] addressed to a hostile or, at least, potentially hostile audience. As Lausberg notes, the rhetor may use such classes as θαυμάζω, as Paul does in Galatians, 'through the expression of astonishment, which also leads the listener to pay attention and to be prepared to be astonished'.[13]

In the *exordium* of Philippians, however, unadorned imperatives ('imperatifs purs'[14]) are absent. Instead, one finds periphrastic constructs such as προσεύχομαι ἵνα... εἰς τὸ δοκιμάζειν... ἵνα (1.9-10). Furthermore, Paul refers to his own goodwill vis-à-vis the Philippians (1.3-6, restated in vv. 7, 8, 9-10).[15] In 1.7 Paul rehearses the gracious acts and attitude of the Philippians towards himself,[16] a rehearsal in which he suggests 'clearly and briefly what the essence of the *causa* is' (1.5, 7).[17]

The absence of a hortatory tone in the letter's *exordium* has led some to think that Philippians is addressed to a less than hospitable

---

8. *Inst.* 3.8.6. As Quintilian notes the speaker addresses the audience as ones with whom he is in agreement.
9. *Inst.* 3.8.6.: 'debet habere aliquam prooemii speciem'.
10. Vincent, *Philippians*, p. xxxii.
11. Watson views 1.1-26 as the proem ('Rhetorical Analysis', pp. 64-65).
12. According to Hansen (*Abraham*, p. 67) the *exordium* is 1.6-12. Betz (*Galatians*, p. 44) assigns the *exordium* to 1.6-11.
13. Lausberg, *Handbuch*, p. 153.
14. Steen, 'Clichés', p. 124.
15. Cf. *Inv.* 1.16.22.
16. *Inv.* 1.16.22.
17. *Inv.* 1.16.23.

audience. Yet, as we have seen, Hellenistic letter openings are marvels of spartan austerity. Furthermore, in his other letter openings Paul appears to elaborate only in letters that are highly polemical in nature (cf. Gal. 1–5) or in ambassadorial letters addressed to an audience that does not know him (cf. Rom. 1.1-7). For example, the Galatian *exordium* introduces the *causa* of the letter, namely, according to Betz, the state of the Galatian churches in their desertion of the Pauline gospel through the work of 'opponents' of that gospel.[18] Phil. 1.3-11, in fact, sets the tone and anticipates 'some of the major themes and motifs which bind the whole letter together',[19] such as the theme of the Philippians' increasing love of God,[20] as well as the motifs of joy, of an intimate sense of friendship, and of thanks for financial help in the proclamation of the gospel.[21]

The Philippian *exordium*, then, functions as a *genus causae honestum* in which Paul seeks not to change the view of his readers but uses the occasion more for instruction. Here Paul reaffirms his good relations with the Philippian believers. This reaffirmation occurs in the formulaic introduction where Paul mentions his prayers for the believers (1.3-4). It also occurs in Paul's expression of thankfulness for the Philippians' participation in his ministry (1.5), which involves but also transcends their financial support (1.5, 7; cf. 4.10-20).[22]

The *exordium* of Philippians is a significant feature in Paul's *preparatio* of his audience for the instruction he will deliver. It has remark-

---

18. Cf. Betz, *Galatians*, p. 46; Hansen, *Abraham*, p. 67.
19. P.T. O'Brien, *Introductory Thanksgivings in the Letters of Paul* (Leiden: Brill, 1977), pp. 37-38.
20. O'Brien, *Thanksgivings*, pp. 34, commenting on αἴσθησις (1.9), and 39-40 (on 1.9-11; 2.1-11; and 4.2-9); cf. Barth, *Philipper*, pp. 21-22 (on 2 Thess. 3.12 and 4.1).
21. Cf. Lipsius, *Philipper*, p. 218.
22. Cf. Dibelius, *Briefe*, p. 46; O'Brien, *Thanksgivings*, pp. 23, 25, 41-46 (on 1.3); Staab, *Briefe*, p. 31 (citing Rom. 15.26 and 2 Cor. 9.13); Paul Schubert (citing 4.10-20), in Jewett, 'Epistolary Thanksgiving', p. 53; Panikulam, *Koinonia*, p. 85; Dewailly, 'Part prise', pp. 252-54; Hawthorne, *Philippians*, p. 19. This does not mean that 1.7 is either merely a spiritualized reference (e.g. the Authorised Versions' 'my bonds-in-Christ' [1.13]). (Michael, *Philippians*, p. 31) or that they imply Paul's 'grateful recognition that [the Philippians] are with him in spirit, sustaining him by their sympathy and by their prayers, and sustained themselves by his cheerful steadfastness' (Beare, *Philippians*, p. 53).

6. *The Rhetorical Functions of Philippians* 123

able similarities with the *exordium* of 1 Thessalonians.[23] In 1 Thess. 1.3 (cf. also 2 Thess. 1.11) Paul thanks God that the gospel has taken root in the midst of the Thessalonians, whose faith is not merely an adherence to the gospel but a giving of themselves 'qui se poursuit et engendrer l'ἔργον πίστεως'.[24] In Phil. 1.5 Paul thanks God for the Philippian believers who received the gospel, who live it, and who are now spreading it abroad themselves, perhaps with even greater zeal given Paul's inability to do so (cf. 1.14).[25] In both 1 Thessalonians and Philippians it is in the *exordium* that we first discover Paul preparing his readers for what he is going to say. And in both cases these preparatory remarks have to do with suffering and Paul's confident expectation.[26]

Narratio (1.12-14)

The *narratio* follows the *exordium* and is the place where the facts of the *causa* are set forth. So Philippians' *narratio* is coterminous with its epistolary body opening, viz., 1.12-14.

In line with rhetorical demands, Paul's *narratio* is brief.[27] Yet the

---

23. Dewailly, 'Part prise', p. 256; cf. Lightfoot, *Philippians*, p. 82.
24. Dewailly, 'Part prise', p. 256.
25. According to N. Walter ('Die Philipper und das Leiden: Aus den Anfängen einer heidenchristlichen Gemeinde', in *Die Kirche des Anfangs: Festschrift für Heinz Schürmann zum 65. Geburtstag* [ed. R. Schnackenburg, J. Ernst and J. Wanke; Leipzig: St Benno, 1977], p. 430 n. 42) λόγος (1.14) is a *terminus technicus* for mission, as in 1 Thess. 1.6 and Gal. 6.6; cf. Mk 4.14-20 and Acts *passim*.
26. Cf. Watson, 'Rhetorical Analysis', pp. 63-64.
27. *Rhet. ad Alex.* 1438a22. Cf. Betz's suggestion regarding the Galatian *narratio*, namely, 1.12-2.14, corrected to 1.11-2.14 (Betz, *Galatians*, p. 58: Gal. 1.12-2.14; Hansen, *Abraham*, p. 67: Gal. 1.13-2.14). It is neither brief nor free from digression—Paul begins with his birth! Betz glosses over the problem by stating that Paul had to go back to his birth to state the facts of the case (Betz, *Galatians*, p. 61). If, however, as Hansen has suggested, the *narratio* does not give us the facts of the case but only facts 'which have a bearing on the case', then it might be better to view the *narratio* as very brief—1.11-12—and 1.13-2.14 as a *digressio*, which may be included at this point in the *narratio* (Hansen, 'Abraham Story', p. 77; cf. Lausberg, *Handbuch*, p. 187). Hansen assumes, prior to analysis, that the facts introduced are not the facts of the *causa* but rather that they are facts 'which have a direct bearing on the case'. Both Betz and Hansen may have leapt too quickly to the conclusion concerning the *causa*, for if 1.11-12 is the *narratio*, then the *causa* is not the Galatians' desertion of the gospel—which is, admittedly, the rhetorical and emotional thrust of the *exordium*—but the challenge to Paul and to the Pauline gospel.

ordered nature of Philippians' *narratio* is apparent in its development from Paul's imprisonment (1.12) to the word reaching others because of his imprisonment (1.13-14).

The matter that caused Paul to write Philippians, however, is treated with utmost, almost perplexing, dispatch and so is anything but clear. Some have tried to read Philippians as simply an expression of thanks for financial aid with appended notes.[28] But would a *narratio*, such as we find here, have begun a letter of thanks? From all that we know of ancient rhetorical conventions, probably not—at least not simply a letter of thanks.

Although admittedly little can be gathered from the letter's telegraphic *narratio* about what impelled Paul to write to the Philippians, the little we can discern concerns his present imprisonment. Yet here we can see the function of the Philippian *narratio* and, consequently, identify the 'overriding rhetorical problem to which the discourse is addressed'.[29] For the issue (*stasis*) revealed in the *narratio* is the question as to whether the gospel has been preached in vain and whether as a result Paul has experienced his present circumstances in vain—and thus, by extension, whether the Philippians have sent their gift in vain.

Partitio (1.15-18a)
As noted above, controversy surrounds 1.15-18a. Even a cursory reading reveals a break between vv. 14 and 15. Yet scholars are divided over whether 1.15-18a is part of the letter's body opening or body middle. What can rhetorical analysis say in the light of this dilemma?

Rhetorically, a *propositio* or *partitio* follows a *narratio* as the place in the discourse where either the matters to be dealt with are set forth methodically (thus representing a clear continuation of the *narratio*) or where it is first shown 'where he agrees with his opponents and where controversy remains'.[30] In the former case, the necessary qualities of the *narratio* obtain—viz., clarity, brevity and order—

---

28. Against, e.g., Vincent, *Philippians*, p. xxv; Mackay, 'Further Thoughts', pp. 168-70.
29. Black's paraphrase of Kennedy's third step in his rhetorical analysis of New Testament texts (Black, 'Rhetorical Criticism', p. 254; cf. Kennedy, *New Testament Interpretation*, pp. 39-156).
30. *Inv.* 1.22.31.

along with *absolutio* and *paucitas*; in the latter, what is sought is an underscoring of the speaker's case.

That Paul uses the *propositio* to introduce the *confirmatio* has been suggested by Betz for Gal. 2.15-21.[31] A *propositio*, however, may also finalize the *narratio* by summing up what has been said.[32] As such the *propositio* not only finalizes the *narratio* but also introduces the *confirmatio*.[33]

I propose that 1.15-18a is Philippians's *partitio*.[34] As such it consists of a double *propositio*.[35] The double nature of the *propositio* is clear from its chiastic form in which Paul contrasts two different kinds of preaching of Christ.

Now Paul may indeed have (wittingly or unwittingly) mixed rhetorical *genera* by moving out of the sphere of strictly deliberative rhetoric into that of forensic rhetoric by his introduction of a *partitio*. Yet it remains true that a *partitio* can be useful in deliberative rhetoric. For deliberative rhetoric is concerned with honour or repute (*honestum*),[36] with what is useful or beneficial (*utile*),[37] and, possibly, with what is necessary or inevitable (*necessarium*).[38] Paul's situation, though required by necessity, provides the opportunity to choose how both he and the Philippians will view his experience. The resulting contradiction in the scenario, namely, an imposed necessity and yet a task that still lies before, is one that leads to deliberation.[39]

---

31. Betz, *Galatians*, p. 113.
32. Cf. Hansen, *Abraham*, p. 68.
33. *Inst.* 4.4.1.
34. Cf. *Inv.* 1.22.31-23.33; *Inst.* 4.5.1-28.
35. Cf. *Inst.* 4.3.1-9. According to Watson, the confirmation is 2.1–3.21 ('Rhetorical Analysis', p. 67). It would be less objectionable to say that 2.1–3.21 are the limits of the *argumentatio*. Nevertheless, even this statement would have to be seriously modified.
36. *Inst.* 3.8.22; *honestum* includes 'fas, iustum, pium, aequum, mansuetum', i.e., τὸ ἥμερον (*Inst.* 3.8.26).
37. *Inst.* 3.8.22; *utile* includes 'an sit autem facile, magnum, iucundum, sine periculo' (*Inst.* 3.8.27).
38. *Inst.* 3.8.22. Quintilian can understandably find no place for *necessarium* in deliberative rhetoric, which is concerned with persuasion and choice: 'Quantalibet enim vis ingruat, aliquid fortasse pati necesse sit, nihil facere; de faciendo autem deliberatur'.
39. Cf. *Inst.* 3.8.27.

Argumentatio: Confirmatio (1.18b-26)

The *argumentatio* proper begins with the *confirmatio*, which is coterminous with the first sub-section of Philippians's epistolary body middle, viz., 1.18b-26.[40] Epistolary guidelines also enable us to discern the first part of the *confirmatio*, viz., 1.18b-20, the first epistolary segment of 1.18b-26. In these opening verses of the *confirmatio* Paul uses an inductive type of argumentation in setting himself forth as an example.[41] Such a practice is consistent with Quintilian's assertion that deliberative rhetoric is concerned at this point with 'to whom appeal to authority is made and to whom it applies'.[42] Accordingly, 1.19 posits a statement that will serve as the basis for an analogy that 'is of such a kind that it must necessarily be conceded'.[43]

The second half of the *confirmatio*, 1.21-26, presents a deductive argument whose premise is taken from the conclusion of the first half, viz., 1.20b-c.[44] In deliberative fashion Paul sets out the choices that are available to him (life and death, 1.21) and then acknowledges that there is indeed a choice to be made (1.22-24). According to Quintilian,

> almost all deliberative oration is based on comparison, and one sets forth what is to be obtained and how, such that it be possible to evaluate whether it is more suitable or unsuitable to pursue our aims.[45]

The consequences of this choice are made known in 1.25-26.

Argumentatio: Exhortatio (1.27–2.18)

In all likelihood the second epistolary sub-section of 1.15–2.18, viz., 1.27–2.18, represents a hortatory conclusion to the rhetorical *confirmatio* of 1.18b-26. Furthermore, as we noted above, 1.27–2.18 is

---

40. Betz contends that 3.1–4.31 forms the *confirmatio* of Galatians (*Galatians*, p. 128). In this extensive portion of the letter, Betz (p. 129) finds six arguments that lead the Galatians to affirm the truth of Paul's *causa*. These arguments, mixed in style, are based on an appeal to the Galatians' own spiritual experience (3.1-5), to Scripture (3.6-14), to common human practice (3.15-18), to Christian tradition (3.26–4.11), to friendship (4.12-20), and to allegory (4.21-31). Watson suggests that the *confirmatio* is 2.1–3.21 ('Rhetorical Analysis', p. 67).
41. *Inv.* 1.32.53; cf. *Rhet.* 1.2 (1356b1).
42. *Inst.* 3.8.36.
43. *Inv.* 1.32.53.
44. Cf. *Rhet.* 1.2 (1356b1); *Inv.* 1.34.57-41.77.
45. *Inst.* 3.8.34.

6. The Rhetorical Functions of Philippians 127

divided into three parts: 1.27-30; 2.1-11; 2.12-18. Each sub-section commences with parallel motifs centring on Christian conduct (1.27; 2.1-2, 5, 12). Likewise, each of the motifs is spelled out by means of a series of exhortations concerning common thought and conduct (1.27; 2.2-4, 5, 14). Finally, 1.27–2.11 contains echoes of the παρακαλῶ-Satz of 1 Thess. 2.12.[46]

Phil. 1.27	Phil. 2.1	1 Thess. 2.12
μόνον ἀξίως τοῦ εὐαγγελίου τοῦ Χριστοῦ πολιτεύεσθε	εἴ τις οὖν παράκλησις ἐν Χριστῷ, εἴ τι παραμύθιον ἀγάπης	παρακαλοῦντες ὑμᾶς καὶ παραμυθούμενοι καὶ μαρτυρόμενοι εἰς τὸ περιπατεῖν ὑμᾶς ἀξίως τοῦ θεοῦ τοῦ καλοῦντος ὑμᾶς εἰς τὴν ἑαυτοῦ βασιλείαν καὶ δόξαν

The exhortation then continues in 2.12-18, an admittedly problematic sub-section of the hortatory unit 1.27–2.18. It has been noted that 2.12, which opens the final portion of this extended paraenetic section of 1.27–2.18, seems to disregard either the whole of 2.1-11 or just the words of the hymn preceding it, picking up the thought of 1.27-30.[47] Furthermore, the structure of 2.12 seems strangely incomplete, lacking a οὕτως-clause to correspond with the καθώς clause. A οὕτως-clause is to be found at 4.1, as is a variation of the ὥστε + ἀγαπητοί μου which introduces the phrase! Is it possible that the protasis should be separated from the apodosis by 2.13–3.21? Is it possible that within the larger sections of 1.27–2.18 and 3.17–4.7, 2.12-18 corresponds somehow to 4.1?[48] As we will see, there is something to be said for such a view.

In that 2.12 contains lexical echoes of 1.27 (1.27b: ἵνα εἴτε ἐλθὼν καὶ ἰδὼν ὑμᾶς εἴτε ἀπὼν ἀκούω τὰ περὶ ὑμῶν and 2.12b: μὴ ὡς ἐν τῇ παρουσίᾳ μου μόνον ἀλλὰ νῦν πολλῷ μᾶλλον ἐν τῇ ἀπουσίᾳ μου), it may be viewed as part of the practical body middle begun at 1.27, and so understood in the context of Paul's immediately preceding exhortation. The use of ὑπήκοος and ὑπακούω in 2.8 and

---

46. Cf. C.J. Bjerkelund, *Parakalō* (Oslo: Universitetsforlaget, 1967), p. 175.
47. T.J. Deidun, *New Covenant Morality in Paul* (Rome: Pontifical Biblical Institute, 1981), p. 64; cf. Collange, *Philippiens*, p. 97.
48. Hawthorne (*Philippians*, p. 98) glosses over the problem.

12, respectively, which is one of Paul's favourite word groups,[49] would seem to support this.[50]

Argumentatio: Exempla (2.19-30)

As noted earlier at various points, 2.19-30 represents a problematic section in terms of the structure of Philippians. While it has a clear epistolary function as a body closing, does it also have a rhetorical function? Watson suggests that 2.19-30 should be understood as a *digressio*.[51] Cicero cites Hermagoras, according to whom the *digressio*

> consists of an oration that is removed from the *causa* and the judgment, containing a praise of self or a rebuke of the adversary, or that leads to another *causa* from which some kind of *confirmatio* or *reprehensio* may be built up, not by argumentation but by addition through amplification[52]

Yet while it is true that 2.19-30 draws attention away from the immediate concern of the *narratio* and *confirmatio* by pointing to the behaviour of Paul's co-labourers, more significant is its function of adding to or amplifying the *confirmatio*. For in that Timothy and Epaphroditus are (or will be) known to the Philippians, Paul uses them to further the *argumentatio* by pointing to these men as further examples of the Christ-like behaviour Paul sets before the Philippians in the *exhortatio* (1.27–2.18). Therefore it seems more appropriate to view 2.19-30 rhetorically as *exempla* through which Paul illustrates his *argumentatio*.

Both Timothy and Epaphroditus are discussed in the context of their mission to the Philippians—Timothy in the midst of a sending formula (2.19, 23), viz., 2.20-22; Epaphroditus by means of a similar contextualization. For 2.25-26 and 30 represent an *inclusio*, while 2.27 represents an elaboration on Epaphroditus and 2.30 a further development of that elaboration.

---

49. ὑπακούω: 11× Paul; 1× Mark and par.; 1× Q; 1× Luke; 2× Acts; 2× Hebrews; 1× 1 Peter; ὑπακοή: 11× Paul; 1× Hebrews and 3× 1 Peter; ὑπήκοος: 2× Paul: 1× Acts.
50. *Pace* Deidun, *New Covenant*, p. 64.
51. Watson, 'Rhetorical Analysis', p. 71. Nevertheless, Watson argues that 2.9-30 as a whole is a rhetorical digression within the confirmation. Though there is disagreement on the specifics, my view and that of Watson are close on the passage's function.
52. *Inv.* 1.51.97.

6. The Rhetorical Functions of Philippians 129

This rhetorical *exempla* is at the structural centre of the *argumentatio*. If the *partitio* is a means of presenting the matter in dispute, then the *confirmatio* is the actual beginning of the *argumentatio*. It is followed by the hortatory conclusion to the *confirmatio*. The latter side of the *argumentatio* mirrors this arrangement, with the *reprehensio* and its hortatory conclusion. The *exempla* falls neatly in the middle, approximately 29 verses of the *argumentatio* falling on either side of it. This centrality of the *exempla* in the *argumentatio* reflects Paul's desire to portray Timothy and Epaphroditus as perfect types or examples of the kind of behaviour Paul urges his Philippian converts to assume in 1.27–2.18 and which he sets out against his 'opponents' in 3.17–4.7.

Argumentatio: Reprehensio (3.1-16)

The *reprehensio* of an *argumentatio* deals with potential objections to a *causa* as introduced in a *narratio*. Philippians's *reprehensio* appears to be a sub-section of the epistolary section 3.1–4.7, namely 3.1-16. That it functions as the second main part and conclusion of the *confirmatio* is clear from the introductory words of the *reprehensio* (3.1), which, following Holladay,[53] should be translated 'in conclusion', 'as a result', or 'in consequence of what has been said'.

The *reprehensio* uses the same type of argumentation as does the *confirmatio*, 3.2-11 being inductive argumentation with 3.12-16 deductive. It also employs *indignatio*: 'an oration whose end result is that great hatred or grave disfavour is excited against some person or thing'.[54] This is not surprising in a case such as Philippians where the speaker has made himself the *causa* and appeals to his audience from the premise of his own character. In *indignatio* Cicero counselled the speaker to stress the offence as it relates to the speaker and the speaker's immediate audience.[55]

Paul's inductive argumentation in 3.2-11 begins from the agreed but implicit premise of the community's own theological purity. As well, in 3.2-4a Paul uses *negatio* argumentation to deprive his 'opponents'[56]

---

53. Holladay, 'Paul's Opponents', p. 77 n. 1, citing 2 Cor. 13.11; Phil. 4.8; 1 Thess. 4.1; 2 Thess. 3.1. He could have added 1 Cor. 7.29; Gal. 6.17; Eph. 6.10.
54. *Inv.* 1.53.100-105.
55. *Inv.* 1.54.104-105. *Loci* eleven to fifteen, used here, are unique to Cicero; *loci* one to ten are shared with *Rhet. Her.* 2.48-49.
56. On the opponents of Paul at Philippi, see Appendix.

of their argument that they are true worshippers of God. He does this by opening his polemical anticipation with a tripartite introductory rebuttal (3.2, βλέπετε... βλέπετε... βλέπετε...) and then advancing to a contrast of ἡμεῖς γάρ ἐσμεν ἡ περιτομή (3.3a) with τὴν κατατομήν (3.2c).

The main point of Paul's argumentation here does not concern circumcision versus uncircumcision. Most today maintain that the message of 3.2-3 is that the gospel cannot rest on any presumed human perfection, as evidenced by a mark in our fleshly bodies.[57] Yet it is clear from the language he employs[58] that circumcision versus uncircumcision is primarily a rhetorical *topos*[59] that Paul uses to negate the arguments of his 'opponents' concerning his own experiences and those of his followers. Accordingly, the dichotomy, circumcision versus uncircumcision, reveals a more fundamental difference between Paul and his 'opponents', namely two distinctly different modes of existence: existence ἐν σαρκί, which Paul mentions in 3.3 (καὶ οὐκ ἐν σαρκὶ πεποιθότες [3.3bγ]) and develops in 3.4-8, and existence ἐν Χριστῷ, which Paul also mentions in 3.3 (ἡμεῖς γάρ ἐσμεν ἡ περιτομὴ οἱ πνεύματι θεοῦ λατρεύοντες καὶ καυχώμενοι ἐν Χριστῷ Ἰησοῦ [3.3bα-β]) and then develops in 3.7-11.[60]

In 3.4b-6 Paul sets out an outline of life ἐν σαρκί, that is, the kind of life to which Paul could in fact have made appeal himself and which he accuses his 'opponents' of living. These verses are more than mere autobiography,[61] for in them Paul sets forth a stronger argument (*argumentatio firmior*) than that of his opponents. Significant here is Cicero's suggestion that *argumentatio firmior*

> is especially employed in deliberations when we concede that something that is said against us is fairly said but shows that what we defend is necessary; or when we confess that what they defend is indeed acceptable but show that what we say is honourable.[62]

Thus the rhetorical intention of Paul's autobiographical comment in 3.4b-6 is not merely to show that he once stood where his 'opponents'

57. E.g. Panikulam, *Koinonia*, p. 100.
58. Benoit, *Philippiens*, p. 31; Collange, *Philippiens*, pp. 111-12.
59. See Watson, 'Rhetorical Analysis', p. 73, for a discussion of *topoi*.
60. Cf. Dibelius, *Briefe*, p. 60.
61. As, e.g., Collange, *Philippiens*, p. 114; Lyons, *Pauline Autobiography*, p. 153.
62. *Inv.* 1.51.96; cf. 3.18-21.

6. The Rhetorical Functions of Philippians 131

now stand.⁶³ Nor do these verses merely represent Paul's rejection (*negatio*) of his opponents' accusations that he pays insufficient attention to the flesh (specifically to circumcision), or that he considers himself sufficient before God on the basis of his pedigree as summed up in the expressions ἄμεμπτος and δικαιοσύνη ἐν νόμῳ (3.6). Such a defence would only put him on an equal footing with his opponents. Rather, in 3.4b-6 Paul sets forth his own status with the aim of ridiculing those who hold tenaciously to any status ἐν σαρκί, for in so doing they fall short of the goal of life ἐν Χριστῷ.

But who are these 'opponents'? Their identity in Philippians has been hotly debated. Are they Jews, Christians, Gnostics? Do they exist at all? Although controversy has raged (and still does) over the issues raised here,⁶⁴ new light has recently been shed on the question of the function if not the identity of the 'opponents' in Philippians.

The difficult question of the opponents' identity has been touched on by George Lyons who uses rhetorical analysis to discuss some of Paul's autobiographical statements.⁶⁵ In doing so, he has provided some help in answering questions regarding Paul's opposition. For Lyons argues that Paul's letters do not so much evidence actual, historical opposition as they do Paul's use of a rhetorical device of fictitious, hypothetical opposition by means of which Paul can set forth his case autobiographically.

Undoubtedly Lyons has gone too far in all but dismissing the historical reality of opposition to Paul. Yet Lyons has brought to light certain central issues of great importance in the discussion of Paul's opponents, namely, (1) how do we discern how Paul *perceived* this opposition, and (2) how do Paul's words regarding opposition function in the context of what he desires to say to his readers? In the light of Lyons's study and my own rhetorical analysis of the letter, I would suggest that though the opponents of Paul spoken of in Philippians did in fact exist, and though there is much in the letter to suggest that they were some kind of Jewish Christian pneumatics,⁶⁶ their historical identity is veiled by Paul's own rhetorical polemic in which they are

63. So Lightfoot, *Philippians*, p. 146.
64. See Appendix.
65. Lyons, *Pauline Autobiography*.
66. See Appendix.

depicted in terms of the common opponents of God in rabbinical Judaism, namely Epicureans.[67]

Jerome Neyrey has shown that the same tagging of opponents also underlies the argument of 2 Peter.[68] Neyrey compares the 'fictive occasion' of Plutarch's *De sera numinis vindicta* with 2 Peter and argues that the key to understanding the opponents in 2 Peter is to be found in viewing them as Epicureans, who were considered a threat to piety—whether in Judaism (for example, in Josephus's description of the Sadducees as Epicureans)[69] or in 2 Peter[70] because of their rejection of providence.[71] The Epicureans held, for example, that God did not make the world, does not determine it in the present or future, and does not right wrongs either in the here-and-now or in the hereafter.[72]

Neyrey's argument regarding 2 Peter is persuasive. The opponents of that letter seem to be clearly described in Epicurean terms. Yet were they historically Epicureans? Neyrey himself holds that the occasion of Plutarch's work is 'fictive'. What is more, he argues that Josephus was led to describe the Sadducees as he does in part because they were already his opponents.[73] Thus, on analogy, nothing demands that the opponents of 2 Peter be historically Epicureans.

Likewise, given that in rabbinic Judaism and Josephus, as well as in Plutarch's Middle Platonism, Epicureanism was a catch-all title for all opposing views that dismissed providence—and given that almost all theological discussion revolves in some way around the question of theodicy—it is likely that contemporary authors of polemics, influenced either by rabbinic theology or Stoicism, would describe their historical opponent(s) of whatever stance in terms of the acknowledged opponents of divine providence, namely, the Epicureans. While Neyrey may not have helped us draw closer to an accurate assessment of who the opponents in 2 Peter were historically, he has given inestimable help in sorting out the description of those opponents and their function.

---

67. See E.E. Urbach, *The Sages* (trans. I. Abrahams; Jerusalem: Magnes Press, 1979), I, p. 29. See also above, p. 90.
68. J. Neyrey, 'The Form and Background of the Polemic in 2 Peter', *JBL* 99 (1980), pp. 407-31.
69. Josephus, *War* 2.164-165, cited in Neyrey, 'Polemic', p. 414.
70. Neyrey, 'Polemic', pp. 415-31, on 2 Peter.
71. Neyrey, 'Polemic', pp. 408-409; so, too, Urbach, *Sages*, p. 29.
72. Neyrey, 'Polemic', p. 409.
73. 'Polemic', pp. 413-14.

6. The Rhetorical Functions of Philippians 133

And it is possible that what we have in Paul's treatment of his historical opponents in Philippians, whose identity, except in the broadest of outlines, is now veiled, is a tarring with the brush of Epicureanism, a description and label readily available to Paul.

Such an explanation has the virtue of explaining why Paul's opponents have the apparently contradictory form they do. It would explain, for example, how rigorist opponents could be called libertines: not because their behaviour revealed their libertine tendencies, but because as deniers of the providence of God, as Paul perceived it, they fell under the same heading as the well-known libertine deniers of providence, the Epicureans. There is no reason, therefore, to posit different opponents here from those mentioned in the *partitio* of 1.15-18a, for the *reprehensio* of 3.1-16 develops the *partitio*.

Thus, just as Paul in Philippians is not seeking to set forth a historical picture of his imprisonment but rather the meaning of it, so he is not attempting to set forth a historically accurate picture of who his opponents are but rather attempting to convince his followers in Philippi of the value of *his* position. He sets up his 'opponents' in order to delineate more fully his own position, *not* theirs.[74]

Likewise, the depiction of Paul's opponents as Epicureans fits admirably with Paul's intended goal in the letter, namely, to reassure the Philippians—and himself—of resurrection transformation, following sufferings, at the parousia. Whatever the actual, historical case, Paul's 'opponents' in Philippians are entirely this-worldly in terms of their hope. What is more, if Paul's actual historical opponents were Jews or Jewish Christians, Paul has turned the tables on them by painting them with the colours with which they, drawing from their rabbinical tradition or a Stoic tradition, would paint their own opponents.

Now if my estimation of the form and function of Paul's polemic is correct, then we are not amiss in seeing in 3.7-11 Paul's conclusion to the inductive argumentation of 3.2-4a (*negatio*) and of 4b-6 (*argumentatio firmior*), where Paul shifts from a polemical portrayal of Epicurean perfection ἐν σαρκί,[75] to true existence ἐν Χριστῷ (3.8b-11)—with ἐν Χριστῷ functioning as a catch-phrase for Paul's understanding of what it means to reflect in one's experience the Christ type. This shift takes place in 3.7-8a.

74. See above p. 90.
75. Cf. Jewett, *Anthropological Terms*, p. 118.

Structurally, 3.7-8a is a carefully crafted rhetorical axis in the form of an *inclusio*, bound by the words κέρδος and κερδήσω.[76] With these words, Paul expresses how being ἐν Χριστῷ surpasses existence ἐν σαρκί. Although loss is not necessarily implicit in gain—one *could* gain in addition to what one has—Paul contrasts the gain of being ἐν Χριστῷ (expressed by triple διά clauses: διὰ τὸν Χριστόν, διὰ τῆς γνώσεως Χριστοῦ Ἰησοῦ,[77] and δι' ὄν)[78] with his loss (here expressed three times by the structurally dependent word-group ζημια-). The use of ζήμιαν in parallel phrases (twice using the substantive and the third time using the verb) serves Paul's purpose of highlighting the term σκύβαλα (with the accompanying ἥγουμαι) by leaving that term uncomfortably isolated and stark: any allegiance to σάρξ, as opposed to Χριστός, is simply useless garbage. Thus Phil. 3.7-8 brings Paul to the conclusion of his argument inaugurated in 3.3, namely, to the ἐν Χριστῷ pole of the contrast.

Beginning with the ἵνα purpose clause at the end of 3.8, Paul elucidates further on what he means by the phrase ἐν Χριστῷ in the following phrases: (1) ἵνα Χριστὸν κερδήσω (3.8), (2) ἔχων... δικαιοσύνην διὰ πίστεως Χριστοῦ ἐκ θεοῦ ἐπὶ τῇ πίστει (3.9), and (3) τοῦ γνῶναι αὐτόν (3.10), which as a gerundive explicates both (1) and (2).[79] Starting from the basis of his experience of Christ, Paul has denied the experience of his 'opponents' (3.2-4a), has provided a stronger argument for his own position (3.4b-6), and, following the rhetorical axis (3.7-8), has concluded that life in Christ is the future goal of the believer (3.8-11).

In the second part of the *reprehensio* (3.12-16) Paul argues deductively. As in 3.2-4a, in 3.12a-b he uses a *negatio* form of argumentation, which, as in 3.2-4a, allows him to separate himself even further

---

76. Against Beare, *Philippians*, p. 116, who takes ἵνα Χριστὸν κερδήσω as 'dependent upon the two verbs in the present tense: *I count everything as loss... I count it all rubbish, that I may gain Christ*'.

77. Beare offers no reason for taking γνώσεως as a genitive of apposition (*Philippians*, p. 112).

78. Dibelius, *Briefe*, p. 59.

79. On (1), see Huby, *Saint Paul*, p. 348; K.T. Kleinknecht, *Der leidende Gerechtfertigte* (Tübingen: Mohr, 1984) p. 307; Barth, *Philipper*, p. 59; on (2), see P. Jouön, 'Notes philologiques sur quelques versets de l'épître aux Philippiens', *RSR* 28 (1938), pp. 305-306 (apparently following Loisy); Friedrich, *Philipper*, p. 119. The earliest understanding of the verses in this way may be found in John Damascene, *In epistulam ad Philippenses*, PG 95.873D.

6. The Rhetorical Functions of Philippians 135

from his 'Epicurean' opponents. Specifically, Paul argues enthymemetically to the conclusion that he has not yet arrived at perfection. He argues thus by contrasting the goals of 3.8-11 with what he has not yet accomplished, namely, οὐχ... ἔλαβον (3.12a, cf. ἵνα κερδήσω, 3.8c), (οὐ) τετελείωμαι (3.12a, cf. [ἵνα] εὑρέθω, 3.9a), εἰ καὶ καταλάβω (3.12b, cf. τὸ γνῶναι, 3.10). In this way he is able to argue against a hidden premise that the counting of all things as loss is somehow sufficient for perfection.

The *negatio* conclusion, spelled out in 3.12a-b, is reiterated in 3.13a. Each of these *negationes*, however, is followed by another conclusion, in this case, a *conclusio non necessaria*, in which Paul states positively what he does in order to accomplish his goal. Thus, in 3.12b Paul says διώκω δὲ εἰ καὶ καταλάβω (3.12), which seems to be picked up in 3.14: κατὰ σκοπὸν διώκω εἰς τὸ βράβειον. In 13b he says ἕν δέ, τὰ μὲν ὀπίσω ἐπιλανθανόμενος τοῖς δὲ ἔμπροσθεν ἐπεκτεινόμενος. The goals are to be striven for, says Paul using the language of athletic exertion.[80] Finally 3.15-16 provides a hortatory conclusion to the section in preparation for the exhortation contained in 3.17–4.7.

Argumentatio: Exhortatio (3.17–4.7)

I have already noted the presence of a hortatory conclusion to the *confirmatio* in 1.27–2.18. Another exhortation, however, is to be found in 3.17–4.7, the epistolary sub-section of the larger section 3.1–4.7. It, too, functions as a hortatory conclusion. But there are two differences. First, while both portions are part of the larger *argumentatio*, 1.27–2.18 is a conclusion to the *confirmatio*, while 3.17–4.7 is a conclusion to the *reprehensio*. Secondly, while the exhortation of 1.27–2.18 is tripartite (1.27-30; 2.1-11; 2.12-18), 3.17–4.7 is bipartite.

In terms of rhetorical function, however, the two portions have much in common. Specifically, the hortatory conclusion to the *confirmatio* employs the example of Paul himself and Christ in so far as Paul 'impersonates' Christ. The hortatory conclusion to the *reprehensio* also employs the example of Paul, but now as distinguished from his 'opponents'. In 1.27–2.18 Paul's desire is to underscore his choice of suffering in this world for the sake of the community, rather than glorification. So he invokes the Christ hymn of 2.6-11 to show how Christ is personified in himself. In 3.17–4.7 Paul's intention is to point

80. Pfitzner, *Agon Motif*, pp. 139-40.

to the ultimate goal of all faithful servants of God, namely, resurrection transformation. In order to show this he again invokes a hymnic portion, that of 3.20-21.

In the latter half of 3.17–4.7, viz., 4.1-7, Paul's concern is to ensure that the behaviour of his community evidences that they belong ultimately to the heavenly world through resurrection transformation rather than to a perishing earth, as is the case of his 'opponents'. Accordingly, Paul's words here are dependent on the first part of the exhortation in 3.17-21.[81]

Peroratio (4.8-20)
The *peroratio* occurs in 4.8-20.[82] Following the introductory formulae of 4.8, 9, Paul in 4.10-20 summarizes the concerns of his address, a key feature of a *peroratio*. Various themes scattered throughout the letter are brought together, not least of which is Paul's thank-you to the Philippians, expressed by means of an *inclusio* between the *proem* (1.5, 7) and the *peroratio* (4.15).

True, an *indignatio* is absent from the *peroratio*, probably because of Paul's inclusion of the *indignatio* in the *reprehensio* (3.1–4.7). Cicero notes 'that an indignation can be dealt with in whatever place is most suited for it'.[83] This might further help to explain why Paul breaks with rhetorical conventions[84] and separates the anticipation (3.1-16) from the summary (4.8-20) by the interjection of an exhortation (3.17–4.7), which in 3.17-21 develops in hortatory fashion the theme of the anticipation as *indignatio*.

Yet the most striking feature of the *peroratio* is the presence of a clear *conquestio* (4.10-14). Here Paul follows closely the *loci* prescribed by Cicero for an effective concluding *conquestio* by further

81. Against Bjerkelund, *Parakalo*, pp. 175-76, according to whom the paraenesis is a critique of the situation of disunity at Philippi. Cf. Lipsius, *Philipper*, p. 243, citing Rom. 15.33; 16.20; 2 Cor. 13.11; 1 Thess. 5.23.
82. Watson sees 4.1-20 as Paul's summary ('Rhetorical Analysis', p. 76-79). According to him, 4.1-9 is a rhetorical repetition within the summary. According to Betz the Galatian *peroratio* is 6.11-18 (*Galatians*, p. 312). While one does expect a *peroratio* in a rhetorical address, Betz's identification leaves one with the uncomfortable feeling that a rigorous control over the assignation of rhetorical parts in Paul's letters is still lacking. For why should the epistolary *post*script have a specific rhetorical function when the epistolary *pre*script does not?
83. *Inv.* 1.53.100.
84. *Rhet. ad Alex.* 1439b11-13.

endearing himself to the Philippians. He does this by stressing in *inclusio* fashion their gift to him (4.10, 14) and, within the *inclusio*, his deprived state and response to it (4.11-13). Paul thus utilizes in 4.11-13 Cicero's sixteenth *locus* for the *conquestio*, namely, the *ostensio animi*:

> we show that our soul is compassionate towards others and nevertheless we demonstrate that it is and will be high-minded, excellent, and patient in all discomforts, should they arise.[85]

In the second half of the *peroratio* Paul appears to hint that he had expected some support from other churches but that this was not forthcoming (4.15-16, 17). The presence of this note in the *peroratio* represents a twist of Cicero's sixth *locus*, namely, the *summae miseriae*:

> where the speaker is shown to experience griefs beyond hope, and when he expects something, not only does he not obtain it, but he falls into the very depths of grief.[86]

Paul follows this with a restatement of the *ostensio animi* (4.18a) and then singles out the gift of the Philippians (4.18b-19), even as he had done in the *proem*.[87] The doxology of 4.20 brings the rhetorical address to a close. This is immediately followed by the epistolary postscript of 4.21-23.

3. Conclusion

In the light of the above rhetorical analysis, I suggest that the rhetorical functions of the component parts of Philippians are as follows:

(Epistolary Prescript 1.1-2)
1.3-11   *Exordium*
1.12-14   *Narratio*
1.15-18a *Partitio*
1.18b–4.7 *Argumentatio*
    1.18b-26   *confirmatio*
    1.27–2.18 *exhortatio* (conclusion to *confirmatio*)
    2.19-30   *exempla*
    3.1-16   *reprehensio*
    3.17–4.7   *exhortatio* (conclusion to *reprehensio*)
4.8-20   *Peroratio*
(Epistolary Postscript 4.21-23)

---

85. *Inv.* 1.56.109.
86. *Inv.* 1.55.108.
87. Cf. *Inst.* 6.1.12.

Epistolary guidelines provide us with a measure of scientific control over the assigning of rhetorical functions in the letter. By understanding the epistolary structure of Philippians we are able to understand the letter on its own terms rather than in those presented by modern exegetes.

So in Philippians we discover a rhetorical address, the focus of which is entirely on Paul. Paul appeals to others whose type he embodies (Christ) or who embody the Paul type (Timothy, Epaphroditus and the Philippian community) in order to make his case. He also radically contrasts himself with his 'opponents', who are characterized by another type opposed to that of Christ.

PART III

EXEGETICAL AND THEMATIC STUDIES

Chapter 7

THE THEME OF SUFFERING IN THE *PREPARATIO*

1. *Epistolary Prescript (1.1-2)*

That the very *stasis* of Philippians concerns suffering can be argued from Paul's description of himself and Timothy as δοῦλοι (1.1). It is an interesting designation in that Paul mentions Timothy along with himself as senders (as also in the letter openings of 2 Cor. 1.1; Phlm 1; cf. Col. 1.1). Yet the practice of mentioning other senders is not alien to the non-literary papyri (e.g. PTebt 1.48). Paul, in fact, names not only himself but also one or two others in all of his letter openings except Rom. 1.1 and Gal. 1.1 (cf. Eph. 1.1).[1] Nor is it unusual in the papyri to find senders identifying themselves by a known appellative, as in PTebt 2.289.

Yet, why δοῦλοι? Custom is unfortunately no guide to the meaning of the term. In his acknowledged letters, Paul appears to have been reticent to use δοῦλος. It is used by Paul of himself in letter openings only here and at Rom. 1.1 (cf. Tit. 1.1; Jas 1.1; Jude 1; 2 Pet. 1.1 and Rev. 1.1), and only in 2 Cor. 4.5 and Gal. 1.10 outside of letter openings. But it appears with reference to both Paul and another only here—breaking with Paul's general approach of putting 'a distance between himself and his colleagues'.[2]

What leads Paul to choose this particular term to describe this situation? Moreover, why would he break with his normal practice and apply the same term to Timothy? Gnilka's suggestion, that Timothy's name is mentioned because of his good relations with the Philippian congregation, rightly rejects the view that Timothy is mentioned as amanuensis.[3] But it nevertheless must be discarded. For though Gnilka

---

1. Cf. Doty, *Letters*, p. 30.
2. Hawthorne, *Philippians*, p. 3.
3. Gnilka, *Philipperbrief*, pp. 29-30.

7. The Theme of Suffering in the Preparatio 141

adduces as proof for his contention the examples of Romans and Galatians—which are agreed to be authoritative but where Paul's name stands alone—he conveniently neglects to explain why Paul asserts that οἱ σὺν ἐμοὶ πάντες ἀδελφοί were responsible for Galatians (cf. 1.2). That δοῦλοι is used to highlight the theme of suffering has been suggested by a number of scholars. Some, for example, have conjectured that Paul, writing in a Hellenistic setting, speaks of himself and Timothy as subservient, dependent, redeemed property, that is, as slaves,[4] who though imprisoned are free in that they are slaves of Jesus Christ. G. Barth, for example, writes 'that what Paul and Timothy are and say, they are and say not of their own right and power, but as slaves of their Lord'.[5]

Now this explanation, though it takes into account the overtones of suffering suggested by δοῦλοι, is patently insufficient. For why, we may ask, does Paul not then use δοῦλος in 1 and 2 Thessalonians, letters which, though not reflecting a prison setting, are certainly directed to a Hellenistic audience, or in Philemon, which does, in fact, reflect a prison setting? Or, again, though meaningful, would not Paul's theological use of δοῦλος in a letter have been off-putting to this Hellenistic congregation attuned to the word's social and economic overtones?[6]

The view that δοῦλος is used here with specific reference to Paul's sufferings while in prison was suggested some 50 years ago by Lohmeyer,[7] who, as we have seen, believed that Paul wrote a treatise on martyrdom. According to Lohmeyer the use of δοῦλοι fits ideally into a martyrological understanding of Philippians. Lohmeyer did not draw this conclusion because the word necessarily refers to Paul's imprisonment or sufferings, for it is absent in the other Prison Epistles. Rather, according to Lohmeyer, δοῦλοι functions as Paul's substitute in Philippians for the more normal designation ἀπόστολος,[8]

---

4. J.L. Houlden, *Paul's Letters from Prison: Philippians, Colossians, Philemon and Ephesians* (PNTC; Harmondsworth: Penguin Books, 1970), p. 47; BAGD, pp. 205-206.
5. Barth, *Philipper*, p. 4; cf. Vincent, *Philippians*, p. 2; V.P. Furnish, *Theology and Ethics in Paul* (Nashville: Abingdon, 1968), p. 179.
6. So K. Grayston, *The Letters of Paul to the Philippians and to the Thessalonians* (CBC; Cambridge: Cambridge University Press, 1967), pp. 11-12.
7. Lohmeyer, *Philipper*, p. 5.
8. Lohmeyer, *Philipper*, pp. 5, 9.

a designation absent only in the letter openings of Philippians, 1 and 2 Thessalonians and Philemon.[9] Clearly some reason for the absence of ἀπόστολος in 1.1 needs to be suggested. And suggestions have indeed been forthcoming. For example, some have argued that Philippians is an essentially personal letter with no point to drive home, and therefore no appeal to apostolic authority needed—as compared with, say, 1 Corinthians or Romans.[10] Others have suggested that ἀπόστολος is omitted because Paul's 'office as an apostle had not been challenged at Philippi'.[11]

The first suggestion, however, founders on the evidence of the public nature of Philippians, which can be seen in Paul's inclusion of Timothy as co-worker and witness.[12] And the second suggestion overlooks the absence of the term in the letter opening of 1 Thessalonians, although 1 Thess. 2.1-20 is a clear defence of Paul's apostolic ministry.

Few suggestions have been as compelling as that of Lohmeyer, namely, that δοῦλος was Paul's word in Philippians for ἀπόστολος. Nevertheless, Lohmeyer's view, insightful as it is, is vitiated by the fact that both ἀπόστολος and δοῦλος are present in Rom. 1.1 and that δοῦλος is present in Gal. 1.10. Furthermore, the term δοῦλος is used in none of the other so-called Prison Epistles, but appears in letters in which Paul is not necessarily thought to have been in prison[13]—as well as in the letter openings of James, Jude and 2 Peter, letters that are apparently free of prison or martyrological overtones.[14]

In spite of this critique of Lohmeyer's insight into the relationship between δοῦλος and ἀπόστολος, attempts have been made to salvage it. G. Sass, followed by E. Best, offered the intriguing suggestion that

9. Cf. 1 Cor. 1.1; 2 Cor. 1.1; Col. 1.1; Eph. 1.1.
10. For a survey of opinion, see E. Best, 'Bishops and Deacons', in *Studia Evangelica* (ed. F.L. Cross; Berlin: Akademie, 1968), IV.1, pp. 473-75. Even Lohmeyer (followed by Gnilka) stresses that Paul's words in 1.1 serve to drive home Paul's heart-ties to the Philippian congregation (*Philipper*, pp. 9-10; Gnilka, *Philipperbrief*, p. 31).
11. E.g. Martin, *Philippians*, p. 56. The earliest instance of this theory seems to be that of Ambrosiaster, *In Epistolam ad Philippenses*, PL 17.403C, followed later by Haymo. See above, p. 26.
12. 1 Thess. 2.2; 3.1; 2 Thess. 1.1; cf. Acts 16.1 and 17.14; *pace* Hawthorne, *Philippians*, pp. 3-4, who rejects the public nature of the letter with no justification at all.
13. E.g. Rom. 1.1; cf. Tit. 1.1.
14. Though cf. Rev. 1.1!

7. The Theme of Suffering in the Preparatio 143

Paul uses δοῦλος in place of ἀπόστολος in order to stress (1) his role as a chosen member of a distinguished group of leaders and (2) his subservience to the community consequent upon such a high calling.[15] On the basis of its use in the LXX, it is argued that Paul draws δοῦλος from the Old Testament to highlight his prophetic identity as a leader entrusted by God with a specific task and as the one through whom God acts, but also to signal his lowliness and so to criticize in a veiled way those who seek power and, consequently, divide the Philippian congregation.[16] According to Best, the same down-playing of position is at work in Paul's mocking reference to the Philippians' ἐπίσκοποι and διάκονοι.[17]

That Paul directs his attention to the divided nature of the Philippian community, however, raises the question as to whether the Philippian community was, in fact, divided. The answer to that question is by no means self-evident. Nothing in the epistolographic or rhetorical structure of the letter itself necessitates such a view. At best, such an argument is deduced from Paul's call to unity in 2.1-4.

Furthermore, Sass's elaborate theory raises another question about the Philippians' background. Would they have been able to draw from the use of δοῦλοι this subtle argument against a supposed disunity? As converts from a Gentile or predominately Gentile community or even from Hellenistic Jewish communities, they probably would not have been as conversant with the intricacies of LXX vocabulary as Paul was or modern scholars are. And this, it seems, it one reason why Hawthorne opts for a 'Hellenistic' understanding of δοῦλοι.[18]

Thus in the light of the present impasse concerning the interpretation of this term, I suggest that Lohmeyer was probably correct to discern a connection between δοῦλοι and the absence of ἀπόστολος,

---

15. G. Sass, 'Zur Bedeutung von δοῦλος bei Paulus', ZNW 40 (1941), pp. 24-32; Best, 'Bishops and Deacons', pp. 374-76; Beare, Philippians, pp. 50-51; Martin, Philippians, pp. 57-58.
16. LXX δοῦλοι κυρίου or θεοῦ, e.g., Abraham (Ps. 104.42 LXX), Moses (Exod. 14.31; Num. 12.7; Josh. 14.7; 4 Kgs 18.12; Ps. 104.26 LXX; Mal. 3.24), David (2 Kgs 7.5; Ps. 88.4 LXX), Jacob (Isa. 48.20; Jer. 26.27), the prophets (Amos 3.7; Jer. 25.4; Dan. 9.6, 10), and other pious men (Ps. 27.9; Job 1.8; Jer. 7.25); cf. Gnilka, Philipperbrief, p. 30; Beare, Philippians, pp. 50-51; Beker, Paul, p. 115. Note Vincent's early intuition: the 'LXX δοῦλος θεοῦ or κυρίου is often applied to the OT prophets in a body' (Philippians, p. 2).
17. Best, 'Bishops and Deacons', pp. 374-76.
18. Hawthorne, Philippians, pp. 4-5.

though, contrary to Sass, not in a substitutionary way. In all probability the absence of ἀπόστολος in 1.1 is to be explained as due to the early date of Philippians. For ἀπόστολος as an ascription is also absent in the letter openings of Paul's earliest extant letters, namely 1 and 2 Thessalonians. It may simply be, therefore, that at this early point in Paul's career the controversies that focused on apostolicity and that rocked Paul's later years had not yet taken shape in the communities addressed by 1 and 2 Thessalonians and Philippians.

True, ἀπόστολος is used in 1 Cor. 1.1, a letter that precedes the writing of Philippians, indicating in all probability that Paul perceived his authority to be in question there. We cannot, however, deduce from the slightly later date of Philippians that the same situation necessarily obtained at Philippi. For although Paul's dialogue with the Philippian believers overlaps chronologically the Corinthian sequence, and Philippians is later, the two letters do not necessarily address the same situations. In 1 and 2 Thessalonians and Philippians, then, Paul's self-conscious identity as minister of the gospel of Christ is communicated to Macedonian believers semantically by terms other than the later, polemical use of ἀπόστολος. And one of these terms is δοῦλος.

Furthermore, there is truth to Lohmeyer's contention that δοῦλοι functions in what may be a martyrological context, for Paul's use of δοῦλος does speak of how lowly, humble service makes no self-centred claim to position or dignity.[19] Where I differ from Lohmeyer's assessment of the situation, however, is in the *locus* of the perceived problem. For Paul's words do not illuminate the situation of the community as much as they do Paul's own mind. In Philippians Paul communicates his perception of *his* ministry and its reception,[20] for, as becomes clear in the letter body, it is the experiences of his ministry that Paul wants to set before the Philippians.

For these reasons I believe that Paul's intention in using δοῦλοι follows the rhetorical practice of the day as he sought to establish himself and his co-workers—in this case, Timothy—before his audience as ones worthy of belief. Paul makes himself a credible speaker by presenting himself in terms of Christ, who in 2.7 will also be called δοῦλος. He does the same for Timothy, whose own work will again be spoken of in 2.22 by the verbal form δουλεύω. Clearly,

19. So Müller, *Philippians*, p. 34; cf. D. Garland, 'Philippians 1.1-26', *RevExp* 77 (1980), p. 328, though for different reasons; Hawthorne, *Philippians*, pp. 3-4.
20. *Pace* Houlden, *Paul's Letters*, p. 48.

7. The Theme of Suffering in the Preparatio 145

neither δοῦλος (2.7) nor δουλεύω (2.22) have to do with imprisonment. Rather, as 2.7 suggests, they may very well have something to do with how Christ is pictured.

So Paul accomplishes in telegraphic fashion the same end as his lengthy *apologia* of 1 Thess. 2.1-20, where he stresses his sufferings and labours on behalf of the community. Sass was not entirely incorrect in his examination of δοῦλοι: however, he lacked the rhetorical context that would have elucidated the letter. For sufferings and labours in Philippians, as in 1 Thessalonians, both endear Paul's audience to him and make him credible, in particular over against 'opponents' who appear diametrically opposed to Paul.

But what role do the Philippians play in all this? Are they simply an audience, addressed by Paul? The answer begins to be given in the *exordium*.

2. *Exordium (1.3-11)*

Like the epistolary prescript, the Philippian *exordium* also suggests that the rhetorical *stasis* or specific question at issue has to do with suffering. This is most clear in 1.5 and 7. Although the close relationship between 1.5 and 7 is not immediately apparent, it is nevertheless the case that if 1.3-4a is a formulaic unit[21] and 1.4b (μετὰ χαρᾶς τὴν δέησιν ποιούμενος) is an explanatory clause,[22] then 1.7 must be related to the entire unit 1.3-6 and not only to 1.6 or 1.4.

Furthermore, given that the participation envisioned in 1.5 is active ('your cooperation [in aid of] the gospel'), not passive ('your participation in the gospel'),[23] it is likely that Paul's words on the Philippians' participation with him in 1.7 are a fuller expression of his words in 1.5. As Michael says:

> Paul thought of the Philippians, in virtue of their sharing with him in the divine grace, as co-partners with him in his imprisonment, and as co-operating with him in his defence and vindication of the gospel.[24]

---

21. Cf. Rom. 1.8-10; 1 Cor. 1.4; Col. 1.3; 1 Thess. 1.2.
22. Lightfoot, *Philippians*, p. 82. For a summary of opinion, see Dewailly, 'Part prise', p. 248; Omanson, 'Translation of Philippians 1.3-5', p. 244; Panikulam, *Koinonia*, pp. 81-82.
23. O'Brien, *Thanksgivings*, pp. 23-24.
24. Michael, *Philippians*, p. 15.

In the *exordium*, as in the epistolary prescript, suffering functions as a *captatio benevolentiae*. The words, however, also reveal the foundation of Paul's *inventio*. For Paul's stress on their love, which was manifest in their gift, suggests that he will appeal directly to the audience for confirmation. The Philippian believers will not only be the tribunal before whom what Paul says will be believed or disbelieved but also the very evidence of the Pauline *causa*, since their acceptance of the gospel confirms Paul's hopes by evidencing the effectiveness of the gospel.[25]

In fact, because the gospel has become implanted in the Philippian community—as in the Thessalonian community—Paul's labours and sufferings are shown not to have been in vain but to have been truly efficacious.[26] The Philippians' faithfulness 'ist keine Selbstverständlichkeit, sondern blankes Wunder, für das Paulus nicht aufhören kann zu danken'.[27] Thus Paul can speak of these believers as εὐδοκία, a term he later uses to emphasize his confidence in the accomplishment of God's purposes according to God's agenda (cf. 1.15b; 2.13).

Paul's perception of the Philippians is due not only to their gift but also to that which the gift manifests, namely, their share in Paul's work of proclamation (1.7). Paul expresses joy because in the Philippians' fulfilment of his work they prove that regardless of his fate the gospel will advance.[28] According to Karl Barth, Paul in 1.5, 7 is thinking of

> the active collaboration of the Philippians in the *proclaiming* of the Gospel, of their earnestness in letting it *be* the Gospel in their own midst, of their *prayers* for its progress through the world and *to that extent* their company on his own high, hard apostolic way.[29]

While Barth does show how Paul's words transcend a mere thanksgiving for monetary relief, he does not go far enough. For Paul's involvement of the audience in the *causa* not only indicates his

---

25. Cf. Barth, *Philipper*, p. 21.
26. Vincent, *Philippians*, p. 9.
27. Barth, *Philipper*, p. 18.
28. Cf. Ellicott, cited in Michael, *Philippians*, p. 32; M. Bouttier, *En Christ: Etude d'exégèse et de théologie pauliniennes* (EHPR, 54; Paris: Presses Universitaires de France, 1962), p. 130, relating Phil. 1.13 to 2 Cor. 2.14; 3.1, 18; and 4.10; Martin, *Philippians*, p. 68; P.T. O'Brien, *Introductory Thanksgivings in the Letters of Paul* (NovTSup, 49; Leiden: Brill, 1977), p. 25 n. 30 (citing Rom. 1.5; Eph. 3.2 and 8).
29. Barth, *Philippians*, p. 16 (emphases his).

conviction that the Philippians are participants in his work,[30] but also that they vividly embody his own style. This is hinted at by Dewailly, who notes that Paul's use of κοινωνία and πᾶς (1.3, 9)—as well as εἰς and τὰ εἰς τὰ αὐτά (1.27; 2.2-3; 4.2), ἰσοψύχης (2.20), and the συν-compounds—speaks of union between Paul and his co-workers, between Paul and the Christians, and between all Christians and Christ.[31]

This is not, however, an *imitatio Pauli*. Using Patte's conceptual framework and my own discovery of the rhetorical function of the *exordium*, we can see how in the *exordium* Paul appeals to the Philippians' 'proclamation' of the gospel by the embodiment in their lives of the Christ and Paul 'types'.[32] This is especially true in relation to the term φρονέω found here, and again in 2.5 and 3.15 (cf. 2.2 [twice], 3; 3.15, 19; 4.2, and 10 [twice]). Although Paul does not here directly address the Philippians' own suffering, he does suggest that their sufferings, as well as their embodiment of the task of proclamation,[33] mirror his experiences.

Furthermore, as in the case of Christ, Paul and his co-workers, the Philippians not only participate in or reproduce the 'type' in terms of suffering, but they also reiterate the triumph of the gospel reflected in Christ's experience and in Paul's confidence, a triumph to the fulfilled at the parousia. The strongly eschatological tone of the *exordium* in Philippians—manifest in the concluding eschatological climax[34] and in the parallels between the thanksgiving of Philippians and that of 1 Corinthians—highlights Paul's confidence in the parousia, a confidence that is in large part due to the faithfulness of the Philippians.[35] It is in this light that Paul speaks to the Philippians about suffering.

3. *Narratio (1.12-14)*

The disclosure formula of the body opening (1.12a) testifies to Paul's awareness that the *narratio*'s optimistic estimate of his sufferings

---

30. Cf. Gnilka, *Philipperbrief*, p. 45.
31. Dewailly, 'Part prise', p. 259.
32. Cf. Panikulam, *Koinōnia*, p. 85; Lipsius, *Briefe*, p. 217.
33. Cf. Grayston, *Philippians*, p. 17.
34. Cf. Dewailly, 'Part prise', p. 258; Panikulam, *Koinōnia*, pp. 85-86.
35. Cf. Barth, *Philipper*, p. 18; D.M. Stanley, *Christ's Resurrection in Pauline Soteriology* (Rome: Pontifical Biblical Institute Press, 1961), p. 95.

would come as a surprise to the Philippians.[36] Behind this *narratio* one may discern the Philippians' expectation of a tragic outcome to Paul's imprisonment and Paul's desire to redress that fear. The majority of commentators, therefore, are correct when they hold that the occasion of Philippians has to do first of all with the congregation's communication to Paul of some form of concern over his personal fate.[37]

One would have expected, however, in what has been called Paul's most personal letter and in what we have discovered to be a deliberative address, more personal information intended, at least in part, to support this perception.[38] This is, in fact, what we find, for example, in the *ostensio animi* of the *peroratio*. Yet even there Paul's intention seems to have been otherwise.

Or we might have expected some details to explain Paul's situation. True, Timothy or Epaphroditus may have been charged with this information. Nonetheless, the absence is striking.

Rather, in the *narratio* Paul appears to have suppressed the *facts* surrounding his sufferings and to have stressed the *meaning* of those sufferings, specifically the meaning for the progress of the gospel.[39] He responds to their concerns by communicating to them not the details of his personal imprisonment, which beyond the simple statement of them (τὰ κατ' ἐμέ) are never elaborated in personal terms, but the meaning of his imprisonment for the advance of the gospel (1.12-14).[40]

In fact, he writes to the Philippians not personally but rather in terms of his role and function as their father (cf. 1 Thess. 1.5; 2.7; 1 Cor. 4.14, 15). As such, he writes to them of his confidence in the advance of the gospel. This confidence, manifest here in the *narratio*, represents a development of verses 1.7 and 9 in the *exordium*:

---

36. Cf. Michael, *Philippians*, pp. 27-28.
37. Cf. Hawthorne, *Philippians*, p. 34.
38. Cf. Funk, 'Apostolic Parousia', p. 262 n. 1; against Jerome, *Commentarii in epistolam ad Philippenses*, *PL* 30: 842B-C; G.B. Caird, *Paul's Letters from Prison* (Oxford: Oxford University Press, 1976), p. 109; Lohmeyer, *Philipper*, pp. 51-52; Gnilka, *Philipperbrief*, pp. 55, 66; Friedrich, *Philipper*, p. 103; cf. Houlden, *Paul's Letters*, p. 53.
39. Cf. Caird, *Letters*, p. 109; Bouttier, *En Christ*, p. 130 (on Phil. 1.13 in relation to 2 Cor. 2.14; 3.1, 18; and 4.10).
40. Lohmeyer, *Philipper*, p. 51.

7. The Theme of Suffering in the Preparatio 149

Narratio	Exordium
1.12	1.9
... ὅτι τὰ κατ' ἐμὲ μᾶλλον εἰς προκοπὴν τοῦ εὐαγγελίου ἐλήλυθεν	... ἵνα ἡ ἀγάπη ὑμῶν ἔτι μᾶλλον καὶ μᾶλλον περισσεύῃ
1.13-14	1.7
ὥστε τοὺς δεσμούς μου φανεροὺς ἐν Χριστῷ γενέσθαι ... καὶ τοὺς πλείονας τῶν ἀδελφῶν ἐν κυρίῳ πεποιθότας τοῖς δεσμοῖς μου περισσοτέρως τολμᾶν ἀφόβως τὸν λόγον λαλεῖν	... ἔν τε τοῖς δεσμοῖς μου καὶ ἐν τῇ ἀπολογίᾳ καὶ βεβαιώσει τοῦ εὐαγγελίου συγκοινωνούς μου τῆς χάριτος πάντας ὑμᾶς ὄντας

As in the *exordium*, so here, too, Paul involves the believers in his task. Thus in the *narratio* Paul expresses his confidence by noting how, on the one hand, his preaching has reached the very heart of imperial Rome (1.13),[41] and, on the other, how believers are taking up the task of preaching (1.14):[42]

ὥστε	καὶ
τοὺς δεσμούς μου	τοὺς πλείονας τῶν ἀδελφῶν
φανεροὺς [γενέσθαι]	[τολμᾶν λαλεῖν τὸν λόγον]
ἐν Χριστῷ	ἐν κυρίῳ
ἐν ὅλῳ τῷ πραιτωρίῳ	περισσοτέρως
καὶ τοῖς λοιποῖς πᾶσιν	ἀφόβως

The reason for inclusion of this parallelism here in the *narratio* again has to do with Paul's emphasis on his role as the apostolic founder of the community rather than on any supposed personal address to the Philippians. Paul perceives that because of his imprisonment the word (1) has extended beyond its expected bounds and (2) is preached more boldly by other believers (1.14).[43] For him, this is evidence for his confidence that the gospel will advance, regardless of the fate of the one who has preached it. This brief opening, then, reveals Philippians to be primarily intended as an authoritative letter of comfort in which Paul reassures the Philippian believers of the gospel's advance in the light of Paul's imprisonment.

Is it possible, however, that Paul's words to the Philippians are

41. On which see Hawthorne, *Philippians*, p. 35.
42. See the overview in Michael, *Philippians*, p. 32; recently reaffirmed by Pobee, *Persecution*, p. 97.
43. H.G. Herklots, *The Epistle of St Paul to the Philippians* (London, 1947), p. 43; Grayston, *Philippians*, p. 17.

intended to carry a further message? Are the Philippians' concerns exhausted by their fears for the personal security of Paul—concerns that are answered by Paul in terms of his mission—or does the letter also reflect fears over their own fate? Was the situation in Philippi comparable to that at Thessalonica? For the Thessalonians had accepted the gospel as Paul preached it.[44] They did so, in fact, in spite of persecutions,[45] which increased in severity shortly after Paul's departure.[46] Not without reason, the new believers of that city feared the worst.[47] They communicated that concern to Paul,[48] who, in response, sent Timothy to them, carrying 2 Thessalonians, to encourage them.[49]

It is not impossible that the Philippian believers may also have experienced some kind of persecution after Paul's departure, especially in the light of Paul's words in 1.29. And, as the Thessalonians turned to Paul in their need,[50] so the Philippians would have turned to Paul in their need. Philippians may then represent not only Paul's words of confidence but also a message of reassurance to the Philippian believers, even as 2 Thessalonians was to the Thessalonian believers.[51]

4. *Partitio (1.15-18a)*

That Paul's imprisonment was not universally acknowledged in the way Paul understands it is clear from the *partitio* (1.15-18a). Here Paul

---

44. Phil. 1.5; 4.15-16, 19 and 1 Thess. 2.2; cf. Acts 16.12-15. The pre-history of Paul's mission beyond Asia Minor is found only in Gal. 1.13–2.1; cf. Acts 9.1–13.12. In Gal. 1.21 we read that he had been in Syria and Cilicia, but where he was during the 14 years of Gal. 2.1 (cf. 2 Cor. 12.2) is unknown.
45. 1 Thess. 2.2; Phil. 1.30; cf. Acts 16.16-40.
46. 1 Thess. 2.14-16. On this point, see E. Bammel, 'Preparation for the Perils of the Last Days', in *Suffering and Martyrdom in the New Testament* (ed. W. Horbury and B. McNeil; Cambridge: Cambridge University Press, 1981), pp. 91-100.
47. 2 Thess. 2.1-3.
48. 1 Thess. 2.18.
49. Cf. 1 Thess. 3.2.
50. On Paul as comforter, see now A. Malherbe, *Paul and the Thessalonians: The Philosophic Tradition of Pastoral Care* (Philadelphia: Fortress Press, 1987), pp. 61-99.
51. Cf. Gundry, *SOMA*, p. 152, following P. Hoffmann, *Die Toten in Christus* (Munster: Aschendorff, 1966), pp. 217-18.

7. *The Theme of Suffering in the* Preparatio 151

presents the Philippians with two differing approaches to his imprisonment among those who are emboldened to preach Christ (1.14). The two positions are set out by means of a chiasm:

```
        a       1.15a
        b       1.15b
        b'      1.16
        a'      1.17
```

On the one hand, there are those who preach Christ διὰ φθόνον καὶ ἔριν (1.15a) and ἐξ ἐριθείας..., οὐχ ἀγνῶς, οἰόμενοι θλῖψιν ἐγείρειν τοῖς δεσμοῖς μου (1.17). On the other, there are those who preach Christ δι' εὐδοκίαν (1.15b) and ἐξ ἀγάπης (1.16a), probably towards Paul, in light of 1.16b. This twofold *propositio* underscores Paul's case and establishes an actual or hypothetical conflictive point centred on Paul himself.

In accord with the function of the *partitio* in rhetorical address, Paul uses the actions of his opponents to his own advantage. First of all, he posits that there are two sides, rather than one unified front. Then, without applauding the means of those who in the light of his imprisonment preach Christ ἐξ ἐριθείας and so seek to augment Paul's suffering, he rejoices, not because he suffers as a result, but because Christ is preached where he has never been preached and by those who never before, for whatever reason, preached him or who preached him less boldly. In this the *partitio* clearly concludes the *narratio* and, as well, leads us to a proof of Paul's words in the *confirmatio*. Clearly, Paul has set the stage for two different approaches to his experience. And, as we shall see, it is the deliberative nature of the presentation of choices that characterizes Philippians.

Chapter 8

THE THEME OF SUFFERING IN THE *ARGUMENTATIO*, PART I

The *argumentatio* of Philippians appears in five sub-units. Here I will deal exegetically with the *confirmatio* and first *exhortatio*, leaving the *exempla*, the *reprehensio* and the second *exhortatio* for the following chapter.

1. *Confirmatio (1.18b–26)*

The focus of the *confirmatio* is clearly on Paul himself. In the first part (1.18b-20) Paul puts himself forward as the example on which he will build his argument that God's work will not be frustrated through his imprisonment.

Paul's intention is to show the Philippians that, even though he is being pressed by necessity into an adverse situation, God will prove victorious regardless of the outcome (1.20). Clearly Paul found himself in a situation in which doubt and anxiety would have been more realistic. In fact, some have suggested that 1.18b-26, particularly the concluding, deductive section 1.21-26, evidences something less than confidence or, at least, something less than the kind of absolute confidence that faces earthly difficulties with resolution. It is argued, for example, that Paul was aware of his imminent departure from this earthly context of suffering and of a moving on to fullness in Christ (1.24),[1] and that consequently he equated life with a less-than-desirable state separate from full fellowship with Christ (ἐν σαρκί, 1.23).

Now if τὸ ἀποθανεῖν is understood as antithetical to τὸ ζῆν,[2] the

1. Gnilka, *Philipper*, pp. 75-81.
2. *Pace* Jouön, 'Notes', pp. 89-90; cf. Lightfoot, *Philippians*, pp. 92-93, and Vincent, *Philippians*, p. 27. For ἀναλῦσαι as a parallel to ἀποθανεῖν, see esp. Dibelius, *Briefe*, p. 50.

8. The Theme of Suffering in the Argumentatio, Part I 153

traditional interpretation that takes Paul's words in 1.21 to mark a differentiation between life for Paul in the here and now (associated with τὸ ζῆν Χριστός)[3] and life to come (associated with τὸ ἀποθανεῖν κέρδος) would be the correct one.[4] And, accordingly, authors who have suggested that 1.21-26 reflects Paul's personal, emotional suffering, stemming from his emotional insecurity at the unknown outcome of his trial, would be correct. Paul, it could then be suggested, was caught between, on the one hand, a desire for release from prison and from death so as to continue the service of the gospel (1.19) and, on the other, a desire to be with Christ by being released from death through death (1.21).[5] Lexical proof has even been adduced to show that Paul's words in 1.21-26 reflect not hope and confidence, but anxiety.[6]

Such a conclusion, however, is both unnecessary and misleading. First of all, it can only be reached by abstracting Paul's words from their epistolary and rhetorical context. For 1.21-26 is not some isolated portion of the letter but the conclusion to the rhetorical *confirmatio* that begins at 1.18b. And, indeed, 1.18b-26 would be a strange rhetorical confirmation of 1.12-18a if Paul suddenly turns from a triumphant note of confidence in 1.12-18a in order to discuss his own sorry future in 1.18b-26.

In fact, just the opposite is true.[7] Paul here confirms his confidence in the triumph of the gospel by analogy with his statements in the *partitio*. For in the *partitio*, Paul proposes to the Philippians that both those who support Paul *and* those who stand opposed to him preach Christ, while in the *confirmatio*, he affirms that whether he lives or dies, God will be victorious.

---

3. Assuming that Χριστός is the correct reading in 1.21. For an original, but highly debatable, suggested textual emendation, see A. Giglioli, 'Mihi enim vivere Christus est', *RivB* 16 (1968), pp. 305-15.
4. C.-H. Hunzinger: Paul speaks of his death 'nicht nur als einer drohenden, sondern als einem ersehnten Ziel' ('Die Hoffnung angesichts des Todes im Wandel der paulinischen Aussagen', in *Leben angesichts des Todes* [ed. B. Lohse and H.P. Schmidt; Tübingen: Mohr, 1968], p. 70).
5. Esp. Lightfoot, *Philippians*, p. 92; G. Delling, 'Philipperbrief', *RGG*, V, p. 334.
6. G. Bertram, ''Αποκαραδοκία', *ZNW* 49 (1958), pp. 269-70, citing post-Christian Hellenistic literature and the commentaries of Theodore Mopsuestia and Luther; followed by Gnilka and Collange.
7. Cf. Staab, *Briefe*, p. 33.

Paul's words throughout the *confirmatio* evidence confidence, not doubt. (Whether Paul is at this time trying to convince himself that the outcome will be positive goes beyond the task of historical investigation and enters the realm of motivism.[8]) Lexical and thematic motifs stressing reassurance and confidence are scattered throughout the inductive section: χαρήσομαι, 18b; οἶδα γάρ + future + εἰς σωτηρίαν, 19; ὅτι ἐν οὐδενὶ αἰσχυνθήσομαι... καὶ νῦν μεταλυνθήσεται Χριστός, 20.[9] Furthermore, Paul's verbatim use of Job 13.16 LXX in 1.19 hints at his desire to adduce scriptural data having to do with confident expectations of vindication.[10] His use of ἀποκαραδοκία (1.20) is intentionally paired with ἔλπις, which in Scripture and Paul (cf. Rom. 8.19-25) always manifests a 'confident and certain expectation... whatever may have been the case with the cognate verb in secular Greek'.[11] As Denton notes, Paul's confident view of the future contrasts with pagan views of the future that speak of something uncertain and about which one is anxious.[12] Or as Paul Antin observes,

> the apostle Paul's optimism contrasts with the pessimism of the elaborate stories of Sophocles. In the latter's work, death is a sinister descent; in that of the former, it becomes a joyful ascent.[13]

Likewise even in the more debated deductive argumentation of 1.21-26 there is the same note of confidence. The reference to prayer in 1.19, when compared with the letter's other references to prayer (1.4 in the *exordium* and 4.6 in the *exhortatio*) confirms that in

---

8. On which, cf. W.C. Booth, *Modern Dogma and the Rhetoric of Assent* (University of Notre Dame Ward-Phillips Lectures on English Language and Literature, 5; Notre Dame, IN: University of Notre Dame Press, 1974).
9. Jerome: 'non solum credo sed etiam certissime novi' (*Commentarii, PL* 30.843 D).
10. Grayston, *Philippians*, p. 18; Houlden, *Paul's Letters*, p. 61; *contra* Collange, *Philippiens*, p. 58.
11. D.R. Denton, "'Ἀποκαραδοκία', *ZNW* 73 (1982), pp. 139-40, citing Chrysostom, the majority of Greek Fathers, and Calvin; cf. *idem*, 'Hope and Perseverance', *SJT* 34 (1981), p. 315; A.M. Denis, 'L'apôtre Paul, prophète "messianique" des gentils', *ETL* 33 (1957), pp. 254-55 n. 45 (on 1 Thess. 2.1-6 and 2 Cor. 3.12 and 7.4); Vincent, *Philippians*, p. xxiv.
12. Denton, ''Ἀποκαραδοκία', p. 139.
13. P. Antin, '*Mori Lucrum* et *Antigone* 462, 464', *RSR* 62 (1974), pp. 259-60.

8. The Theme of Suffering in the Argumentatio, Part I 155

Philippians prayer is a matter of assurance and victory. Robert Funk correctly notes the harmony between 1.18b-20 and 1.21-26:

> since [Paul] is confident (πεποιθώς, 1.25) that it is necessary for him to remain in the flesh (1.24), he knows (οἶδα, 1.25, of his certainty in faith; cf. 1.19) that he will remain (1.25) in order to continue his fruitful labor (1.22), which, through his presence again to them, will benefit their progress and joy in faith (1.25b-26). The prayers of the Philippians (1.19) thus eventually come to bear upon Paul's presence again to them.[14]

So the future is confidently viewed by Paul in 1.25, with reasons for that confidence given in 1.26.

In sum, in spite of the current of suffering on which Paul's tone of triumph rides,[15] 1.18b-20 and 21-26 evidence confidence—not in Paul's person but rather in the advance of the gospel. Paul has no doubt that God will triumph by his grace,[16] whether through Paul[17] or through the Philippians, who, as we have seen, are perceived by Paul as mirroring his own experiences (cf. also Paul's use of εὐδοκία 1.15b; 2.13). Paul is confident that the 'historical and apocalyptic spread of the gospel through the known world before the parousia' will happen.[18] Consequently, his *confirmatio* majestically crowns the *narratio* and *partitio* with 'triumphal certitude'.[19]

Yet what is the point of the deliberative element in Paul's *confirmatio*? If Paul's confidence is in God's ultimate victory, and if the indisputability ('res quasi non dubias')[20] of 1.18b-20a is clear from Paul's conclusion that μεγαλυνθήσεται Χριστός... εἴτε διὰ ζωῆς εἴτε διὰ θανάτου (1.20b-c), why does Paul leave the matter open-ended in 1.20c—especially if in the latter part of the *confirmatio* (1.25-26) he expresses confidence that he will indeed be delivered by God? To what does Paul want his readers to assent? Or as Cicero

---

14. Funk, *Parables*, p. 96 n. 15; cf. idem, 'Apostolic Parousia', p. 262 n. 1.
15. Bouttier, *En Christ*, pp. 40-42, *contra* J. Dupont.
16. Gnilka, *Philipperbrief*, p. 46; Collange, *Jésus à Paul*, p. 200.
17. Cf. Bouttier, *En Christ*, pp. 55, 60, concerning the phrase ἐν κυρίῳ in Phil. 1.14 as used to express the actual, sovereign intervention of Jesus, against Neugebauer's exclusively ethical interpretation of the ἐν κυρίῳ motif.
18. Jewett, *Anthropological Terms*, p.117; cf.Gundry, *SOMA*, p. 58. According to Walter ('Die Philipper', p. 430 n. 42) λόγος (1.14) is a *terminus technicus* for mission, as in 1 Thess. 1.6 and Gal. 6.6; cf. Mk 4.14-20 and Acts *passim*.
19. Bouttier, *En Christ*, pp. 60-61.
20. Bouttier, *En Christ*.

puts it, to what does he lure his readers?[21]

Although God will be victorious through those who preach the word, no matter what their motives or fate, it is up to those who find themselves in such a situation—that is, persons such as Paul—to decide what to do. Paul is assured not only of the progress of the gospel,[22] but also of resurrection transformation either at death or at Christ's return.[23]

What Paul writes reveals both his desperate situation and his confidence in the power of the God of resurrection to accomplish his purposes, whether through Paul himself or not. So what Paul sets out here is his own understanding of his situation.

Although his personal desire is to be with Christ (1.23, τὴν ἐπιθυμίαν ἔχων εἰς τὸ ἀναλῦσαι καὶ σὺν Χριστῷ εἶναι) probably through death,[24] Paul opts to remain ἐν σαρκί where suffering continues to be a reality (cf. 1.22, 24),[25] in order to work for and with the Philippian Christians. He opts for continued personal suffering as an evangelist and as the pastor of the Philippian congregation because it is ἀναγκαιότερον for them (1.24), as opposed to his own desire (1.23). This decision will not only ensure the fruit of his labours (1.22, καρπὸς ἔργου),[26] but, in line with the deliberative genre, will also present the Philippians with a credible example that demands their respect.

His conclusion ('probabile aliquid'),[27] then, found in 1.25-26, represents not merely an intellectual or forensic proof but the choice he will make presented didactically. It is more than a simple restatement of the premise of the inductive conclusion, for life and death are both choices precisely because of the inductive conclusion, namely, that God will prove victorious whatever the fate of the preacher. The conclusion of the deductive argumentation, however, is that, though that is true, Paul chooses to continue labouring for the good of the

21. *Inv.* 1.32.54.
22. Pesch, 'Theologie des Todes', p. 12: 'Nur der Glaube spricht von Gewinn, wo die Erfahrung des Menschen von Verlust redet'.
23. Cf. Bouttier, *En Christ*, p. 41.
24. Cf. Collange, *Philippiens*, p. 65.
25. So Jewett, *Anthropological Terms*, p. 116. So also Lightfoot, *Philippians*, p. 92. Lightfoot's translation of ἐπιμένειν τῇ σαρκί is questionable but does not affect his argument.
26. Lohmeyer, *Philipper*, p. 60; cf. Jewett, *Anthropological Terms*, p. 116.
27. *Inv.* 1.34.57.

8. The Theme of Suffering in the Argumentatio, Part I 157

gospel in the community because this is what will bring the greatest benefit to others.

2. Exhortatio (1.27–2.18)

In the first *exhortatio* section of Philippians, that which serves as the hortatory conclusion to the *confirmatio*, the theme of suffering has appeared to some to be not very prominent. In fact, it has been argued that suffering has a merely parenthetical role in this section.[28] Yet 1.29, 2.7-8 and 2.17 have directly to do with suffering. We must ask, therefore, regarding the place of suffering in this *exhortatio*, and in particular in terms of these verses in their respective contexts.

Philippians 1.27-30

A *prima facie* reading of 1.29 suggests that not only did Paul suffer persecution through his imprisonment but also that the Philippians were suffering some type of persecution as well. Paul goes so far as to connect their suffering with his in 1.30: τὸν αὐτὸν ἀγῶνα ἔχοντες.

Not all commentators, however, have viewed the Philippian Christians' suffering in terms of external persecution. Ralph Martin, for example, writes,

> The church at Philippi is suffering with [Paul] by entering into the afflictions of his apostolate... It is doing this by the gifts and prayers of the members, and by their unswerving devotion to Christ in the face of common adversaries (1.28-30: 'the same conflict').[29]

Beare argues against seeing 1.29-30 as evidence for a persecution of the Philippian believers at the time of the letter because, as he says, such a view 'depends upon a prior acceptance of the notion that the epistle as a whole is a tractate on martyrdom'.[30] According to Gnilka, Paul is speaking about their lot in life as a result of having shared with Christ the sacramental death of baptism.[31]

---

28. Cf. Vincent, *Philippians*, p. 53; Walter, 'Die Philipper', p. 432, according to whom 1.12-26 is connected to 2.1-18 by the parenetical section 1.27-30.
29. Martin, *Philippians*, p. 63.
30. Beare, *Philippians*, p. 53; cf. Gnilka, *Philipperbrief*, pp. 101-102, who argues that the Philippians share Paul's 'spirit' in their trials. See also Caird, *Paul's Letters*, pp. 116, 127, who argues that 1.30 refers to the blameless life the Philippians are to lead and the struggle they are to wage against spiritual enemies.
31. Gnilka, *Philipperbrief*, p. 101.

Yet the evidence that has been marshalled in support of the contention that the earliest believers experienced widespread physical attacks and personal harrassments similar to what Paul describes in 1.15, 17 and 2 Cor. 11.23-29, as well as police actions and persecution, is compelling.[32] Furthermore, there is no *a priori* reason why 1.27-30 cannot refer to the Philippians' experience or expectation of persecution.[33]

Likewise internal evidence makes it probable that the Philippians were indeed undergoing suffering as a result of persecution. For 1.29 needs to be understood in the light of 1.7, where the Philippians are called συγκοινωνοί of Paul's grace as he writes from prison.

Thus the place of suffering in the larger context of Paul's rhetoric is not difficult to discover. For in this hortatory conclusion to the *confirmatio* Paul's intent is to relate the Philippians even more closely to his own *causa*. Although the *exordium* focuses on himself, it also points to this *exhortatio* in which Paul speaks of how the κοινωνία of the Philippians in his ministry involves their suffering. So Paul's suffering in bringing the gospel is now mirrored in the Philippians,[34] for they are as willing to give of themselves for the sake of the gospel as Paul is.[35] According to Baumeister, 'Paul's letters show that persecution and suffering do not only happen to the apostle but also to the apostle's communities'.[36] In all likelihood the Philippians suffered in a similar fashion as did the Thessalonians in receiving the gospel (cf. 1 Thess. 1.6; 2.14; 2 Thess. 1.5). One may set out parallels between the hortatory conclusion of the Philippian *confirmatio* and the *exordia* of the two Thessalonian letters to demonstrate this:

---

32. Cf. J.E. Stambaugh and D.L. Balch, *The New Testament in its Social Environment* (Philadelphia: Westminster Press, 1986), pp. 32-36.

33. Lightfoot, *Philippians*, p. 58 (citing 2 Cor. 8.2); Lohmeyer, *Philipper*, pp. 22-27 (followed in part by Houlden, *Paul's Letters*, p. 53).

34. Cf. Michael, *Philippians*, p. 19; Lightfoot, *Philippians*, p. 85, according to whom ἐναρξάμενος (1.6) implies the beginning of sacrifice; Grayston, *Philippians*, p. 15; *pace* Vincent, *Philippians*, p. 8 (citing Gal. 3.3). The exact setting for the positive outworking of God's grace in Paul's suffering, whether in his defence at his trials or in his teaching and influence both in prison and elsewhere, is discussed by Michael in relation to 1.7 (*Philippians*, p. 15).

35. Cf. Vincent, *Philippians*, p. 7; Lightfoot, *Philippians*, pp. 58-59.

36. Baumeister, *Anfänge*, pp. 156-57 (citing 1 Thess. 2.14; Phil. 1.29-30).

8. The Theme of Suffering in the Argumentatio, Part I 159

Phil. 1.27b-29	2 Thess. 1.4-5c	1 Thess. 1.3, 6
... ἵνα εἴτε ἐλθὼν καὶ ἰδὼν ὑμᾶς, εἴτε ἀπὼν ἀκούω τὰ περὶ ὑμῶν ὅτι στήκετε ἐν ἑνὶ πνεύματι μιᾷ ψυχῇ συναθλοῦντες τῇ πίστει τοῦ εὐαγγελίου	ὥστε αὐτοὺς ἡμᾶς ἐν ὑμῖν ἐγκαυχᾶσθαι ἐν ταῖς ἐκκλησίαις τοῦ θεοῦ ὑπὲρ τῆς ὑπομονῆς ὑμῶν καὶ πίστεως	μνημονεύοντες ὑμῶν τοῦ ἔργου τῆς πίστεως καὶ τοῦ κόπου τῆς ἀγάπης καὶ τῆς ὑπομονῆς τῆς ἐλπίδος τοῦ κυρίου ἡμῶν Ἰησοῦ Χριστοῦ ἔμπροσθεν τοῦ θεοῦ καὶ πατρὸς ἡμῶν
καὶ μὴ πτυρόμενοι ἐν μηδενὶ ὑπὸ τῶν ἀντικειμένων ἥτις ἐστιν αὐτοῖς ἔνδειξις ἀπωλείας ὑμῶν δὲ σωτηρίας, καὶ τοῦτο ἀπὸ θεοῦ	ἐν πᾶσιν τοῖς διωγμοῖς ὑμῶν καὶ ταῖς θλίψεσιν αἷς ἀνέχεσθε ἔνδειγμα τῆς δικαίας κρίσεως τοῦ θεοῦ εἰς τὸ καταξιωθῆναι ὑμᾶς τῆς βασιλείας τοῦ θεοῦ ὑπὲρ ἧς καὶ πάσχετε	
ὅτι ὑμῖν ἐχαρίσθη τὸ ὑπὲρ Χριστοῦ, οὐ μόνον τὸ εἰς αὐτὸν πιστεύειν ἀλλὰ καὶ τὸ ὑπὲρ αὐτοῦ πάσχειν		καὶ ὑμεῖς μιμηταὶ ἡμῶν ἐγενήθητε καὶ τοῦ κυρίου, δεξάμενοι τὸν λόγον ἐν θλίψει πολλῇ μετὰ χαρᾶς πνεύματος ἁγίου

Suffering, of course, is not the last word for either the Philippians or the Thessalonians, even as it is not for Paul. In that Paul's converts are direct participants in his *causa*—not just jury, but co-defendants!— they, like Paul, experience suffering. But they are encouraged by Paul to look to the goal,[37] that is, 'l'avancement de l'Evangile'.[38] So Paul urges the Philippians to view his fate and theirs in terms of confidence in the gospel's triumph, as expressed in both the *narratio* (1.12-14) and the *confirmatio* (1.18b-26); and he is encouraged to think that his confidence is well placed in the light of their faithfulness (cf. 1.3-11). Although they, like Paul, may die, the gospel will prove victorious. His confidence concerning them mirrors his confidence concerning his own case. It is God's grace that has enabled the Philippian community to believe the gospel (1.7), and it is God's grace that has enabled both

37. Caird, *Paul's Letters*, p. 108.
38. Collange, *Philippiens*, p. 68.

him (1.21) and them (1.29-30) to be fruitful in their service. Such a confidence, however, is not to lead to a careless attitude but rather to such an attitude as Paul himself epitomizes. In other words, Paul urges the Philippian believers to follow his example: in the midst of their suffering and pressed by circumstances, they are to choose what is honourable and worthy, even as Paul does, confident of God's victory.[39] They are to serve not in spite of their situation but precisely because of it. In so doing they are to reflect true service or *diakonia*[40] such as found in Paul and Jesus (cf. 1 Thess. 2.14; Phil. 1.30).[41]

Philippians 2.1-11

It is the portrayal of Jesus' service or *diakonia* that Paul builds on in 2.1-11. Specifically vv. 6-11 form a crucial nucleus within the letter,[42] and so must be examined in context more closely. Critical questions concerning vv. 6-11 are primarily whether these verses comprise a hymn or not,[43] who the author of the hymn was,[44] and what the pre-Pauline background of the hymn is.[45] Although important, such questions are not crucial to our study. For though the great majority of commentators view these verses as a pre-Pauline hymn and discuss them as such,[46] the way in which Paul uses these lines within the letter demands that we interpret them first of all in terms of their function within their present epistolary and rhetorical contexts—namely, as part of the hortatory conclusion to the *confirmatio* and, specifically, as part of the second segment, 2.1-11, which (1) follows as a consequence of Paul's words in the first segment, 1.27-30, as is indicated by the

---

39. Cf. Collange, *Philippiens*, p. 71.
40. B. Reicke, 'Unité chrétienne et diaconie', in *Neotestamentica et Patristica* (Leiden: Brill, 1962), pp. 204-205; cf. Michael, *Philippians*, p. 79.
41. Cf. Murphy-O'Connor, 'Philippiens', p. 1222; M. Carrez, *De la souffrance à la gloire* (Neuchâtel: Delachaux & Niestlé, 1964), p. 98; S.J. Hafemann, *Suffering and the Spirit: An Exegetical Study of 2 Cor. 2.14–3.3 within the Context of the Corinthian Correspondence* (WUNT, 2.19; Tübingen: Mohr, 1986), p. 73.
42. Cf. Kleinknecht, *Gerechtfertigte*, p. 306.
43. For an exhaustive study of the options, see R.P. Martin, *Carmen Christi* (Grand Rapids: Eerdmans, 2nd edn, 1983), pp. 15-38.
44. Cf. *Carmen Christi*, pp. 42-62, 297-309.
45. Cf. *Carmen Christ*, pp. 63ff.
46. Cf. the recent discussion by J.A. Fitzmyer, 'The Aramaic Background of Philippians 2.6-11', *CBQ* 50 (1988), pp. 470-83.

8. *The Theme of Suffering in the* Argumentatio, *Part I* 161

introductory οὖν (2.1); and (2) is parallel to the other two hortatory sub-sections, 1.27-30 and 2.12-28.[47]

Also alien to our task is the debate between those who believe that in these verses Paul exhorts to ethical imitation of Christ[48] and those who believe that Paul engages in 'a recital of soteriology, a dramatic story of the odyssey of Christ whose "way" led from one eternity to His ultimate glory by acts of obedience, exaltation and acclamation', on which basis ethical appeal can then be made.[49] Both positions have arisen largely as a result of a preliminary theological judgment of the text in question rather than as a result of an examination of the text in its literary context.

Our task is to discern (1) the outline of the figure depicted in 2.6-11, and (2) the relationships between vv. 6-11 and the rest of Philippians. We shall then be in a position to discuss the implications of these findings.

As for discerning the outline of the figure in 2.6-11, a variety of figures have been posited as *religionsgeschichtliche* models. Lohmeyer argues that the figure in view is the Son of Man.[50] Others suggest that the figure behind the hymn is the heavenly man contrasted with disobedient Adam.[51] Still others have suggested that the figure behind the hymn is that of the righteous man.[52]

---

47. *Pace* Bjerkelund, *Parakalō*, p. 175; Beare, *Philippians*, p. 53; cf. Collange, *Philippiens*, p. 71.
48. As found, for example, in a variety of authors and translations, including the Authorised Version, Hawthorne, *Philippians*, pp. l-li; Panikulam, *Koinōnia*, p. 177; Reicke, 'Unité', p. 210; Furnish, *Theology and Ethics*, p. 218; cf. Collange, *Philippiens*, p. 55; Martin, *Carmen Christi*, pp. 84-88.
49. Paraphrase of E. Käsemann, 'Kritische Analyse von Phil. 2.5-11', *ZTK* 47 (1950), pp. 313-60, in Martin, *Carmen Christi*, p. xv; cf. pp. viii-xxxiii; R. Scroggs, Review of Martin, *Carmen Christi, Int* 22 (1968), p. 352; R.B. Strimple, 'Philippians 2.5-11 in Recent Studies', *WTJ* 41 (1979), p. 253; H.H. Schade, *Apokalyptische Christologie bei Paulus* (Göttingen: Vandenhoeck & Ruprecht, 1981), p. 125. See, also, Dibelius, *Briefe*, p. 53; Bultmann, Review of Lohmeyer, *Philipper* and *Kyrios Jesus, DLZ* 51 (1930), p. 780.
50. E. Lohmeyer, *Kyrios Jesus: eine Untersuchung zu Phil. 2.5-11* (Darmstadt: Wissenschaftliche Buchgesellschaft, 1961 [1928]), pp. 8, 38-39.
51. A.M. Hunter, *Paul and his Predecessors* (London: SCM Press, rev. edn, 1961), p. 43; B. Rey, *Creados en Cristo Jesús* (Madrid: FAX, 1968), pp. 93, 97; J. Bligh, Review of Martin, *Carmen Christi, Bib* 49 (1968), p. 129; J. Menard, Review of Martin, *Carmen Christi, RHR* 175 (1969), pp. 215-17.
52. C.H. Talbert, 'The Problem of Pre-Existence in Phil. 2.6-11', *JBL* 86

Some years ago, however, Cerfaux argued convincingly that the figure of the Isaian suffering servant (Isa. 45, 52, 53) underlies 2.6-11.[53] He noted the following parallels between the Isaian Servant Songs and Phil. 2.6-11:

Phil. 2.6-11	Correspondence in Isaiah
μορφή (2.6, 7)	Isa. 52.14 and 53.2.
οὐχ ἁρπαγμὸν ἡγήσατο (2.6)	Isa. 53.12 LXX; 49.24-25 or Isa. 53.12 Aquila
δοῦλος (2.7)	δοῦλος (Isa. 49.3, 5 LXX) or δουλεύοντα (Isa. 53.11 LXX) or παῖς (Isa. 52.13 LXX) or δοῦλος as found in the Aquila and Symmachus text variants (Isa. 41.3-5; 53.11; 52.13)
ἑαυτὸν ἐκένωσεν (2.7)	Isa. 53.12, or 49.4: κενῶς ἐκοπίασα καὶ εἰς μάταιον καὶ εἰς οὐδὲν ἔδωκα τὴν ἰσχύν μου
ἐν ὁμοιώματι ἀνθρώπων γενόμενος καὶ σχήματι εὑρεθεὶς ὡς ἄνθρωπος (2.7)	Isa. 53.3 LXX; τὸ εἶδος αὐτοῦ ἄτιμον ἐκλεῖπον παρὰ πάντας ἀνθρώπους ἄνθρωπος ἐν πληγῇ ὤν
ἐταπείνωσεν ἑαυτόν (2.8)	Isa. 53.7-8 LXX: ἐν τῇ ταπεινώσει (αὐτοῦ)
μέχρι θανάτου (2.8)	Isa. 53.8 LXX: εἰς θάνατον; Isa. 53.12 LXX: παρεδόθη εἰς θάνατον
διὸ καί (2.9)	Isa. 53.12
ὑπερύψωσεν (2.9)	Isa. 52.13 LXX: ὑψωθήσεται
πᾶν γόνυ κάμψῃ. . . καὶ πᾶσα γλῶσσα ἐξομολογήσηται (2.10-11)	Isa. 45.23

There have, of course, been objections to these parallels. Certain terms in the hymn do not accord with the LXX Isaian Servant Songs; as well, various elements germane to the Servant Songs, such as sin-bearing and vicarious elements, are missing in Phil. 2.6-11.[54] Yet

---

(1967), pp. 141-53; J. Murphy-O'Connor, 'Christological Anthropology in Phil. 2.6-11', *RB* 83 (1976), pp. 25-50; G. Howard, 'Phil. 2.6-11 and the Human Christ', *CBQ* 40 (1978), pp. 368-87; J.D.G. Dunn, *Christology in the Making* (Philadelphia: Westminster Press, 1980), p. 120.
   53. L. Cerfaux, 'L'hymne au Christ—serviteur de Dieu (Phil. 2.6-11 = Isa. 52.13–53.12', in *Recueil Lucien Cerfaux* (Gembloux: Duculot, 1954), II, pp. 426-30; cf. Menard, Review of Martin, *Carmen Christi*, pp. 215-17; Strimple, 'Phil. 2.5-11', p. 260; Hunter, *Paul and his Predecessors*, pp. 43-44.
   54. Cf. Schade, *Apokalyptische Christologie*, p. 65.

8. The Theme of Suffering in the Argumentatio, Part I   163

there are a number of factors in these hymnic strophes of Philippians to suggest a modelling after the outline of the Isaian suffering servant. For one, the understanding of ἑαυτὸν ἐκένωσεν (2.7a) in terms of the Isaian servant provides a way out of the impasse concerning whether the subject of the verb is a pre-incarnate divine being as traditionally held or a human figure.[55] The κενο- word group is found in LXX Isa. 49.4 (κενῶς ἐκοπίασα καὶ εἰς μάταιον καὶ εἰς οὐδὲν ἔδωκα τὴν ἰσχύν μου). Understood in the light of this wording,[56] being emptied of rightful power 'le Christ se rend "vain", "vide" '.[57]

So, too, the term δοῦλος (2.7) is clarified, in part, by understanding it in terms of the Isaian hymns. δοῦλος in 2.7aβ probably picks up δοῦλος from LXX Isa. 49.3, 5; from the Aquila or Symmachus variants of Isa. 41.3-5, 53.11, 52.13; or from LXX Isa. 52.11 δουλεύοντα. Understood in the light of the Isaian Servant Songs, the Philippian hymn presents a picture of the righteous one (cf. 3.9) who does not turn the situation to his own advantage but permits himself to be put to death or to suffer.[58] Thus, 2.8 develops Christ's 'self-humiliation in the days of his flesh',[59] contrasting δοῦλος and κύριος.[60]

The structure of 2.6-11 clearly reveals this contrast,[61] or what might be called an abasement–exaltation pattern.[62] Suffering, experienced as hopelessness or abandonment, is not the servant's final experience. The one reassurance the servant has is the triumph of God's grace, understood in terms of exaltation. Thus the servant, though despised by humanity because of his powerlessness, is in fact the one through whom the grace of God is proclaimed and who is vindicated. In both Christ's case (2.9-11) and Paul's (cf. 1.20, 24-26), what is humanly doomed to failure (κενός) is vindicated by God.[63]

---

55. As held, e.g., by E. Schweizer, *Lordship and Discipleship* (London: SCM Press, 1960), pp. 62-63; Murphy-O'Connor, 'Anthropology', pp. 30-31. For a study of the history of the kenotic doctrine, cf. P. Henry, 'Kénose', *DBSup*, V, pp. 7-161.
56. Cf. Lohmeyer, *Philipper*, p. 94; Cerfaux, 'Hymne au Christ', p. 428.
57. Collange, *Philippiens*, p. 91; cf. Grayston, *Philippians*, p. 28.
58. Murphy-O'Connor, 'Anthropology', pp. 32-41.
59. Michael, *Philippians*, p. 92.
60. Collange, *Philippiens*, p. 94.
61. Benoit, *Philippiens*, p. 27 (citing Gal. 4.1 and Col. 3.22-23).
62. Martin, *Carmen Christi*, p. 229.
63. Significantly the one exception to the absence of κενόω–κενός language

With regard to our second task, that of discerning relationships between 2.6-11 and the rest of Philippians, we need to understand 2.6-11 in its literary context. For the language of 2.6-11 is spread throughout the letter—especially throughout the *argumentatio*, but also in the epistolary prescript and *exordium*. The only exceptions are the *narratio* and the *partitio*.[64] Schematically, this spread of vocabulary and themes can be laid out as on the following page.

The implications of such a contextual reading of 2.6-11 are significant. So, for example, the verb κενόω in 2.7 may be understood in terms of Paul's use of κενός in 2.16 (οὐκ εἰς κενὸν ἔδραμον οὐδὲ εἰς κενὸν ἐκοπίασα).[65] This would mean that the traditional attempt to discern in κενόω (2.7) a reference to abandonment is not wholly incorrect. For in 2.7 it is the Christ-figure who is referred to, while in 2.16 it is Paul, whose words suggest that fruitlessness would have been one possible understanding of his fate. Yet in that the κενο-word group touches on two different figures, the important thing in either case seems not to be the particular state abandoned, but abandonment or fruitlessness *per se*.

Likewise, close observation of the recurrence of the language and imagery of 2.6-11 throughout the letter reveals the way the experience of Christ, the experience of Paul, and the experiences of Paul's co-workers are interwoven. For example, our understanding of δοῦλος in 2.7 ought to be arrived at in the context of Paul's use of the term in 1.1 and of the verbal form in 2.22. Accordingly, δοῦλος in 2.7 probably does not mean simply slave in a physical or social sense;[66] nor is it to be taken as a synonym for ἄνθρωπος, as if the writer were seeking to set down a general anthropology or metaphysic in which the human state as such is characterized by suffering[67]—a

---

clusters in Paul is 1 Cor. 15, a section that, like Phil. 1.27–2.18, points clearly to Paul's resurrection hope.
 64. Cf. Culpepper, 'Co-Workers', p. 350.
 65. κενόω is used by Paul elsewhere only four times: Rom. 4.14; 1 Cor. 1.17; 9.15; 2 Cor. 9.3; κενός is used elsewhere in 1 Cor. 15.10, 14, 58; 2 Cor. 6.1; Gal. 2.2; Eph. 5.6; Col. 2.8; 1 Thess. 2.1; 3.5.
 66. Staab, *Briefe*, p. 36.
 67. Pace e.g., H. Riesenfeld, 'La descente dans la mort', in *Aux sources de la tradition chrétienne* (Neuchâtel: Delachaux & Niestlé, 1950), p. 210; cf. Lightfoot, *Philippians*, p. 112; Gnilka, *Philipper*, p. 120; Barth, *Philipper*, p. 42; E. Schweizer, 'Paul's Christology and Gnosticism', in *Paul and Paulinism* (ed. M.D. Hooker and S.G. Wilson; London: SPCK, 1982), p. 119.

8. The Theme of Suffering in the Argumentatio, Part I

	Prescript	Exordium	Narratio	Partitio	Confirmatio	Exhortatio	Exempla	Reprehensio	Exhortatio	Peroratio
	1.1-2	1.3-11	1.12-14	1.15-18a	1.18b-26	1.27-2.18	2.19-30	3.1-16	3.17-4.7	4.8-20
2.6-11		1.7				2.2, 5		cf. 3.15	3.17; cf. 3.19	cf. 4.10
φρονέω										
ἐν Χριστῷ Ἰησοῦ		1.11		1.26; cf. 1.19		2.5		3.3, 14	4.7	4.19, 21
μορφή						2.6, 7		cf. 3.10	cf. 3.21	
ὑπάρχει						2.6			3.20	
ἡγέομαι						2.6		3.7, 8		
ἴσα						2.6	2.25			
κενόω						2.7; cf. 2.16	cf. 2.20			
δοῦλος 1.1						2.7	cf. 2.22			
σχῆμα						2.7		cf. 3.21		
εὑρίσκω						2.7		3.9		
ταπεινόω						2.8; cf. 2.3			cf. 3.21	cf. 4.12
ὑπήκοος						2.8; cf. 2.12				
θάνατος					1.20	2.8	2.27, 20	3.10		
μέχρι						2.8	2.30			
θανάτου										
σταυρός						2.8			3.18	
χαρίζομαι						1.29; 2.9				
ἐπουρανίων						2.10			cf. 3.20	
ἐπιγείων						2.10			3.19	
κύριος Ἰ. Χ.						2.11			3.20	
δόξα		1.11								
θεός 1.2						2.11		cf. 3.8	3.19, 21	4.19, 20
πατήρ						2.11				4.20
πᾶς						2.9-11			3.20	

view that is further made possible when the hymn is structured so that μορφὴν δούλου λαβών (2.7αβ) parallels ἐν ὁμοιώματι ἀνθρώπων γενόμενος (2.7b) alone or plus καὶ σχήματι εὑρεθεὶς ὡς ἄνθρωπος (2.7c) following a division of the hymn into three parts: 2.6-7a; 2.7b-8; 2.9-11.[68] Rather, understood in the light of 1.1 and 2.22, as well as the κενο- word group,[69] δοῦλος points to one who has no power in himself to avoid apparent failure, no human means of escaping his inevitable destiny.

Phil. 2.6-11, therefore, presents Christ as the servant whose single-minded obedience leads him to give of himself and so jeopardize his life.[70] Christ, like Paul, has been pressed by necessity into the situation in which he finds himself, and so the depiction of Christ in 2.6-11 appears in its literary context as intentionally pointing to Paul's own ministry. There are too many instances where the language of 2.6-11 is also used to describe Paul or Timothy to suggest that Paul was ignorant of the implication of these verses.

Of significance here, I believe, is Quintilian's discussion of *prosopopoeia*, that is, of impersonation or taking on a role in deliberative rhetoric.[71] For in *prosopopoeia* a speaker impersonates famous historical personages and puts himself in the cultural context of that day rather than his own.[72] Furthermore, *prosopopoeia* has a wider significance that I do not believe was lost on Paul, for it necessitates that the one who speaks speak in character.[73] Quintilian notes 'that an oration is clearly vitiated if it does not agree with the person or thing which it is supposed to fit'.[74]

Now, Paul appeals to the Philippians in familiar terms, terms which are also in keeping with his character and theirs. We have seen how in 1.30 Paul does not ask of them something they cannot see in him. Furthermore, we have seen how in 1.29 he ties his own experience of suffering to that of the Philippians themselves, putting himself in their

---

68. So J.T. Sanders, *The New Testament Christological Hymns* (Cambridge: Cambridge University Press, 1971), pp. 9-10; Cerfaux, 'Hymne au Christ', p. 426; Murphy-O'Connor, 'Anthropology', pp. 26-28.
69. So intended by the writer according to Gnilka, *Philipperbrief*, p. 118.
70. So Müller, *Philippians*, p. 34.
71. *Inst.* 3.8.49.
72. *Inst.* 3.8.50.
73. *Inst.* 3.8.51.
74. *Inst.* 3.8.51.

8. *The Theme of Suffering in the* Argumentatio, *Part I*   167

place and them in his. Paul's use of *prosopopoeia*, then, first of all establishes the grounds of his appeal.

But Paul's attempt in the *exhortatio* goes further, for, as suggested above, here he depicts himself as a fulfilment of the Christ type.[75] What is involved in 2.6-11 is an interplay of 'types', that is, the Isaian suffering servant, Christ and Paul himself.[76] Paul's *prosopopoeia Christi* is not, then, as Lohmeyer had thought, martyrological, but rather rhetorical. Paul's address to the Philippians is intended first of all to point to the analogy between the ἦθος of Paul's life and that of Christ. In other words, in the same situation, both he and Christ act the same way.

So when understood in light of its epistolographic and rhetorical contexts, it seems clear that 2.6-11 is not a presentation of Christology—that is, reflection on the abasement of the Lord and his exaltation after death[77]—but a depiction of the suffering of God's servant in the light of the servant's mission.[78] Paul depicts not only Jesus' experience in terms of the Isaian suffering servant, but also his own experience, the experiences of his co-workers, and those of the Philippians in terms of the same figure. This explains why Murphy-O'Connor could argue that one of the evidences of the pre-Pauline nature of 2.6-11 is that Paul normally uses the Servant Song material of himself, not of Christ.[79] The fact is that the referents are multiple, nor univocal: Paul uses the Servant Song material to depict servants.

Such an analysis, borrowing heavily from Patte, has the virtue of taking us beyond the dialogical or syntagmatic level of the text to the warranting or paradigmatic level by raising the question whether the one depicted by Paul in 2.6-11 is Christ or Paul's experience reflecting the experience of Christ. In that both are 'types', reflecting the experience of the other, we need not say that their experiences are indistinguishably merged (which, as we have seen, is Güttgemanns's critique of Christ-mysticism). Rather, as J.O. Tuñí reminds us, there is no Paul without Jesus—but neither can we know Jesus unless we take into account the fact that Paul only explains himself in relation to

---

75. Patte, *Paul's Faith*, p. 177.
76. Cf. Lohmeyer, *Philipper*, p. 96.
77. *Pace* Leon-Dufour, *Resurrección de Jesús*, pp. 72-73.
78. Collange, *Philippiens*, p. 91; *pace* Gnilka, *Philipperbrief*, p. 120.
79. Murphy-O'Connor, 'Philippiens', pp. 1226-28, following D. Stanley.

Jesus.[80] In Patte's terms, Paul becomes one in whom the experiences of the Christ type are visible, just as in Christ one sees the expected fulfilment in another, namely, the Paul type.

Within 1.27–2.18, then, 2.6-11 expresses succinctly the fate of the Christ type or the servant. Paul exhorts the Philippian believers to see in Christ's experience, in Paul's experience, and consequently in their own experiences, 'Christ-like manifestations'.[81] He does not, however, do so as a rebuke.[82] Rather, Paul writes to the Philippians to encourage them. For in seeing in their experience the experience of Christ, they will recognize that God has not abandoned Paul who, like Christ, 'renounced all past achievements and gains—who has made himself "poor" (cf. [2.]7)'.[83]

As Christ advanced the gospel and the gospel had not ceased with his death, so Paul—and believers, including the Philippians—advanced a gospel that will not cease with their death.[84] It is not because Paul as servant dies that the gospel advances,[85] but because the experience of Christ is relived by God's grace in Paul and in the Pauline communities. Furthermore, it is relived in a way that culminates by being crowned by Christ's resurrection, or exaltation.[86] In sum, the reason for Paul's appeal to the example of Christ in 2.6-11 becomes now clear: it is meant to clarify the appeal to his own example in 1.27-30 and 2.12-18 as a fulfilment of the Christ type.

Philippians 2.12-18

Phil. 2.12-18 concludes the first *exhortatio* directed to the entire community. In the light of my analysis of 2.1-11 the references to

80. J.O. Tuñí, 'Pau i Jesus', *RCT* 12 (1987), pp. 48-49.
81. Patte, *Paul's Faith*, pp. 185, 187.
82. As claimed, e.g., by Patte (*Paul's Faith*, p. 177), the Philippian congregation was a divided one in which believers were unwilling to discern 'types' in their midst, an attitude that results in a hostile attitude towards other believers in the community and so effectively denies God's working as mediated through others in the community. As a result, says Patte, the Philippians were denying the faith itself (cf. 2.12-18).
83. Furnish, *Theology and Ethics*, p. 221.
84. Bouttier, *En Christ*, p. 58; cf. Michael, *Philippians*, p. 35.
85. Cf. Jewett, *Anthropological Terms*, p. 253; N. Baumert, *Täglich sterben und auferstehen* (Munich: Kösel, 1973), p. 112.
86. Cf. Bonnard, *Philippiens*, p. 27. Weinrich reaches a similar conclusion on the basis of Paul's quote of Job 13.16 LXX in 1.19 (*Spirit and Martyrdom*, pp. 55-56).

8. *The Theme of Suffering in the* Argumentatio, *Part I* 169

suffering in 2.12-18 can now be clarified. For Paul's intention in 2.12-18 is clearly not to theologize concerning the visibility of Christ in his life or in the Philippians' community life, either because of ontological identification with Christ in suffering, as Christ-mysticism and its followers would have led us to believe, or otherwise. Throughout 2.12-18 no appeal is made to christological argumentation—as we should expect if we followed a soteriological interpretation of the Philippian hymn. Rather, Paul's intention is motivated by his desire to present his case concerning his own situation, and his presentation is shaped by the rhetorical patterns available to him.

Thus, while it has frequently been maintained that in 2.12-18 Paul shifts 'the basis of appeal from the example of Jesus (2.3-15) to himself and to the judgment he must face at the day of Christ',[87] when judged on epistolographic and rhetorical bases, no such shift is required. In the light of the integral nature of 1.27–2.18, it seems correct to see that the one to whom obedience is due throughout 1.27–2.18 is, in fact, Paul. Not, I hasten to add, because Paul seeks to impose an incipient, apostolic hierarchy to resolve the matter.[88] The thrust of Paul's exhortation here does not rest on an appeal to apostolic authority. Rather, it rests on the analogy that has been created between himself and Christ.

Obedience to Paul does not imply veneration of a master or participation with the apostle in religious mysticism, but proclamation: 'he invites people to join with him in the journey on the gospel road'.[89] The same necessity that presses him into a situation that is not necessarily of his plan or desire is that which pressed Christ. And though caught by necessity, Paul, like Christ, is confident of God's ability to bring victory out of apparent tragedy. Again like Christ, Paul seeks simply to act honourably to the end (1.18b-26 and 1.27-30). And so like the one described in 2.6-11, though forced by necessity into a situation not of his own choosing and ultimately

---

87. Hawthorne, *Philippians*, p. 103.
88. Such a position has been maintained by those who view Paul's use of the Old Testament citations in 2.14-16 as intended to be read as signs that the Christian community of Philippi has rebelled against God and God's appointed leader as the Old Testament people of the wilderness had. See, e.g., Patte, *Paul's Faith*, p. 101.
89. Collange, *Jésus à Paul*, p. 200.

confident of God's grace, Paul gives of himself freely and willingly. In the words of Theodoret of Cyr:[90]

οὐ γὰρ ὡς δοῦλος δεσποτικὸν πεπλήρωκε πρόσταγμα, ἀλλ' ἑκὼν τὴν ὑπὲρ ἡμῶν ἀνεδέξατο σωτηρίαν, καὶ ὑπήκουσεν ὡς υἱός, οὐχ ὡς δοῦλος.

We have seen how in 2.1-11 Paul uses a rhetorical strategem that allows him to present himself before the Philippian congregation as a model in so far as he mirrors Christ's ministry, death and resurrection. Here, now, in 2.12-18 he encourages the Philippians, as he has done incipiently in 1.27-30 and 2.1-11, to view themselves in the same light. Phil. 2.12-18 is not a rebuke of divisiveness but an encouragement to the Philippian congregation as a body to 'hold firmly to the gospel message that he had preached'.[91] For they, too mirror Christ's destiny in their lives as a congregation, both Christ's sufferings[92] and Christ's vindication by the grace of God. Paul sets before the Philippians his own experiences and those of Christ,[93] and exhorts 'those who will be his boasting on the day of Christ'[94] to envision in their lives the same grace and humility.

E. Schweizer's suggestion regarding 2.6-11 may also be applied to 2.12-18, at least in part:

> the meaning of obedience... is: acceptance of suffering. And this is explicitly indicated by the concept that we find so infrequently in the OT and in Judaism: it is 'humbling himself'.[95]

Schweizer, however, is only partially correct, for Paul's emphasis is not on suffering itself but on the experiences of Christ in their totality. For in 2.12-18 Paul's intention is to cap his case with the assertion that his servanthood is a type of theirs: both stem from God's gracious-

---

90. *Interpretatio epistulae ad Philippenses*, PG 82.569 C.
91. Hawthorne, *Philippians*, p. 104.
92. Cf. Collange, *Philippiens*, p. 100; Cerfaux, 'Hymne au Christ', p. 434 (citing Phil. 2.5-11; 1 Pet. 2.21-25 [cf. Isa. 53.4-12]; *1 Clem.* 16.1-17 [cf. Isa. 53.1-12]; Rev. 14.4, 5; Ignatius, *Eph.* 1.2; 10.3; *Trall.* 5.2; *Rom.* 4.2; 5.3; the Letter to the Churches of Lyon, in Eusebius, *Hist. Eccl.* 5.1.10; 5.2.2; 5.1.23 [citing Phil. 2.4-11, Isa. 53, and Rev. 14.4-5]); Schade, *Apokalyptische Christologie*, p. 65 (on the use of Isa. 53 in 1 Cor. 15.3-5; Rom. 4.25; 8.32).
93. Cf. Collange, *Philippiens*, p. 98 (citing Rom. 1.5; 15.18; 16.19).
94. Collange, *Philippiens*, p. 100.
95. Schweizer, *Lordship*, p. 62.

8. *The Theme of Suffering in the* Argumentatio, *Part I* 171

ness: both are manifested in humble and honourable service;[96] both are rewarded with resurrection transformation.

The *confirmatio* concludes as Paul invokes a final impersonation, this time in terms of sacrifice (2.17-18).[97] As in the case of servant imagery, the levels of meaning surrounding Old Testament sacrifice are multiple. So Paul writes of himself as destined for suffering, and possibly martyrdom, though not immediately (cf. 2.24).[98] Paul fully expects to be martyred for the gospel and for his communities, including the Philippian community (cf. 1.23-26),[99] and thus to be a sacrifice. His is 'the blood of the priest... poured out upon the sacrifice which he is offering',[100] an understanding paralleled by the priestly language found in Rom. 15.8, 16, 17. There Paul speaks of his apostolic office as a priestly service ordained by Christ, who himself was made a minister that the Gentiles might glorify God for his mercy. Here Paul speaks in terms of a sacrificial worship that is not perfected in the Jerusalem temple[101] but in the proclamation of the gospel to the Gentiles, a 'sacrifice' that demands his all, as it does that of his co-workers and communities, even as it did Christ's all.[102]

The focus in 2.16-18, however, is on the sacrificial offering brought by the Philippians themselves. They are the ones who are 'making the offering, perhaps their devotion and support for the apostle'.[103] Or, as Michael notes,

---

96. Collange, *Philippiens*, p. 98; Dibelius, *Briefe*, p. 55.
97. Cf. R.G. Hamerton-Kelly, 'A Girardian Interpretation of Paul', *Semeia* 33 (1985), pp. 65-81.
98. Müller, *Philippians*, pp. 95-96; H.C.G. Moule, *The Epistle to the Philippians* (Grand Rapids: Baker, repr. 1981 [1890]), p. 76.
99. Funk, *Language*, p. 105 (on the basis of εἰ καί + indicative); cf. Gnilka, *Philipperbrief*, p. 154.
100. Cf. Vincent, *Philippians*, p. 71, though rejected by Vincent.
101. *Pace* Vincent, *Philippians*, p. 72. Clearly, the sacrifice Paul alludes to here is to be understood by his readers in terms of the sacrificial worship of Israel, not Gentile worship. Given that the language of 2.12-18 is outstandingly full of Old Testament imagery and citation, a sudden shift to a Hellenistic context would be both unexpected and unclear.
102. Barth, *Philipper*, p. 51.
103. Vincent, *Philippians*, p. 71; cf. Grayston, *Philippians*, p. 30; Gnilka, *Philipperbrief*, p. 155; *pace* Hawthorne, *Philippians*, p. 116, according to whom these verses refer to Paul's sacrifice completing that of the Philippians.

[the Philippians'] adherence to the new faith entails the offering of a sacrifice to God which is at the same time the rendering of a service to Him... What the Philippian Christians sacrifice is their comfort, their ease, their worldly prosperity, and possibly in some cases their very lives.[104]

Paul's joy here is twofold: (1) the Philippians' action evidences the Christ type;[105] and (2) the Philippians' sacrifice provides for Paul further grounds for his confidence in the advance of the gospel,[106] in spite of his ignorance of his own personal destiny.[107]

In sum, Paul concludes this first *exhortatio* and, accordingly, the *confirmatio*, by again placing himself before the Philippians as a fulfilment of the Christ type, the one whose blood is poured on the altar. In this he continues the *prosopopoeia Christi* begun in 2.1-11. Here in 2.12-18, however, he also includes the Philippians in the impersonation for they, like he, are sacrifices, at least in their actions. Throughout the Pauline mission, then, the Christ type is found, depicted primarily in terms of suffering.

104. Michael, *Philippians*, p. 110.
105. Cf. Collange, *Jésus à Paul*, p. 182.
106. Lohmeyer, *Philipper*, p. 113.
107. Lipsius, *Briefe*, p. 231; Gnilka, *Philipperbrief*, pp. 154-55.

Chapter 9

THE THEME OF SUFFERING IN THE *ARGUMENTATIO*, PART II

1. *Exempla (2.19-30)*

As is clear from a rhetorical analysis of Philippians, 2.19-30 is central to Paul's *argumentatio*. It serves to join the *confirmatio*, including its hortatory conclusion, to the *reprehensio* and its hortatory conclusion. It does double duty: (1) as *exempla*, presenting the Philippians with well-known and visible apostolic emissaries who exemplify the servanthood depicted in 2.6-11, and (2) as *digressio*, presenting the Philippians with those who also embody the Christ type.

Although the theme of suffering appears most clearly in the body closing of 2.25-30, it is also present in 2.19-24. Much attention has been paid to the place of Paul's co-workers in his letters.[1] Within the literature that has appeared, however, the specific function of suffering vis-à-vis Paul's co-workers has not been highlighted. Timothy's role in Philippians, for example, has frequently been overlooked or misunderstood. An example of this misunderstanding is Lightfoot's statement that 'beyond the association of his name in the salutation, Timotheus takes no part in the letter'.[2]

That Timothy is an emissary to the Philippians is clear from the announcement of his arrival in 2.19-24.[3] As envoy he brings Paul's message to the Philippians. His role as emissary, however, transcends the purely postal nature of message delivery, for he serves as a physical embodiment of the servanthood Paul depicts before the Philippians.

Strikingly, Paul's depiction of Timothy is drawn largely from the

---

1. See esp. W.H. Ollrog, *Paulus und seine Mitarbeiter* (Neukirchen–Vluyn: Neukirchener Verlag, 1979).
2. Lightfoot, *Philippians*, p. 81.
3. White, *Body*, pp. 87-88.

exhortatio of 1.27–2.18.[4] Paul's use of εὐψυχῶ (2.19) ties 2.19-24 to 1.27–2.18 by recalling μιᾷ ψυχῇ (1.27) and σύμψυχοι (2.2). The verb does not speak of an individualistic 'bonne disposition générale de l' âme',[5] but rather continues the note of confidence and joy picked up from 1.18b-26 and 1.27–2.18. So Paul abounds with joy because of the expected good report from the Philippian congregation that Timothy will bring back with him, which report will further confirm in Paul's mind the accuracy of his estimation of events.

Furthermore, Paul's depiction of Timothy is drawn from 2.6-11. Given its rarity, Paul's appellation ἰσόψυχος (2.20) must be seen as recalling the equally rare ἴσα (2.6). Jewett, following Fridrichsen, correctly argues that ἰσόψυχος implies solidarity, much more than Timothy's personal feelings.[6] Yet the solidarity that Jewett rightly sees to be signified by the word must be understood in the light not just of social solidarity.[7] For Timothy mirrors in his life the Christ type, a mirroring that as emissary he passes on to the Philippians *viva voce* and *vivo exemplo*.

Likewise, Paul's explication of ἰσόψυχος by ὅστις γνησίως τὰ περὶ ὑμῶν μεριμνήσει (2.20) points to Timothy's experience as contrasted with that of those who seek τὰ ἑαυτῶν not τὰ Ἰησοῦ Χριστοῦ (2.21), a contrast that, according to Culpepper, is a distinct echo of 2.4-5: 'let not each look out for τὰ ἑαυτῶν, but τὰ ἑτέρων; have the mind which was also in Christ Jesus'.[8] More than a messenger, therefore, Timothy is one in whom Paul's experiences of suffering and expected glorification are visible, a further living embodiment of the Christ type—even as Paul is.

Finally, the use of ἐδούλευσεν (2.22) recalls not only the letter opening in which Paul calls himself and Timothy δοῦλοι (1.1), but also 2.7 where the servant *par excellence* is depicted as one who takes upon himself the form of δοῦλος.[9] Thus, even as Christ is pictured as serving and suffering, so now Timothy is described in terms used to depict the suffering servant. Although shorn of immediate reference

---

4. Cf. Culpepper, 'Co-Workers', pp. 350, 353.
5. *Pace* Joüon, 'Notes', pp. 302-303.
6. Jewett, *Anthropological Terms*, p. 349, following A. Fridrichsen, 'ἰσόψυχος = ebenbürtig, solidarische', *Symbolae Osloenses* 18 (1938), pp. 42-49.
7. Cf. Jewett, *Anthropological Terms*, p. 349.
8. Culpepper, 'Co-Workers', p. 350.
9. Culpepper, 'Co-Workers'; Collange, *Philippiens*, p. 104.

9. The Theme of Suffering in the Argumentatio, Part II 175

to suffering, the epistolary context indicates that Timothy is depicted in terms common to the suffering servanthood of the ones I have already examined, namely, Paul and the figure of 2.6-11 drawn from Isaiah.

True, Paul's commendation of Timothy and disregard for the others around him is hyperbolic, especially, as Vincent notes, 'in view of the high commendation of Epaphroditus which follows'.[10] The import of Paul's words, however, is clear. As Lipsius notes, 'no one around Paul is of the same mind as Timothy, namely, in his true, heartfelt concern for this community, a concern he will show when he comes to them'.[11] That for which Timothy, like Paul, is zealously and faithfully concerned—even to the point of suffering—is the welfare of the Philippian community. In this Timothy mirrors Paul's selfless concern, a concern that Paul identifies as reflective of Christ. Paul's ringing commendation of Timothy, set in contrast with his stinging condemnation of those who care only for themselves, not only mirrors his representation of himself in his desperate situation but also prepares the readers for the *reprehensio*.

Before turning to that *reprehensio*, however, Paul notes the suffering that Timothy's co-worker and Paul's, Epaphroditus, has undergone.[12] Epaphroditus receives special mention in this letter because, like Timothy, he is an emissary. Furthermore, he appears to have a special relationship with the Philippian congregation.[13] But Epaphroditus is also significant because he, too, is a type of the one depicted in 2.6-11. In the light of his special relationship to the Philippians, Epaphroditus brings the picture of the suffering servant into their very midst, very possibly as a mirror to them not just of suffering servanthood as such but of their own suffering servanthood.

Evidence of Paul's perception of Epaphroditus as a servant is first of all found in the appellations ἀδελφός, συνεργός and συστρατιώτης of 2.25—all of which identify Epaphroditus as a specially recognized co-worker. These same three terms occur in this same order in Phlm 1-2.[14] There, however, they are applied to three different people (ὁ ἀδελφός to Timothy, ὁ ἀγαπητὸς καὶ συνεργὸς ἡμῶν to

---

10. Vincent, *Philippians*, p. 74.
11. Lipsius, *Briefe*, p. 231; cf. Dibelius, *Brief*, p. 57.
12. Cf. Lipsius, *Briefe*, p. 231.
13. Hawthorne, *Philippians*, p. 114.
14. Culpepper, 'Co-Workers', p. 355.

Philemon, and ὁ συστρατιώτης to Archippus); here they refer to Epaphroditus's share in Paul's suffering service.

Especially noteworthy, as well, are the subsequent ascriptions ἀπόστολος and λειτουργός (2.25). When read in the light of 1.5, 7, 29 and 2.17, λειτουργός (2.25) and λειτουργία (2.30) probably denote priestly action,[15] again mirroring Paul's self-depiction in 2.17-18 as priest offering both the sacrifices of the Philippian community and his own blood. Epaphroditus, as priest, enables the Philippian believers to do Paul service, something they would have been unable to do without him.[16]

Epaphroditus is, thus, their ἀπόστολος (2.25). This use of ἀπόστολος confirms our earlier suspicions that the usage of the term is not fixed in this letter. Paul does not call Epaphroditus an ἀπόστολος in the absolute sense used in 2 Corinthians or Romans, but in the sense of one who represents the Philippians to Paul (2.30), possibly also including their sufferings. Accordingly the word ἀπόστολος used of Epaphroditus functions not so much lexically as performatively.[17]

The use of ἀπόστολος here, however, also confirms our suspicion that its substitution by δοῦλος in 1.1 and its connection to λειτουργός in the context of 2.25 imply a suffering context. Paul pictures Epaphroditus as one who over-exerts himself in the service of Christ[18] and, as a result, was at death's door. Paul expresses this by the phrases ἠσθένησεν παραπλήσιον θανάτῳ, 2.27 and μέχρι θανάτου ἤγγισεν, 2.30.

Now the fact that 2.30 contains a verbatim repetition of the expression used of Christ only a few verses earlier (cf. 2.8), namely, μέχρι θανάτου, is not accidental. In fact, it is hailed by Culpepper as 'the most striking echo of [Phil. 2.5-11 in 2.19-30]', for 'the phrase

---

15. Dibelius, *Briefe*, p. 57; Lipsius, *Briefe*, p. 232 (citing Rom. 13.6; 15.27; 2 Cor. 9.12).

16. Lightfoot, *Philippians*, p. 125; Beare, *Philippians*, p. 99.

17. The phrase 'performative utterances' is attributed to J.L. Austin, *How to Do Things with Words* (Cambridge, MA: Harvard University Press, 1962) and D. Evans, *The Logic of Self-Involvement* (London: SCM Press, 1963), by D.H. Kelsey, *The Uses of Scripture in Recent Theology* (Philadelphia: Fortress Press, 1975), pp. 78-79, 87 n. 47.

18. Lightfoot, *Philippians*, p. 125; D.A. Black, *Paul, Apostle of Weakness* (New York: Peter Lang, 1984), p. 212.

9. The Theme of Suffering in the Argumentatio, Part II 177

appears nowhere else in the New Testament except Philippians 2.8'.[19] Furthermore, in that μέχρι θανάτου (2.8, 30) appears to pick up either LXX Isa. 53. 8 ἤχθη εἰς θάνατον or LXX Isa. 53.12 παρεδόθη εἰς θάνατον, it may be suggested that as the imagery of the Servant Songs underlies the depiction of the Christ type in 2.6-11, so too that imagery runs through the depiction of those who reflect the Christ type, such as Epaphroditus.[20] Paul sets Epaphroditus before the Philippians as one in whom the experiences of the Christ type are clearly visible. For, like Paul and Christ, Epaphroditus risks his life in the service of the gospel[21] in order to 'fill what is lacking in your service towards me'—words that recall in a striking way Col. 1.24, where Paul is depicted as suffering imprisonment as an apostle on behalf of the Gentiles and where his sufferings are said to fill up the measure of Christ's sufferings on behalf of his church (cf. also 1 Cor. 16.17; 2 Cor. 11.9; and later *1 Clem.* 38).[22]

As with Paul and Christ, however, Epaphroditus's suffering alone is not evidence of his embodiment of the Christ type. Thus I disagree with Houlden who sums up much of the current, scholarly consensus when he writes that 'suffering, for Paul, is always the mark of real Christian service'.[23] What Paul actually depicts rhetorically before the Philippians is a picture of a situation of necessity, a hostile setting where fatigue and sickness from over-exertion are the norm. In this situation suffering is a cipher for necessity. For it is here, caught in the midst of suffering, that one is forced to choose either to reflect God's action in the world as that action is reflected in Christ, or to flee to safety.

Nevertheless, Paul does not leave servants of the gospel without hope. According to Paul, underlying the actions of God's servants is the confidence that those who choose to reflect God's action in Christ will inevitably know the triumph of God's grace that breaks the powers of sin. For this reason, rather than concluding his words of exhortation and example with Epaphroditus's sickness, Paul writes to the Philippians to encourage them with the news of his recovery (2.27), a recovery that is for Paul not only a natural relief and cause

19. Culpepper, 'Co-Workers', p. 350; cf. Black, *Paul*, p. 214.
20. Cf. Collange, *Philippiens*, p. 90.
21. For παραβουλεύομαι, see Hawthorne, *Philippians*, p. 120.
22. On Col. 1.24, see esp. Kremer, *Was an den Leiden?*, *passim*.
23. Houlden, *Paul's Letters*, p. 93 (citing Phil. 3.8; 2 Cor. 11.23-30).

for joy at a co-worker's well-being but also a further sign of the victory of God's grace among God's servants.[24]

μέχρι θανάτου, therefore, is not the final word in the fulfilment of the Christ type. It does not mark 'the bitter end' of the course. For what awaits Christ, as is clear from 2.9-11[25]—but also Paul, Epaphroditus and Timothy—is not simply a course of suffering but transformation and exaltation, which is more commonly expressed by Paul as resurrection. As Karl Barth comments:

> The emptying and humbling must take its course to the bitter end, *mechri thanatou* (to death), the door must be bolted, till in fact *nothing* remains but the word God alone can speak—the word *resurrection*.[26]

All who have served obediently and faithfully will, like Christ, be exalted even over the powers (cf. 3.10-11, 20-21). So Paul stresses victory through God's grace, the *ultimate* fulfilment of the type, which Paul expects to take place at the parousia.

2. Reprehensio (3.1-16)

A *reprehensio* in classical rhetoric attempts to defuse objections that could be raised by real opponents, perhaps those mentioned in an earlier *partitio*, or hypothetical opposition to an argument. The objections met in Philippians seem to be determined by the Epicurean nature of Paul's 'opponents'. That this is the case is seen in that Paul's first steps in the *reprehensio* are to establish the Philippian community's purity and, through *negatio* argumentation in 3.2-4a, to deny the same purity to his 'opponents' (cf. 3.2). This *tour de force* requires Paul's 'opponents' to prove the validity of their own experience of being ἐν Χριστῷ.

One possible implication of Paul's actions may be that Paul felt his experience of being ἐν Χριστῷ was under attack. More likely, however, is the understanding of Paul's intention that can be drawn from his *argumentatio firmior* in 3.4b-6, where Paul ridicules those who prize status ἐν σαρκί. In Paul's argumentation his opponents demon-

---

24. Cf. Lipsius, *Briefe*, p. 233.
25. Cf. Martin, *Carmen Christi*, p. xviii; D.M. Hay, *Glory at the Right Hand: Psalm 110 in Early Christianity* (Nashville: Abingdon, 1973), p. 86, who compares Phil. 2.9-11 with 1 Tim. 3.16; Rev. 4–5; and Heb. 1.8-13.
26. Barth, *Philippians*, p. 67 (emphases his).

9. The Theme of Suffering in the Argumentatio, Part II   179

strate that they are really Epicureans who fall far short of life ἐν Χριστῷ. So Paul's *argumentatio firmior* exalts his own—and the community's—existence ἐν Χριστῷ, while at the same time suggesting grave deficiencies in that of those who seek to ensure existence ἐν σαρκί.

Paul's argument is consistent. Pressed into a situation of necessity, he is able to choose. Admittedly, he could have chosen escape, flight, or an option for a comfortable life. What he chooses, however, is anything but comfort. Thus when he concludes his inductive argumentation of 3.2-11 in 3.7-11, he does so by focusing on the suffering of Christ, which is called gain (cf. 3.8-10).

The focus of the inductive portion of the *reprehensio* is 3.10-11. There is, however, a problem with these verses, for Paul's argument seems to be reversed. Rather than speaking first of resurrection and then of suffering, Paul should have spoken of suffering and then of resurrection. The existing order, it is suggested, contradicts Paul's expression of Christian existence as found in, say, Rom. 6.5—a situation that led some early critical commentators to question the authenticity of the letter.[27] It would not be amiss to suggest that much of the history of interpretation has laboured under the weight of attempts to harmonize Paul's theology here in Philippians with that of his other letters.[28]

Phil. 3.10-11 represents the development of τοῦ γνῶναι αὐτόν, a gerundive that explicates both 3.8 (ἵνα Χριστὸν κερδήσω) and 3.9 (καὶ εὑρεθῶ ἐν αὐτῷ).[29] As is clear from the bipartite explication of αὐτόν in 3.10, where the double καί structure is epexegetical, explicating the preceding αὐτόν, rather than coordinate, and the definite article governs both accusatives,[30] knowledge of Christ involves both ἡ δύναμις τῆς ἀναστάσεως αὐτοῦ (viz., of Christ) and ἡ κοινωνία τῶν παθημάτων αὐτοῦ (viz., of Christ). But, how?

---

27. See the survey in Vincent, *Philippians*, p. xxviii. According to Vincent himself, the order in Phil. 3.10 is 'the true one' (p. 105).
28. Cf. Huby, *Saint Paul*, p. 350.
29. Explicating 3.8: Huby, *Saint Paul*, p. 348; Kleinknecht, *Gerechtfertige*, p. 307; Barth, *Philipper*, p. 59. Explicating 3.9: Joüon, 'Notes', pp. 305-306, apparently following Loisy; Friedrich, *Philipper*, p. 119. The earliest understanding of the verses in this way may be found in John Damascene, *In epistulam ad Philippenses*, PG 95.873D.
30. BDF 442.9, followed by Proudfoot, 'Imitation?', p. 150; Tannehill, *Dying and Rising*, pp. 119-20.

The answer to this question becomes clearer in light of the parallel nature of these verses:

A καὶ τὴν δύναμιν
        τῆς ἀναστάσεως αὐτοῦ
  B καὶ (τὴν) κοινωνίαν
        (τῶν) παθημάτων αὐτοῦ
  B′ συμμορφιζόμενος
        τῷ θανάτῳ αὐτοῦ
A′ εἴ πως καταντήσω εἰς
        τὴν ἐξανάστασιν
        τὴν   ἐκ νεκρῶν

A carefully designed inverse parallelism suggests that the resurrection of Christ and the sufferings of Christ are integrally bound together. While chronologically one may follow from the other, as is clear in 3.10b-11, Christ's resurrection also presupposes his sufferings (3.10a). So while some authors have found parallels in 3.10-11 to other contemporary depictions—such as, for example, Christ's words in Mt. 16.26,[31] or the *topos* of loss–gain in contemporary Judaism[32]—much more is it the case that here Paul is reflecting on his own experience in terms of the imagery, if not the wording, of 2.6-11.[33] The parallel form of 3.10-11 does not so much provide the Philippians with a depiction of the two primary facets of existence ἐν Χριστῷ, as contrasted with existence ἐν σαρκί,[34] as much as it provides them with a depiction of the Christ type in Paul's present experiences and its consequent fulfilment in Paul's future. For the knowledge spoken of in 3.10 is both experiential[35] and future-oriented:[36] Paul finds in his own experience an enactment of the Christ type because of his present sufferings and his expectation of a future resurrection.

Contrary to the supposition that there can be resurrection transformation or peace without suffering—a position Paul seems to have attributed to his 'Epicurean' opponents, who love pleasure but reject

---

31. Martin, *Philippians*, p. 129.
32. Str-B 3.622. For a further list, see Hawthorne, *Philippians*, p. 135.
33. Cf. Huby, *Saint Paul*, p. 320, following L. de Grandmaison; M.D. Hooker, 'Interchange in Christ', *JTS* ns 22 (1971), p. 356; Martin, *Philippians*, p. 130, following Hendriksen, *Philippians*, p. 161 n. 139.
34. Cf. Hawthorne, *Philippians*, p. 145.
35. Forestell, 'Christian Perfection', p. 124; Huby, *Saint Paul*, p. 348.
36. Forestell, 'Christian Perfection', p. 124.

9. *The Theme of Suffering in the* Argumentatio, *Part II*   181

anxiety and suffering, whether in the here-and-now or in the beyond[37]—Paul insists that there is no resurrection transformation without suffering. Paul's Epicurean 'opponents' reject suffering and cling to all they have—that is, fleshly existence—because for them there is no after-life.[38] What Paul so passionately sets before the Philippian congregation is a view of present suffering that will enable them to see meaning in that suffering *sub specie resurrectionis*, as opposed to a view of static existence ἐν σαρκί that makes present suffering meaningless.

Thus suffering, though a crucial component of the argumentation of Philippians, is not the main thrust of Paul's argument. True, suffering provides the occasion for the letter and the setting of necessity that elicits Paul's decision and action. Second Temple Judaism could have provided Paul with ways of viewing his sufferings—for example, as loving chastisements,[39] as martyr sufferings, as atoning sufferings,[40] as evidences of a share in the world to come,[41] etc. The basis, however, of Paul's action is not suffering itself but resurrection transformation. Paul's attention is centred not on the cross but on the resurrection hope of the parousia.[42] Paul does not contrast existence ἐν Χριστῷ with existence ἐν σαρκί in terms of the involvement in sufferings of the one versus the lack of sufferings in the other. Rather, what differentiates existence ἐν Χριστῷ from existence ἐν σαρκί is that existence ἐν Χριστῷ expects future transformation because of the 'type' of Christ, while existence ἐν σαρκί awaits failure and destruction.

That the theme of resurrection underlies the *reprehensio* is also clear from Paul's contrast of those πεποιθέναι ἐν σαρκί (3.3) with συμμορφίζεσθαι τῷ θανάτῳ αὐτοῦ (3.10).[43] For Paul the servanthood that implies abandonment of the richness of possibilities and the embrace of a life characterized by the 'gains' of suffering, imprisonment, sickness, harassment, opponents, etc. is the same servanthood

---

37. Neyrey, 'Polemic', p. 408.
38. Neyrey, 'Polemic', pp. 420-22.
39. E.g. *Sanh.* 101a-b.
40. E.g. *Mek. R. Ish.*, *Bahodesh* 10 (on Exod. 20.20); *Mo'ed Qat.* 28a.
41. E.g. *Gen Rab.* 33.1 (on Gen. 8.1).
42. A. Schlatter, *Die Theologie des Apostel* (Stuttgart: Calwer, 1977), p. 351; *pace* Gnilka, *Philipperbrief*, p. 196. Cf. Joüon, 'Notes', pp. 306-307; Beare, *Philippians*, p. 127.
43. H.D. Betz, *Nachfolge und Nachahmung: Jesu Christi im Neuen Testament* (Tübingen: Mohr, 1967), p. 146; Murphy-O'Connor, 'Philippiens', p. 1223.

and the same 'gains' (cf. 1.21) that lead inevitably to the true gain of resurrection transformation (cf. 1.21 τὸ ἀποθανεῖν κέρδος). What is inevitable failure in the eyes of worldly existence, existence ἐν σαρκί, will be future triumph through the grace of God. For those who have found the experiences of the Christ type to be their own, future victory will also be theirs, as it was Christ's.

This resurrection existence is, however, still a future reality, as is clear from the deductive argumentation of the *reprehensio* in 3.12-16. Like 3.2-4a, 3.12a-b uses a *negatio* form of argumentation in which Paul separates himself even further from his 'Epicurean' opponents. Here Paul argues enthymemetically that the state to which his convictions expressed in 3.7-11 have led him is not one of perfection. So he contrasts the goals of 3.8-11 with what he has not yet accomplished, namely οὐχ...ἔλαβον (3.12a, cf. ἵνα κερδήσω, 3.8c), (οὐ) τετελείωμαι (3.12a, cf. [ἵνα] εὑρεθῶ, 3.9a), (οὐ) κατέλαβον (3.12b, cf. τὸ γνῶναι, 3.10). In this way he is able to argue against a hidden premise, which is that the counting of all things as loss is somehow sufficient for perfection.

This *negatio* conclusion, spelled out in 3.12a-b, is reiterated in 3.13a. The *negationes* of 3.12a-b and 3.13a, however, are followed by another conclusion, in this case, a *conclusio non necessaria*, in which Paul picks up the wording of the *negatio* in 3.12 (διώκω δὲ εἰ καὶ καταλάβω) and indicates positively what he does in order to accomplish his goal (3.13b-14): ἕν δέ, τὰ μὲν ὀπίσω ἐπιλανθανόμενος τοῖς δὲ ἔμπροσθεν ἐπεκτεινόμενος, κατὰ σκοπὸν διώκω εἰς τὸ βραβεῖον κτλ. The goals are to be striven for, says Paul using the language of athletic exertion.[44]

The goal Paul has set before him is not Christ himself, at least not Christ alone.[45] In 1.21 Paul spoke of life (τὸ ζῆν) as Christ (Χριστός), implying that he cannot gain Christ simply by death. Nor is Paul's goal a Gnostic-like reaching for 'the ineffable blessedness, beyond which there is nothing more to attain'.[46] Rather, the object of Paul's attainment—κατὰ σκοπόν and εἰς τὸ βραβεῖον—is understood in terms of ἡ ἄνω κλῆσις τοῦ θεοῦ ἐν Χριστῷ Ἰησοῦ (3.14), a phrase that refers specifically to Paul's consciousness of his

---

44. Pfitzner, *Agon Motif*, pp. 139-40.
45. Beare, *Philippians*, p. 130; cf. A. Vitti, '"Comprehensus sum a Christo Jesu" (Phil. 3.12)', *VD* 9 (1929), p. 357.
46. Schmithals, *Paul and the Gnostics*, p. 97.

9. *The Theme of Suffering in the* Argumentatio, *Part II*   183

servanthood that makes him a suffering servant but also a vindicated servant.[47] As such, the primary referent of βραβεῖον is resurrection[48]—that is, the fullness of the Christ type,[49] which is also the seal on Paul's servanthood and God's vindication of his servant.[50]

3. *Exhortatio (3.17–4.7)*

Phil. 3.17–4.7 is the hortatory conclusion to the *reprehensio*. We have already seen the same rhetorical function in 1.27–2.18. In 1.27–2.18, however, Paul urges believers to act even as he acts in a difficult situation; in 3.17–4.7 Paul urges believers to his same action, but in the context of the presentation of the negative 'type' of Paul's opponents ἐν σαρκί as contrasted with his own 'type' ἐν Χριστῷ as an echo of Christ's (cf. 2.6-11).[51]

That a direct relation between the first *exhortatio* of 1.27–2.18 and the second *exhortatio* of 3.17–4.7 exists is clear from the use of related hymnic portions in the two sections. Like 2.6-11, so 3.20-21 does not present christological reflection or ethical discourse on the basis of the Christ-event or of Christ's actions[52] but depicts the servant's destiny.[53] It is Paul who, along with the apostolic team and the Philippians,[54] becomes a living parable of the servant in his projected vindication following suffering. Thus, τὸ σῶμα τῆς ταπεινώσεως of 3.21 parallels ὡς ἄνθρωπος ἐταπείνωσεν ἑαυτὸν γενό-

---

47. Lipsius, *Briefe*, p. 239 (citing 2 Thess. 1.11; Heb. 3.1; and Eph. 4.14), *pace* Beare, *Philippians*, p. 130 (citing Rom. 11.29; 2 Tim. 1.9; 1 Pet. 1.10). τὸ βραβεῖον may be understood as ἡ ἄνω κλῆσις, thus making τῆς ἄνω κλήσεως a genitive of apposition (so Lipsius, *Briefe*, p. 239, following De Wette) or it may be modified by the genitive (so Beare, *Philippians*, p. 130).
48. Dibelius, *Briefe*, pp. 60-61; Lohmeyer, *Philipper*, p. 147; Jewett, 'Conflicting Movements', pp. 386-87; Panikulam, *Koinonia*, p. 100.
49. *Pace* L.P. Trudinger, 'A Further Brief Note on Colossians 1.24', *EvQ* 45 (1973), p. 37 (citing also Acts 14.22 and 1 Pet. 2.21).
50. Vincent, *Philippians*, p. xxix. Cf. Rom. 5.17, 18, 21; 8.38, 39; 2 Cor. 5.1.
51. Collange, *Jésus à Paul*, p. 198; cf. Schade, *Apocalyptische Christologie*, pp. 125-26.
52. Dalton, 'Integrity', p. 100.
53. Jewett, *Anthropological Terms*, p. 252.
54. So Hawthorne, *Philippians*, p. 160, on Paul's use of σκοπέω (2.4; 3.17) and σκόπος in 3.14. Elsewhere in Paul the verb is used only in Rom. 16.17; 2 Cor. 4.18; Gal. 6.1.

μενος ὑπήκοος μέχρι θανάτου of 2.7-8. The subject in both cases is the obedient, suffering servant—though in 2.7-8 the servant is Christ, while in 3.21 the servant is Paul, the apostolic team and the Philippians themselves. Joüon is thus right to see in those spoken of in 3.17-18 certain outstanding co-workers ('des prédicateurs ou des pasteurs qu'il a formés à son image') as contrasted with the opponents ('les mauvais bergers').[55]

Furthermore, in both 2.6-11 and 3.20-21 the stress is not on abasement, as experienced by Christ, Paul, Paul's co-workers, and probably also by the Philippians,[56] but on exaltation, which only Christ has experienced but in which Paul remains confident—largely as a result of the Philippians' faithfulness (cf. χαρὰ καὶ στέφανος μου, οὕτως στήκετε ἐν κυρίῳ, 4.1; cf. 1.27)—and to which he exhorts the Philippians. The believer's assurance is not in that over which Christ has been made Lord, namely, the ἐπίγεια.[57] Indeed, according to Paul, this is the 'hope' of Paul's 'opponents', a hope that Paul is at pains to show is no hope at all. Rather, the believer is assured by the knowledge that the goal that awaits him or her is the one that Christ has reached, namely, resurrection life.[58]

Against a this-worldly understanding of the believer's hope, Paul underscores his future expectation in apocalyptic terms: (1) by the use of ὑποτάξαι αὐτῷ τὰ πάντα (3.21), which is a reflection of ἕως ἂν θῶ τοὺς ἐχθρούς σου ὑποπόδιον τῶν ποδῶν σου of Ps. 109.1 LXX and πάντα ὑπέταξας ὑποκάτω τῶν ποδῶν αὐτοῦ of Ps. 8.7 LXX;[59] and (2) by a conjunction of scriptural references that Paul also uses in 2.9-11 to speak of Christ's lordship over the powers and in 1 Cor. 15.25, 27-28, where the exact word order of Phil. 3.21 is repeated at various points.[60] Paul's emphasis here is on the vindicated suffering servant as the heavenly lord.[61]

55. Joüon, 'Notes', pp. 308-309.
56. Cf. Koester, 'Purpose', p. 325.
57. Phil. 2.10 and 3.19; elsewhere in Paul only 1 Cor. 15.40; 2 Cor. 5.1.
58. Cf. M. Carrez, 'L'herméneutique paulinienne de la résurrection', in *La résurrection du Christ et l'exégèse moderne* (Paris: Cerf, 1969), p. 60; idem, *De la souffrance à la gloire* (Neuchâtel: Delachaux & Niestlé, 1964), p. 162; Beare, *Philippians*, pp. 136-37, citing Gal. 4.26; Heb. 11.13, 16; 1 Pet. 1.1; 2.1; and the Epistle to Diognetus.
59. Beare, *Philippians*, p. 141.
60. Cf. also Rom. 8.34; 16.19-20; Eph. 1.22; Col. 3.1.
61. Tannehill, *Dying and Rising*, p. 108; cf. A. Rolla, 'La cittadinanza greco-

9. The Theme of Suffering in the Argumentatio, Part II   185

Thus Paul's exhortation to his converts concerning the imitation of his lifestyle, including his sufferings, functions within a larger rhetorical framework in which Paul's primary goal is to set forth his own example, to set it forth as a parallel to the example of Christ, and to challenge his Philippian converts to the same approach in the light of a similar situation of necessity. Paul's ultimate purpose is reassurance that is grounded eschatologically, rather than correction grounded ethically or soteriologically,[62] for it is resurrection, not destruction of the flesh, that is the destiny of those who are ἐν Χριστῷ.

The Philippians are brought back to the fore in 4.1-7. Here Paul exhorts his readers to take courage, seeing in themselves a fulfilment of the Christ type, as opposed to the behaviour and 'fulfilment' characteristic of Paul's 'opponents'.

The polemical nature of the paraenesis continues in 4.1-7. For while the mention of the parousia in 4.4-5 clearly reiterates Paul's hope in resurrection transformation, as Baumbach notes, it also underlines the eschatological setting of the warning about false prophets.[63] Furthermore, the blessing of 4.7, set as it is among admonitions regarding mental attitudes and the use of φρονεῖν, indicates 'that the heretical threat is involved here'.[64] Finally, in 4.7 Paul encourages believers to virtues that differentiate them from the opponents: a right attitude, peace,[65] and gentleness (ἐπιεικής).[66]

Yet Paul calls attention to the fact that the Philippians are not like those who think otherwise or who have no peace. They are assured of resurrection life because they witness in their lives the same experiences that characterized the life of Jesus, who was vindicated. Paul's

---

romana e la cittadinanza celeste di Filippesi 3.20', in *Studiorum Paulinorum Congressus Internationalis Catholicus, 1961* (Rome: Pontifical Biblical Institute Press, 1963), II, pp. 75-80; Becker, 'Erwägungen', p. 27; Benoit, *Philippians*, p. 34.

62. Cf. Collange, *Philippiens*, pp. 119-21.
63. G. Baumbach, 'Die Zukunftserwartung nach dem Philipperbrief', in *Die Kirche des Anfanges: Festschrift für Heinz Schürmann zum 65. Geburtstag* (ed. R. Schnackenburg, J. Ernst and J. Wanke; Leipzig: St Benno, 1977), p. 445.
64. Jewett, *Anthropological Terms*, p. 326.
65. *Anthropological Terms*.
66. Elsewhere only 1 Tim. 3.3; Tit. 3.2; Jas 3.17; and 1 Pet. 2.18; cf. ἐπιείκεια 2 Cor. 10.1; Acts 24.4. 2 Cor. 10.1 is set in a polemical context in which the substantive is used in conjunction with παρακαλέω, πραΰτης, ταπεινός, etc., as the modifier is here in Philippians.

urgings to serenity and calm (4.4-9),[67] when read in the context of this letter, are intended to emphasize that anxiety, doubts, questionings, etc. have no place in the experience of believers who see the experiences of Paul and Christ repeated in their own lives.[68] Thus Paul does not end on a polemical note but on a note of joy and encouragement, as well as of assurance.

The goal of Paul's readers contrasts radically with that of the 'opponents'—in whom the worldly 'type' is to be found—who have their minds set on ἐπίγεια (3.19; cf. 2.10)[69] and are enemies of the cross of Christ (3.18; cf. 2.8), which, to them, as 'Epicureans', is meaningless (cf. 1 Cor. 1.18; the use of τέλειος in Phil. 3.15; 1 Cor. 2.6; 3.1).[70] Paul's portrayal of them suggests that they are rooted in σάρξ,[71] not Christ. Consequently, according to Paul, their attachment to 'the temporal and transient character of the things so designated' can only lead to destruction (cf. 2 Cor. 5.1).[72]

---

67. P. Dacquino, 'La gioia cristiana', *BeO* 3 (1961), p. 182 (citing 2 Cor. 7.4b; Col. 1.24); E. Biser, 'Die Idee des Friedens nach den paulinischen Gefangenschaftsbriefen', *GL* 27 (1954), p. 169.
68. Cf. Vincent, *Philippians*, p. 136; Dacquino, 'Gioia', p. 182.
69. Hooker, 'Interchange in Christ', p. 356.
70. Kim, *Origin*, p. 81 n. 2. Cf. Gal. 4.26.
71. *Pace* P.C. Böttger, 'Die eschatologische Existenz der Christen', *ZNW* 60 (1969), pp. 260-61, who argues that in 3.21 Paul combats a false and otherworldly Christanity.
72. Koester, 'Purpose', p. 328.

Chapter 10

THE THEME OF SUFFERING IN THE *PERORATIO*

The *peroratio* of Philippians comprises a summary of the concerns of the letter. Elements of the summary are found in the introductory formulae of 4.8 (cf. 2.1; 3.1) and 4.9 (cf. 1.30; 2.1, esp. 2.5), as well as in the *peroratio* proper, for example, 4.10 (cf. 1.7; 2.29; 3.1; 4.4) and 4.14-15 (cf. 1.5, 7). Several lexical indications in this final body middle demonstrate Paul's consciousness of his sufferings. Paul uses the verb πεινάω, also used in 1 Cor. 4.11 when discussing the apostolic team's sufferings.[1] The verb ὑστερέω (4.12)[2] and the noun ὑστέρησις (4.11)[3] call to mind Paul's use of ὑστέρημα in 2.30—a word rarely used by Paul, but used by him in 2.30 to describe Epaphroditus's sacrifice on his behalf.[4] Furthermore, although Paul uses the verb περισσεύω 26 times, it is especially significant that in this short letter he uses it five times (1.9, 26; 4.12 [twice] and 18) in apparent contrast with a situation of suffering.[5] That contrast is further suggested by the word ταπεινόω,[6] which occurs only here and in 2.8, where, as we have seen, it suggests an element of the Lord's suffering[7]—though there is

1. Also used in Rom. 12.20 (quoting LXX Prov. 25.21); 1 Cor. 11.21, 34 (in the context of the discussion of the Lord's Supper).
2. Only here in Philippians but eight times in total in Paul's letters (Rom. 3.23; 1 Cor. 1.7; 8.8; 12.24; 2 Cor. 11.5, 9; 12.11; Phil. 4.12).
3. Elsewhere in the New Testament only at Mk 12.44.
4. Elsewhere only at 1 Cor. 16.17; 2 Cor. 8.14 (2×); 9.12; 11.9; Col. 1.24; and 1 Thess. 3.10 (cf. Lk. 21.4).
5. Cf. its use ten times in 2 Corinthians. The use in Paul contrasts with its relatively rare use in the Gospels, i.e. twelve times (6× in Matthew, 1× in Mark, 4× in Luke and 2× in John) and once in Acts.
6. Cf. 2.8 and 9; 2 Cor. 11.7 and 1 Pet. 5.6. The parallel ὑστερέω–περισσεύω exists also in 1 Cor. 8.8.
7. Elsewhere in Paul only in 2 Cor. 11.7 and 12.21. Elsewhere in the New

also the use of ταπεινοφροσύνη in 2.3 (elsewhere in Paul only at Eph. 4.2; Col. 2.18, 23; 3.12; cf. Acts 20.19 and 1 Pet. 5.5), ταπείνωσις in 3.21 (which does not recur in Paul, though it is used once in Luke, Acts and James), and the composite word ταπεινοφροσύνη in 2.3. Paul's words here recall τὸ αὐτὸ φρονεῖν and τὸ ἓν φρονοῦντες of 2.2, which introduces the portion containing 2.6-11. Lipsius further draws attention to the use of ταπεινόω here and in 2 Cor. 11.7, and correctly suggests that ταπεινοῦσθαι refers to 'der erniedrigenden Lage, welche die Armuth bereitet, vgl. 2 Kor. 11.7; J. Sir. 6.12'.[8]

Moreover these lexical indicators also reveal something of the meaning that Paul attaches to those sufferings. For Paul's language here states in summary form that he envisions the task of proclaiming the gospel in terms of the work of the suffering servant depicted in 2.6-11 and amplified throughout the letter, as well as in that of his coworkers. According to Collange, 'Paul's apostolate is characterized by a paradox that is simply the reflection of the cross and the resurrection: fullness and hunger, abundance and deprivation'.[9]

The most striking feature of the *peroratio*, however, is the presence of a clear *conquestio* (4.10-14), which begins and ends with the *inclusio* concerning the Philippians' gift to him (4.10, 14). Understanding this section as a *conquestio* explains why Paul seems to be saying that he is not really suffering (4.11-13), an assertion that appears to be at odds with 1.12-18a (and further with 1.26-28b). For in 4.11-14 Paul affirms that in his suffering he is confident, expressed here by the term αὐτάρκης (4.11).[10] In the light of a rhetorical analysis of Paul, it appears that Paul here again refers to the fact that he is able to endure sufferings due to his greatness of soul or to his ability to control his desires and passions that well up within.[11]

As in the case of the thanksgiving period (1.3-11), more is at stake in 4.10-20 than a simple thanksgiving for funds received.[12] Phil. 4.10

Testament five times in the Gospels (Matthew and Luke); Jas 4.10; 1 Pet. 5.6.
 8. Lipsius, *Briefe*, p. 245.
 9. Collange, *Philippiens*, p. 131.
 10. Used only here in the New Testament; cf. Sir. 31.28; 40.18; αὐταρκεία is used in the New Testament in 2 Cor. 9.8 and 1 Tim. 6.6.
 11. So G. Priero, 'Didici...sufficiens esse', *RivB* 10 (1962), pp. 60-62; *pace* Bornkamm, *Paul*, p. 170.
 12. This is not to deny that Paul thanks the Philippians for the gift; *pace* Holsten,

10. The Theme of Suffering in the Peroratio 189

functions as more than just a succinct mention of the Philippian gift, and 4.15-16 does more than reiterate past situations in which the Philippians have provided for him. As noted earlier, 4.15-17 suggests that Paul expected some support, which was not forthcoming, from other churches. As a twist of Cicero's *summae miseriae*, it allows Paul to laud further the Philippians, who embody the Christ–Paul type. And this is further emphasized by his singling out of the gift of the Philippians in 4.18b-19, even as he had done in the *proem*.[13]

Thus one must amplify Gnilka's statement that Paul 'speaks neither of thanks nor of the gift, which would be normal, but rather of his great joy and of their φρονεῖν for him'.[14] True, the Philippians' participation in Paul's ministry is evidenced by their gift to him. By means of the apparent verbal inclusion, represented by 1.5, 7 and 4.14-15, Paul reiterates the way in which his sufferings have been lightened by the loving gifts and aid of his churches. This verbal inclusion further underscores how, on the one hand, the *exordium* and *narratio* and, on the other hand, the *peroratio* bracket the entire letter, and emphasizes Paul's desire to create a well-disposed audience among the Philippians.

But more must be said. For Paul is at pains to note that his joy derives not from monetary assistance but from his congregation's faithfulness. Or as Lipsius notes, 'the reason for his joy is not the satisfaction of his own needs but rather the encouraging situation of the Philippians'.[15] In the light of such expressions as κάρπος in 4.17 (cf. 1.11, 1.22) and ἐν ἀρχῇ τοῦ εὐαγγελίου…ἐκοίνωσεν in 4.15 (cf. 1.5), Glombitza writes that 'Paul recognizes in this gift the fruit of his preaching, the fruit of true belief in the grace given to him in Jesus Christ'.[16]

In effect, the Philippians have manifested servanthood in their own lives[17] and so are living proof to Paul that the gospel is triumphing. This means that his own servanthood has been fruitful, and this, he says, gives him courage—a point that he reiterates in a restatement of

who called Philippians Paul's 'thankless' thanksgiving (cited in Vincent, *Philippians*, p. xxix).

13. Cf. *Inst*. 6.1.12.
14. Gnilka, *Philipperbrief*, p. 173
15. Lipsius, *Briefe*, p. 245.
16. O. Glombitza, 'Der Dank des Apostels', *NovT* 7 (1964), pp. 137-38.
17. Cf. Gnilka, *Philipper*, p. 176; Müller, *Philippians*, p. 148.

the *ostensio animi* in 4.18a. The Philippians' gift to him did much more than help Paul defray expenses incurred. It testified to Paul that the gospel had taken root in the community and, consequently, that his mission had been successful. The Philippians' gift was a testimony to Paul that his work, in spite of the implicit risk of failure, is proving fruitful.

In that 4.15-16 also ties the summary to the *exhortatio* or second, practical half of the body middle (1.27–2.18), we may conclude that, being reassured by the Philippians, Paul can, in turn, reassure the Philippians (cf. 2 Cor. 1.4-7). The Philippians are an encouragement to him to see his own situation and theirs in the light of God's triumph, that is, as experiences of suffering that will be fulfilled at the parousia. Gnilka is correct to note that although Paul suffers and addresses the Philippians in their sufferings, he does not do so out of his own sufferings.[18] Paul, in fact, finishes his rhetorical summary with a flourish as he invokes God's eschatological blessing for the Philippians (4.19)—words that imply that the Philippians, like Paul, ought already to be able to begin to envision the fulfilment of the parousia in their own experiences.

The *peroratio* is not, then, first of all an expression of thanks to the Philippians. It is, rather, primarily the reiteration of Paul's opening thanksgiving to God and the expression of his joy that his preaching has had the intended result of faith in Jesus Christ, as preached by Paul and brought about by God's grace.[19]

---

18. Gnilka, *Philipper*, pp. 174, 176; Müller, *Philippians*, p. 148; contrast Hafemann, *Suffering*, pp. 39, 51.
19. Glombitza, 'Dank', pp. 137-38.

CONCLUSION

As early as Ignatius of Antioch, suffering in Philippians was understood as a means whereby the believer was perfected and could witness to the faith. It effected a union with the suffering, crucified Christ through martyrdom—be it orthodox or Gnostic martyrdom. With the change in the *locus* of suffering, from martyrdom in imperial *stadia* to martyrdom in daily life through conflict with sin and resulting mortification, suffering came to be seen as a means of preparation for resurrection glory as the sufferer dies with Christ to the world. This was a model refined by Augustine, Chrysostom and their respective followers to enable Christians to understand suffering as a means to a fuller or more perfect union with Christ through volitional or practical intention.

In early Christ-mysticism, in Schweitzer and his followers, and in many variants of nineteenth-century studies of Paul's transformative theology, although the form, *locus* and precise goal of this perfection change, the major outlines remain the same. Suffering evidences the ontological union of believers with their Lord. In early Christ-mysticism it evidences the incorporation of the believer in the mystical Christ; in Käsemann and Güttgemanns it reveals Christ.

My work, however, suggests that a new, more scientifically rigorous approach to the text than has previously been offered is necessary. My contention is not that all commentators have mis-read Paul, but that previous discussions of suffering in Philippians have failed methodologically in not dealing with Philippians in its historical context, namely, as a rhetorical address in epistolary form within which suffering fulfils a specific function. Rather than governing our understanding of suffering in Philippians, the theological role of suffering must be understood to be dependent on the epistolary and rhetorical functions of the component parts of the letter and on the role suffering plays in those component parts.

True, the function of suffering in Paul's letters may also be viewed from other angles. Thus, while it would have been impossible to examine every conceivable understanding of function, other methods can and should be employed in order to reveal the threads of Paul's argumentation. For example, one could examine the function of suffering from the angle of the social sciences in their sociological[1] or anthropological variants,[2] or from the angle of communication theory.[3] Recently, for example, K.A. Plank has investigated the function of suffering in 1 Corinthians by using the methodology of P. Ricoeur.[4] The virtue of my choice of the two complementary methods of epistolary and rhetorical analysis, however, is not only that they appear to unlock Paul's textual discourse, but that they are accepted methods that allow us to unlock that textual discourse with a high degree of both scientific and historical rigour.

My analysis has revealed that Philippians has the broad outlines of a private Greek letter, with a readily discernible opening (1.1-2), thanksgiving (1.3-11) and closing (4.21-23). Furthermore, when epistolary analysis and rhetorical analysis are combined we discover that a large portion of the text, which has some of the characteristics of epistolary body middles but does not exactly fit any contemporary models, falls into place in a way that vitiates neither the integrity of the letter nor the broader outlines of epistolary structure uncovered independently of rhetorical analysis.

When examined in terms of its epistolary and rhetorical functions, suffering in Philippians appears in a fourfold way. First, Paul uses suffering as a well-known and widely accepted means of *captatio benevolentiae*. It is through his words on suffering that Paul endears himself to the Philippians, both in the *exordium* (1.5, 7) and the *ostensio animae* of the *peroratio* (4.10-14). This is not, however, mere sophistry, for he himself recognizes the Philippians' already existent concern for him as shown by their gift. Nonetheless, *captatio*

1. Cf., e.g., N. Gottwald, *The Hebrew Bible: A Socio-Literary Introduction* (Philadelphia: Fortress Press, 1985).
2. Cf. B.J. Malina, *The New Testament World: Insights from Cultural Anthropology* (Atlanta: John Knox, 1981) and *Christian Origins and Cultural Anthropology: Practical Models for Biblical Interpretation* (Atlanta: John Knox, 1986). See further, P.J. Richter, 'Recent Sociological Approaches to the Study of the New Testament', *Religion* 14 (1984), pp. 77-90.
3. Cf. V. Tejera, *Semiotics from Pierce to Barthes: A Conceptual Introduction to the Study of Communication, Interpretation, and Expression* (Leiden: Brill, 1988).
4. K.A. Plank, *Paul and the Irony of Affliction* (Atlanta: Scholars Press, 1987).

benevolentiae is a rhetorically accepted practice, and it appears as one of the functions of suffering in this letter.

Secondly, the occasion of Paul's words in Philippians is his imprisonment, a situation which, on the basis of studies such as those of Friedrich, we may assume was one of suffering. Paul refers to his suffering in various ways throughout the letter: in the *exordium* (1.5, 7), the *narratio* in its entirety (1.12-14), the *partitio* (1.17), the *confirmatio* (1.20, 21-26) and its *exhortatio* (1.29-30; 2.17), the *reprehensio* (3.10) and its *exhortatio* (3.21), and finally the *peroratio* (4.10-14).

In that the suffering of others is also to the fore in Philippians, however, the letter is more than just a communication of information. Paul's co-workers, Timothy and Epaphroditus, are said to suffer (2.19-30). In the *exordium* (1.5, 7), the *exhortatio* to the *confirmatio* (1.29-30), and the *peroratio* (4.15-16), Paul also alludes to the Philippians' sufferings. Finally, there is the suffering of Christ, spoken of most clearly in two places: at the centre of the *exhortatio* to the *confirmatio* (2.6-8) and as the culmination of the inductive argument in the *reprehensio* (3.10). A further allusion can be found in the *exhortatio* to the *reprehensio* (3.18).

These examples enable us to see that while suffering is central in Philippians as the occasion of the letter, Paul never limits suffering to himself. This leads me to conclude that Paul never uses suffering or his example of suffering in order to reprove the Philippians or to humble them. He uses suffering to endear them to him, but in a way that is consistent with their gift, which is itself an indication of their sharing with him.

The fact that Paul does not limit suffering to himself would also tend to discount the view that suffering reveals Paul's ontological or revelatory (i.e. proclamatory) union with Christ, a position more consistent with late nineteenth- and early twentieth-century European ontologies than with the text understood according to the epistolographical and rhetorical canons contemporary with Paul.

Thus, thirdly, I suggest that the key to understanding Paul's rhetorical presentation of suffering in Philippians is to be found in his studied use of the Christ type who as servant suffered and was vindicated. Philippians evidences Paul's perception that the Christ type can be discerned in his sufferings, the sufferings of his co-workers, and the sufferings of the Philippians.

My indebtedness to Daniel Patte's structural analysis of Philippians is obvious throughout my exegesis. Using Patte's analysis I have been able to see how Paul perceives that in his own experiences, in those of his co-workers, and in those of the Philippians, the experiences that identified Christ are being fulfilled or re-enacted. Thus, for example, in the rhetorical sections on either side of the *narratio*, where he is primarily concerned with his own suffering, Paul suggests that the experiences of his co-workers (1.1) and of the Philippians (1.5-7; 1.18b-26) mirror his experiences of persecution and imprisonment. True, the conclusion that the Philippians were suffering external persecution may be due more to Paul's desire to tie their destiny to his than to actual events. Nevertheless, whether they suffer actual persecution or not, what is important to see is that Paul stresses that the Philippians mirrored the experiences of himself, of his co-workers, and of Christ in sharing Paul's fate, as well as his hope of the ongoing progress of the gospel and of resurrection transformation. His goal appears to have been to set before the Philippians well-known examples in whom the Christ type was also being fulfilled.

At times it will have seemed that this view comes close to being merely a modern recasting of the earliest, martyrological readings of Philippians. True, there are important insights to be found in the early readings. Yet a fundamental difference separates these early readings from mine. For, whereas for writers from Ignatius to Lightfoot, Christ was the exemplary model held up *before* the Christian whose life then was to imitate that of his master, I have suggested, with Patte, that Paul looked *back* over his life, the life of the co-workers, and the lives of the Philippians and found mirrored in these lives the experiences of Christ.

Unlike Patte, however, I have been able to show that Paul's presentation of the Christ type is not only defensible structurally but that historically it was rhetorically motivated and achieved. So throughout my study I have attempted to show how Paul's attention is focused on himself as one in whom the Christ type is being fulfilled. This focus is consistent with classical rhetorical address where the speaker himself is the *causa*. Furthermore, Paul's presentation is also consistent with the specifically deliberative genre of rhetoric, for Paul presents himself like Christ, namely, as one who finds himself in a situation in which he is forced to choose what is honourable, and so clothes himself in the guise of Christ, that is, of a respected figure from an acknowledged common past whose experience or teaching was similar to—in this case, foundational for—his own.

In Philippians Paul emphasizes that he, like Christ, is a servant who, as such, suffers. Paul points to his own experience as servant in the epistolary prescript and the *narratio*, where he simply states that his suffering is not meaningless. It is, however, in the *confirmatio* that Paul proves rhetorically why his suffering is not meaningless, namely, because it serves as a pointer or guidepost to the victory of God. The reason Paul focuses on suffering in Philippians is in order to stress that, as in the case of Christ, whatever happens to him will not undermine the progress of the gospel. Furthermore, and again as in the case of Christ, suffering prefaces the inevitable vindication of the one suffering.

The centrality of 2.6-11 and the presentation there of Christ as servant alert us to Paul's conviction that his life mirrors the experiences of Christ, especially in terms of suffering. Contrary to most modern commentators who have been unduly influenced by a Lutheran *theologia crucis*, however, the main point of 2.6-11 is its underscoring of the fact that vindication follows suffering. The experiences in Paul's life, reflecting as they do the Christ type, lead him to see that even as Christ as servant suffered and was vindicated, so he too, as well as his co-workers and the Philippians, will be vindicated or exalted. The presentation of the Christ type in 2.6-11, therefore, is not first of all either ethical or soteriological; rather, it is primarily rhetorical.

Here, then, I am able to explain what previous commentators have been unable to explain: the Christ type, identified specifically with Christ (cf. 2.6-11), does not figure more prominently in the letter and is found within the context of the rhetorical exhortation (1.27–2.18)—in some cases (e.g. 2.12) even subordinate to it—because Paul has set before the Philippians the Christ as the cipher in whom the experience of all God's servants is most clearly reflected. The intent is not primarily epideictic—in which case Christ would be hymned—but deliberative. It is a means whereby Paul can communicate meaningfully with those whose experiences mirror the experience of other servants who find themselves in a situation of necessity and are forced to choose—as is clear from the way the language of 2.6-11 is found throughout the letter in descriptions of servants.

Patte's typology and my rhetorical analysis help us to see that Timothy and Epaphroditus, too, are both servants in far more than their suffering. It is, for example, their single-mindedness and the good report from Philippi that Timothy will bring that encourage and reassure Paul. Likewise, the restoration of Epaphroditus and the Philippian congregation's embodiment of the gospel (1.18b-26 and 4.10-20) reassure Paul of God's triumphant grace in so far as they are to him signs of ultimate fulfilment at the parousia.

Thus an important fourth function of suffering in Philippians is that suffering points beyond itself to vindication. While suffering is the occasion of the letter and an occasion for the Philippians to express their love for Paul, it is primarily used by Paul as the occasion for his extended, eschatological confession of faith in God's grace manifested to servants, that is, to those in whom the experiences of the Christ type are found.

It is precisely this eschatological victory and triumph that is in question in the *reprehensio*, the supposedly 'troublesome lapse' or 'clear indication of redactional conflation' (3.1–4.7). In actual fact, this section is a crucial feature of Paul's *argumentatio*. In the *confirmatio*, the first part of the *argumentatio*, Paul sets before the Philippians his proof for the value of his sufferings. He argues that even as Christ suffered and that suffering served to advance the gospel, so too the suffering of Christ's servants, in whom the Christ type is fulfilled, advances the gospel. In the *reprehensio*, the second part of the *argumentatio*, Paul sets before the Philippians a negative 'type', that is, a picture of those in whom the Christ type is not mirrored but who are tied to the experience of the flesh rather than to the advance of the gospel.

I have suggested that the actual historical identity of Paul's opponents does not affect our understanding of Paul's rhetorical argumentation. After all, what is at stake is not who those 'opponents' really were but how Paul saw them, regardless of who they were. Thus the key to understanding the *reprehensio* lies not in understanding who the opponents were but in understanding the rhetorical function of these opponents as not fulfilling the Christ type. The depiction of Timothy in 2.19-24 and of Epaphroditus in 2.25-30 that prefaces the *reprehensio* can only be understood as an intentional, radical contrast with Paul's depiction of those who perish because of their dependence on flesh.

Such an assertion cannot simply be reduced to the statement that these opponents were opposed to suffering. It is not necessary, in fact, to assume that they rejected suffering as such. Rather, in Paul's view these 'Epicurean' opponents rejected the idea that servant suffering has meaning. According to Paul the opponents' expectation of life was exhausted by the here and now (cf. 3.18-19), so denying future vindication or chastisement. But if that be true, says Paul, then the opponents also have to deny the value of the suffering of Paul's co-workers, of the Philippians, and, most decisively, of Christ himself (cf. 3.18)—although whether they ever did this or not is impossible to say given the rhetorical nature of the passage.

Paul sees in his experience of suffering a partial fulfilment of the Christ type, and so he confidently expects that suffering will necessarily be followed by its fuller fulfilment when vindication occurs. Thus he sets out in Philippians the thesis that even as Jesus did not experience suffering in vain, though others thought he had, neither will Christ type servants suffer in vain. There is no attempt in Philippians to equate the actual states of suffering and vindication of Christ and his followers; the equation lies in the dynamic of recompense.

In conclusion, I suggest that my findings will oblige those who approach Philippians to reconsider the inner dynamics of the letter. Not only has the function of suffering in the component epistolary and rhetorical parts been clarified, but we have also been able to see the weight Paul places on the Christ type as a dynamic motor that does not allow believers the complacency of a static existence but moves them, as Christ was moved, by God's grace towards future fulfilment. Philippians portrays Christian servants as part of a dynamic, forward-moving projection that risks all for the sake of an incomparable treasure.

Appendix

THE 'OPPONENTS' OF PAUL AT PHILIPPI

The argument that Paul is attacking Jews is based on Paul's use of polemical terms such as κύνες,[1] ἡ κατατομή as a term of derision for circumcision, αἰσχύνη as a veiled and polemically charged circumlocution for the male sexual organ,[2] an understanding of the κακοὶ ἐργάται as those who bring damnation,[3] and a combat of law-righteousness and knowledge of the law (cf. Rom. 2.19-20) versus Christ-righteousness and knowledge of Christ.[4] The Jews, it is suggested, preached 'a seductive message, because it offered visible and tangible tokens of God's favour in the present, not in the future and invisible world'.[5]

Serious objections, however, have been raised against these conjectures.[6] First, such a view misunderstands the Judaism of Paul's day. For example, Hawthorne's argument that Jews would have spoken of Jewish rightstanding before God on the basis of 'human effort, by painstakingly obeying the law and practicing circumcision' and so would have opposed Paul's abandonment of 'all confidence in those external things and staking one's life wholly upon Jesus Christ'[7] is woefully inadequate. Obedience and circumcision in Second Temple Judaism are no more 'external' than confidence in Christ for Paul, as is clear from rabbinic discussions of Abraham's life of integrity.[8]

Moreover, Hawthorne errs by describing the eschatology of Second Temple Judaism as 'immediate' and 'earth-bound' compared with Paul's conception of

---

1. A.F.J. Klijn ('Paul's Opponents in Philippians', *NovT* 7 [1965], p. 282) cites Mt. 7.6, where the word is used to describe gentility *par excellence*; he also notes Rev. 22.15 and Ignatius, *Eph.* 7.1, where the word implies all those whose lifestyle puts them outside the Christian community. Cf. Beare, *Philippians*, p. 103.
2. Klijn, 'Paul's Opponents', p. 280, citing Paul's reference to Israel as ἡ περιτομή in Rom. 15.8; Gal. 2.7-9; cf. Eph. 2.11. The perception of a veiled reference in αἰσχύνη is long-standing (Ambrose, Hilary, Pelagius, Augustine).
3. Lipsius, *Briefe*, p. 234.
4. Klijn, 'Paul's Opponents', pp. 281-82, 284.
5. Hawthorne, *Philippians*, p. xlvii; Klijn, 'Paul's Opponents', p. 284.
6. W.G. Kümmel, *Introduction to the New Testament* (trans. H.C. Kee; Nashville: Abingdon, 1975), p. 328.
7. Hawthorne, *Philippians*, p. xlvi.
8. Cf. *Mak.* 24a; *R. Nat.* a33; *'Ab.* 1.15.

heavenly transformation.[9] The issue of an immediate, earth-bound perfection versus a future, transcendent perfection is, of course, very much to the fore in Paul's debate. But this does not mean that Paul's view of transcendent perfection stands over against the supposedly Jewish view. For Jewish views of resurrection existence were not uniform. They involved not only physical transformation,[10] but also spiritual resurrection[11] and immortality.[12]

Another serious objection to viewing Paul's opponents as Jews has to do with Paul's use of veiled language in his description, for there is no convincing reason why Paul would have used veiled language here and not elsewhere when referring to Jews. In 1 Thess. 2.14-16, for example, Paul speaks straightforwardly.[13] True, it is possible that Paul perceived the Philippian congregation as siding with the Jewish missionaries and against him and so used veiled language to speak to them so as not to offend those who heeded the Jewish missionaries. Since, however, there is no evidence within the letter itself of Philippian Gentiles converting to Judaism, it seems odd for Paul to attack what could only then be described as a failed mission.[14] It would seem more likely that Paul would attack a movement that had actually achieved some success.

Instead of Jews, some authors have suggested that Paul's 'opponents' are Jewish Christians. Parallels can be found between Philippians, on the one hand, and 2 Corinthians and Galatians, on the other. These parallels suggest that in Philippians Paul has in mind the same opponents.[15] The profile of these opponents can thus be drawn not simply on the basis of Philippians but also using 2 Corinthians and Galatians. These opponents, it is suggested, held firmly to the law of Moses, considering it determinative of faith and action in the life of believers, and sought zealously the conversion of Gentile Christians to obedience to the law.[16] Furthermore, at the heart of their message, particularly as Paul perceived it, lies circumcision (cf. 3.2, ἡ κατατομή).[17] Although acknowledging the Christian faith of the Gentile Philippian believers, the Judaizers required them to move on to 'perfection' expressed by means of acceptance of the law and circumcision.[18]

Objections have also been raised, however, against seeing Paul's opponents as Judaizers, whether Jews by birth or Gentiles who adopted Judaism.[19] It has been

9. Hawthorne, *Philippians*, p. xlvi.
10. Cf. Dan. 12; Isa. 26; 2 Macc. 7; *1 En.* 10; *2 Bar.* 50.2; *4 Sib. Or.* 176-90.
11. Cf. *1 En.* 22; 92.3; 108; *2 Bar.* 30; 51; *Pss. Sol.* 3; *T. Jud.* 25; *T. Benj.* 10.
12. Cf. *Wis.* 1–6; *Jub.* 23; *Ass. Mos.* 10; *4 Macc.* 8; *Apoc. Abr. passim*.
13. Vincent, *Philippians*, p. 93.
14. Wikenhauser–Schmid, *Introducción*, pp. 249-50.
15. Jewett, *Anthropological Terms*, p. 117; cf. Lightfoot, *Philippians*, p. 145; F. Froitzheim, *Christologie und Eschatologie bei Paulus* (FB, 35; Würzburg: Echter, 1979), p. 159.
16. First proposed and widely disseminated by F.C. Baur; cf. Ellis, 'Opponents', pp. 270-72; Jewett, *Anthropological Terms*, pp. 22-23.
17. Barth, *Philippians*, p. 93.
18. Jewett, 'Conflicting Movements', pp. 386-87.
19. That is, where arguments against are actually stated. According to Jewett, Schmithals gives absolutely no grounds for his dismissal of the Judaizing option (Jewett, 'Epistolary Thanksgiving', pp. 44-45).

noted, for example, that Philippians lacks a polemic against circumcision, the law and super-apostles, such as one finds in 2 Corinthians and Galatians.[20] Furthermore, would Paul have criticized the Judaizers for being impure and immoral when, if anything, what characterized them was ethical rigorism?[21]

Some have suggested that Paul's opponents were lapsed Christians, antinomians, libertines, or 'judaizing Gnostics', whose denial of the resurrection led them to live amorally.[22] Beare describes these opponents as 'voluptuaries, whose whole outlook is limited to earthly things'.[23] According to H.D. Betz they were materialistic libertines who act κατὰ σαρκά.[24]

Lightfoot suggests that two different sets of opponents are addressed: the opponents of 3.2-11 (and 1.15-17) are Pharisaic Judaizers, while those attacked in 3.12-19 are 'antinomian reactionists' or Judaizing Gnostics (cf. Rom. 16.17-19 and 6.1-23; 14.1-15.6).[25] Although nothing points to two groups in Paul's integral letter, Lightfoot's observation forces us to take seriously the 'libertine' qualities of the opponents. Again, we are brought face to face with a dilemma: how can the ethical rigorism of Christian Jews coexist with antinomianism?

All the above views point variously to the *this*-worldly nature of Paul's opponents and the *other*-worldly nature of Paul's reaction. As early as 1651 it was suggested that Paul's opposition in 3.2-11 and 17-19 was, in fact, *other*-worldly Gnostic[26] or θεῖος ἄνηρ missionaries.[27] The problem with this view is that unfortunately 'there are no unambiguously Gnostic features in the polemic of 3.2 and 3.17ff., and no christological error can be deduced from the charge "enemies of the cross of Christ" '.[28] The Gnostic characteristics discerned by Schmithals may be due more to what scholars are finding is a root of Gnosticism, namely developing sectarian Jewish apocalypticism,[29] a root they may have shared with Paul. Hawthorne argues that the divine-man idea in Hellenistic antiquity has not yet been fully shown to exist

---

20. Cf. Kümmel, *Introduction*, p. 327.
21. W. Schmithals, *Paul and the Gnostics* (trans. J.E. Steely; Nashville: Abingdon, 1972), pp. 83-86. Schmithals even argues that no Judaizing (or Pharasaic Judaizing) movement ever existed and that such a group is merely a fiction drawn from the fertile mind of F.C. Baur (pp. 86-87)!
22. According to Ellis ('Opponents', p. 272) the view was first suggested by W.M.L. de Wette and D. Schenkel to explain 1 Corinthians.
23. Beare, *Philippians*, p. 101.
24. Betz, *Nachfolge und Nachahmung*, pp. 151-52; cf. Ellis, 'Opponents', p. 274.
25. Lightfoot, *Philippians*, pp. 88-89, 155, followed by Beare, *Philippians*, pp. 101, 133-34; Jewett, 'Conflicting Movements', p. 382; cf. Ellis, 'Opponents', pp. 273-74. For a further list of defenders of this option, see Collange, *Philippiens*, p. 29.
26. Schmithals, *Paul and the Gnostics*, pp. 82-122, followed by Bornkamm, 'Philipperbrief', p. 195. For the history of the attribution of Gnostic identity to the opponents, see Ellis, 'Opponents', p. 264, who traces the theory to H. Hammond (1651).
27. Koester, 'Purpose', p. 324.
28. Kümmel, *Introduction*, p. 328; cf. Jewett, 'Epistolary Thanksgiving', pp. 44-45.
29. See in this regard R.M. Grant, *Gnosticism and Early Christianity* (New York: Columbia University Press, 2nd edn, 1966); B.A. Pearson, 'Jewish Elements in Gnosticism and the Development of Gnostic Self-Definition', in *Jewish and Christian Self-Definition* (London: SCM Press, 1980), I, pp. 151-60.

Appendix 201

and, furthermore, that the concept was certainly not so well developed in the Christian church as to be an alternative theology.[30] Such criticisms call into question the elaborate picture of Gnostic opponents that is often presented.[31]

30. Hawthorne, *Philippians*, pp. xliv-xlv.
31. E.g. Baumbach, 'Zukunftserwartung', pp. 307-10.

BIBLIOGRAPHY

Ahern, B.M., 'The Fellowship of his Sufferings: Phil. 3.10: A Study of St Paul's Doctrine on Christian Suffering', *CBQ* 22 (1960), pp. 1-32.
—'In Phil. 3.10-11', *VD* 37 (1959), pp. 26-31.
—'The Power of his Resurrection and Fellowship in his Sufferings: An Exegetical and Doctrinal Study on Phil. 3.10-11' (Doctoral dissertation, Pontifical Biblical Institute, Rome, 1958).
Aland, B., 'Gnosis und Kirchenväter: Ihre Auseinandersetzung um die Interpretation des Evangeliums', in *Gnosis: Festschrift für Hans Jonas* (ed. B. Aland; Göttingen: Vandenhoeck & Ruprecht, 1979), pp. 158-215.
Aland, K., 'Die Enstehung des Corpus Paulinum', in *idem, Neutestamentliche Entwürfe* (TBNT, 63; Munich: Kaiser, 1979), pp. 302-50.
Aleith, E., *Paulusverständnis in der alten Kirche* (BZNW, 18; Berlin: Töpelmann, 1937).
Alexander, J.N.S., 'The Interpretation of Scripture in the Ante-Nicene Period', *Int* 12 (1958), pp. 272-80.
Allo, E.B., 'L'évolution' de "l'Evangile de Paul"', *VP* 1 (1941), pp. 48-77, 165-93.
Andry, C.F., *Paul and the Early Christians* (Washington, DC: University Press of America, 1981).
Antin, P., '*Mori Lucrum* et *Antigone* 462, 464', *RSR* 62 (1974), pp. 259-60.
Aune, D.E., *The New Testament in its Literary Environment* (LEC, 8; Philadelphia: Westminster Press, 1987).
—Review of H.D. Betz, *Galatians, RelSRev* 7 (1981), pp. 323-28.
Balla, E., 'Das Problem des Leides in der Geschichte der israelitisch-jüdischen Religion', in *Eucharisterion: Studien zur Religion und Literatur des Alten und Neuen Testaments, Hermann Gunkel zum 60 Geburtstage* (ed. E. Balla *et al.*; FRLANT ns, 19; Göttingen: Vandenhoeck & Ruprecht, 1923), pp. 214-60.
Bammel, E., 'Preparation for the Perils of the Last Days: 1 Thessalonians 3.3', in *Suffering and Martyrdom in the New Testament: Studies Presented to G.M. Styler by the Cambridge New Testament Seminar* (ed. W. Horbury and B. McNeil; Cambridge: Cambridge University Press, 1981), pp. 91-100.
—'Zum jüdischen Märtyrerkult', *TLZ* 78 (1953), pp. 119-26.
Barclay, W., 'Phil. 2.1-11', *ExpTim* 70 (1958–1959), pp. 4-7, 40-44.
Barth, G., *Der Brief an die Philipper* (ZBNT, 9; Zürich: Theologischer, 1979).
Barth, K., *The Epistle to the Philippians* (trans. J.W. Leitch; London: SCM Press, 1962 [1928]).
—*Prayer according to the Catechisms of the Reformation: Stenographic Records of Three Seminars* (adapted by A. Roulin; trans. S.F. Terrien; Philadelphia: Westminster Press, 1952).

Bibliography

Baumbach, G., 'Die Frage nach den Irrlehrern in Philippi', *Kairos* 13 (1971), pp. 252-66. Reprinted in *Gnosis und Neues Testament: Studien aus Religionswissenschaft und Theologie* (ed. K.W. Tröger; Gütersloh: Gerd Mohn, 1975), pp. 293-310.

—'Die Zukunftserwartung nach dem Philipperbrief', in *Die Kirche des Anfänges: Festschrift für Heinz Schürmann zum 65. Geburtstag* (ed. R. Schnackenburg, J. Ernst and J. Wanke; Leipzig: St Benno, 1977), pp. 435-57.

Baumeister, T., *Die Anfänge der Theologie des Martyriums* (MBT, 45; Münster: Aschendorff, 1979).

Baumert, N., 'Ist Philipper 4.10 richtig übersetzt?', *BZ* 13 (1969), pp. 256-62.

—*Täglich sterben und auferstehen: Der Literalsinn von 2 Kor. 4.12–5.10* (SANT, 34; Munich: Kösel, 1973).

Baur, F.C., *Paulus, der Apostel Jesu Christi: Sein Leben und Wirken, Seine Briefe und Seine Lehre: Ein Beitrag zu einer kritischen Geschichte des Urchristenthums* (ed. E. Zeller; Leipzig, 1866–1867).

Beare, F.W., *A Commentary on the Epistle to the Philippians* (BNTC; London: A. & C. Black, 1959).

Becker, J., 'Erwägungen zu Phil. 3.20-21', *TZ* 27 (1971), pp. 16-29.

Beker, J.C., *Paul the Apostle: The Triumph of God in Life and Thought* (Philadelphia: Fortress Press, 1980).

—*Paul's Apocalyptic Gospel: The Coming Triumph of God* (Philadelphia: Fortress Press, 1982).

Bengel, J.A., *Gnomon Novi Testamenti* (Tübingen, 3rd edn, 1836).

Benoit, A., 'Ecriture et tradition chez saint Irenée', *RHPR* 40 (1960), pp. 32-43.

Benoit, P., *Les épîtres de saint Paul aux Philippiens, aux Colossiens, à Philémon, aux Ephésiens* (Sainte Bible; Paris: Cerf, 1959).

Benz, E., 'Christus und Sokrates in der alten Kirche: Ein Beitrag zum altkirchlichen Verständnis des Märtyrers und des Martyriums', *ZNW* 43 (1950–51), pp. 195-224.

Berger, K., 'Hellenistische Gattungen im Neuen Testament', in *Aufstieg und Niedergang der römischen Welt* (ed. H. Temporini and W. Haase; Berlin: de Gruyter, 1984), XXV.2, pp. 1031-1432.

Bertram, G., ''Αποκαραδοκία', *ZNW* 49 (1958), pp. 264-70.

Best, E., 'Bishops and Deacons: Philippians 1.1', in *Studia Evangelica* (ed. F.L. Cross; TU, 102; Berlin: Akademie, 1968), IV.1, pp. 371-76.

—*One Body in Christ: A Study in the Relationship of the Church to Christ in the Epistles of the Apostle Paul* (London: SPCK, 1955).

Betz, H.D., *Galatians: A Commentary on Paul's Letter to the Church in Galatia* (Hermeneia; Philadelphia: Fortress Press, 1979).

—*2 Corinthians 8 and 9: A Commentary on Two Administrative Letters of the Apostle Paul* (Hermeneia; ed. G.W. MacRae; Philadelphia: Fortress Press, 1985).

—*Nachfolge und Nachahmung Jesu Christi im Neuen Testament* (BZHT, 37; Tübingen: Mohr, 1967).

Beyschlag, K., 'Das Problem des Leidens in der frühen Christenheit', in *idem, Evangelium als Schicksal: Fünf Studien zur Geschichte der Alten Kirche* (Munich: Claudius, 1979).

Biser, E., 'Die Idee des Friedens nach den paulinischen Gefangenschaftsbriefen', *GL* 27 (1954), pp. 165-70.

Bjerkelund, C.J., *PARAKALO: Form, Funktion und Sinn der parakalō-Sätze in den paulinischen Briefen* (BTN, 1; Oslo: Universitetsforlaget, 1967).

Black, C.C., 'Keeping Up with Recent Studies: 16. Rhetorical Criticism and Biblical Interpretation', *ExpTim* 100 (1989), pp. 252-58.

Black, D.A., *Paul, Apostle of Weakness: Astheneia and its Cognates in the Pauline Literature* (AUS7TR, 3; Frankfurt: Lang, 1984).

Bligh, J., Review of R.P. Martin, *Carmen Christi*, *Bib* 49 (1968), pp. 127-29.

Böttger, P.C., 'Die eschatologische Existenz der Christen: Erwägungen zu Philipper 3.20', *ZNW* 60 (1969), pp. 244-63.

Bonnard, P., *L'épître de saint Paul aux Philippiens* (CNT, 10; Neuchatel: Delachaux & Niestlé, 1950), pp. 5-82.

—'Faiblesse et puissance du chrétien chez saint Paul', *ETR* 30 (1958), pp. 61-70.

—'Mourir et vivre avec Jésus Christ selon saint Paul', *RHPR* 36 (1956), pp. 101-12.

Bornkamm, G., *Paul* (San Francisco: Harper & Row, 1971).

—'Der Philipperbrief als paulinische Briefsammlung', in *Neotestamenica et Patristica: Freundesgabe O. Cullmann* (NovTSup, 6; Leiden: Brill, 1962), pp. 192-202.

Bousset, W., *Kyrios Christos: A History of the Belief in Christ from the Beginnings of Christianity to Irenaeus* (trans. J.E. Steely; Nashville: Abingdon, 1970).

Bouttier, M., *Christianity according to Paul* (trans. F. Clarke; SBT, 49; Napierville, IL: Allenson, 1966).

—*En Christ: Etude d'exégèse et de théologie pauliniennes* (EHPR, 54; Paris: Presses Universitaires de France, 1962).

—'Remarques sur la conscience apostolique de saint Paul', in *OIKONOMIA: Heilsgeschichte als Thema der Theologie: Oscar Cullmann zum 65 Geburtstag gewidmet* (ed. F. Christ; Hamburg: Reich, 1967), pp. 100-108.

Bowker, J., *Problems of Suffering in Religions of the World* (Cambridge: Cambridge University Press, 1970).

Breck, J., 'Biblical Chaismus: Exploring Structure for Meaning', *BTB* 17 (1987), pp. 70-74.

Brown, R.E., *The 'Sensus Plenior' of Sacred Scripture* (Baltimore: St Mary's University, 1955).

Bruce, F.F., *Paul: Apostle of the Heart Set Free* (Grand Rapids: Eerdmans, 1977).

—'St Paul in Macedonia: 3. The Philippian Correspondence', *BJRL* 63 (1981), pp. 260-84.

Brunec, M., ' "Cum timore et tremore vestram salutem operamini" (Phil. 2.12-13)', *VD* 40 (1962), pp. 270-75.

Buchanan, C.O., 'Epaphroditus' Sickness and the Letter to the Philippians', *EvQ* 36 (1964), pp. 157-66.

Buck, C.H., Jr, and G. Taylor, *Saint Paul: A Study of the Development of his Thought* (New York: Charles Scribner's Sons, 1969).

Buckley, F.J., 'Joy in the Midst of Suffering', *BTod* 1 (1966), pp. 1546-47.

Bünker, M., *Briefformular und rhetorische Disposition im 1. Korintherbrief* (GTA, 28; Göttingen: Vandenhoeck & Ruprecht, 1984).

Bultmann, R., 'Ignatius und Paulus', in *Studia Paulina in honorem Johannes de Zwaan Septuagenarii* (ed. J.N. Sevenster and W.C. van Unnik; Haarlem: Bohn, 1953), pp. 37-51.

—*Theology of the New Testament* (2 vols.; trans. K. Grobel; New York: Charles Scribner's Sons, 1951–55).

—Review of E. Lohmeyer, *Der Brief an die Philipper* (Göttingen: Vandenhoeck & Ruprecht, 1928) and *Kyrios Jesus* (Heidelberg: Carl Winter, 1928), *DLZ* 51 (1930), pp. 774-80.

Cai, R. (ed.), *S. Thomas Aquinatis Super Epistolas S. Pauli Lectura*, II (Rome: Marietti, 8th edn, 1953).
Caird, G.B., *Paul's Letters from Prison* (NCB; Oxford: Oxford University Press, 1976).
Carmignac, J., 'La théologie de la souffrance dans les hymnes de Qumrân', *RevQ* 3 (1961), pp. 365-86.
Carr, W., *Angels and Principalities: The Background, Meaning and Development of the Pauline Phrase 'hai archai kai hai exousiai'* (SNTSMS, 42; Cambridge: Cambridge University Press, 1981).
Carrez, M., *De la souffrance à la gloire: De la δόξα dans la pensée paulinienne* (BTh; Neuchatel: Delachaux & Niestlé, 1964).
—'L'herméneutique paulinienne de la résurrection', in *La résurrection du Christ et l'exégèse moderne* (LD, 50; Paris: Cerf, 1969), pp. 55-73.
—'Souffrance et gloire dans les épîtres pauliniennes: Contribution à l'exégèse de Col. 1.24-27', *RHPR* 31 (1951), pp. 343-52.
Casey, M., 'Chronology and the Development of Pauline Christology', in *Paul and Paulinism: Essays in Honour of C.K. Barrett* (ed. M.D. Hooker and S.G. Wilson; London: SPCK, 1982), pp. 124-34.
Cerfaux, L., 'L'antinomie paulinienne de la vie apostolique', in *Recueil Lucien Cerfaux* (BETL, 6-7; Gembloux: Duculot, 1954), II, pp. 455-67. Orig. pub. in *RSR* 41 (Mèlanges Jules Lebreton, 1) (1951–52), pp. 221-35.
—'Las epístolas de la cautividad', in *Introducción a la Bíblia*. II. *Nuevo Testamento* (ed. A. Robert and A. Feuillet; trans. A. Ros; BHSE, 71; Barcelona: Herder, 1965), pp. 438-70.
—'L'hymne au Christ—sérviteur de Dieu (Phil. 2.6-11 = Is. 52.13–53.12)', in *Recueil Lucien Cerfaux* (BETL, 6-7; Gembloux: Duculot, 1954), II, pp. 425-37.
—'Saint Paul et le "sérviteur de Dieu" d'Isaïe', in *Recueil Lucien Cerfaux* (BETL, 6-7; Gembloux: Duculot, 1954), II, pp. 439-54.
Chadwick, H., *The Enigma of St Paul* (London: The Athlone Press, 1969).
Charlesworth, J.H. (ed.), *The Old Testament Pseudepigrapha* (2 vols.; Garden City: Doubleday, 1983, 1985).
Childs, B.S., *The New Testament as Canon: An Introduction* (London: SCM Press, 1984).
Collange, J.F., *L'épître de saint Paul aux Philippiens* (CNT, 10a; Neuchatel: Delachaux & Niestlé, 1973).
—*De Jésus à Paul: L'éthique du Nouveau Testament* (CE, 3; Geneva: Labor & Fides, 1980).
Colombas, G.M., *El monacato primitivo* (2 vols.; Madrid: Biblioteca de autores cristianos, 1974).
Conzelmann, H., *An Outline of the Theology of the New Testament* (trans. J. Bowden; London: SCM Press, 1969).
Coste, J., 'Notion grècque et notion biblique de la "souffrance éducatrice" (à propos d'Hébreux 5.8)', *RSR* 43 (1955), pp. 481-523.
Court, J.M., 'Paul and the Apocalyptic Pattern', in *Paul and Paulinism: Essays in Honor of C.K. Barrett* (ed. M.D. Hooker and S.G. Wilson; London: SPCK, 1982), pp. 57-66.
Cowburn, J., *Shadows and the Dark: The Problems of Suffering and Evil* (London: SCM Press, 1979).
Cullmann, O., 'Le caractère éschatologique du devoir missionaire et da la conscience apostolique de saint Paul: Etude sur le κατέχον (-ων) de 2 Thess. 2.6-7', *RHPR* 16 (1936), pp. 210-45. Reprinted in *Des sources de l'Evangile à la formation de la théologie chrétienne* (REB; Neuchatel: Delachaux & Niestlé, 1969), pp. 51-75.

Culpepper, R.A., 'Co-Workers in Suffering: Philippians 2.19-30', *RevExp* 77 (1980), pp. 349-58.
Dacquino, P., 'Data e provenienza della lettera ai Filippesi', *RivB* 6 (1958), pp. 224-32.
—'La gioia cristiana (Fil. 4.4-9)', *BeO* 3 (1961), pp. 182-83.
—'Il testo cristologico di Fil. 2.6-11', *RivB* 7 (1959), pp. 221-29.
Dahl, N.A., Review of E.P. Sanders, *Paul and Palestinian Judaism*, *RelSRev* 4 (1978), pp. 153-58.
Dalton, W.J., 'The Integrity of Philippians', *Bib* 60 (1979), pp. 97-102.
Damme, D. von, 'Gott und die Märtyrer: Uberleugungen zu Tertullian. *Scorpiace*', *FZPT* 27 (1980), pp. 107-19.
Davies, W.D., *Paul and Rabbinic Judaism: Some Rabbinic Elements in Pauline Theology* (New York: Harper & Row, rev. edn, 1967).
De Boer, Martinus C., 'Images of Paul in the Post-Apostolic Period', *CBQ* 42 (1980), pp. 359-80.
Deidun, T.J., *New Covenant Morality in Paul* (AnBib, 89; Rome: Pontifical Biblical Institute, 1981).
Deissmann, A., *Light from the Ancient East: The New Testament Illustrated by Recently Discovered Texts of the Greco-Roman World* (trans. L.R.M. Strachan; Grand Rapids: Baker, repr. 1965 [1927]).
—*Paul: A Study in Social and Religious History* (trans. W.E. Wilson; New York: Harper & Row, 2nd edn, 1957).
Deissner, K., *Paulus und die Mystik seiner Zeit* (Leipzig: Deichert, 2nd edn, 1921).
Delling, G., 'Philipperbrief', *RGG*, V, pp. 333-36.
—'Der Tod Jesu in der Verkündigung des Paulus', in *APOPHORETA: Festschrift für Ernst Haenchen* (ed. W. Eltester and F.H. Kettler; BZNW, 30; Berlin: Töpelmann, 1964), pp. 85-96.
De Lubac, H., *Exégèse médievale: Les quatre sens de l'Ecriture* (Théologie, 41; Paris: Aubier, 1959).
Denis, A.M., 'La fonction apostolique et la liturgie nouvelle en Esprit', *RSPT* 42 (1958), pp. 617-56.
—'Versé en libation (Phil. 2.17) = Versé son sang? A propos d'une réference de W. Bauer', *RSR* 45 (1957), pp. 567-70.
Denton, D.R., 'Hope and Perseverance', *SJT* 34 (1981), pp. 313-20.
—'Ἀποκαραδοκία', *ZNW* 73 (1982), pp. 138-40.
Dewailly, L.M., 'La part prise à l'Evangile (Phil. 1.5)', *RB* 80 (1973), pp. 247-60.
Dibelius, M., *Die Briefe des Apostels Paulus. II. Die Neun Kleinen Briefe* (HNT, 3.2; Tübingen: Mohr, 1913).
—'Glaube und Mystik bei Paulus', in *Botschaft und Geschichte: Gesammelte Aufsätze* (Tübingen: Mohr, 1956), pp. 94-116.
—'Paulus und die Mystik', in *Botschaft und Geschichte: Gesammelte Aufsätze* (Tübingen: Mohr, 1956), pp. 134-59.
Dodd, C.H., 'The Mind of Paul', in *New Testament Studies* (Manchester: Manchester University Press, 1953), pp. 67-128.
Doty, W.G., *Letters in Primitive Christianity* (GBS; Philadelphia: Fortress Press, 1973).
Downing, J., 'Jesus and Martyrdom', *JTS* ns 14 (1963), pp. 279-93.
Dunn, J.D.G., *Christology in the Making: A New Testament Inquiry into the Origin of the Doctrine of the Incarnation* (London: SCM Press, 1980).

Bibliography

—*Jesus and the Spirit: A Study of the Religious and Charismatic Experience of Jesus and the First Christians as Reflected in the New Testament* (Philadelphia: Westminster Press, 1975).

—'Paul's Understanding of the Death of Jesus', in *Reconciliation and Hope: New Testament Essays on the Atonement and Eschatology* (ed. R. Banks; Grand Rapids: Eerdmans, 1974), pp. 125-41.

Dupont, J., *Gnosis: Le connaissance religieuse dans les épîtres de saint Paul* (Louvain: Nauwelaerts, 1949).

Eichholz, G., 'Bewahren und Bewähren des Evangeliums: Der Leitfaden von Philipper 1-2', in *Tradition und Interpretation: Studien zum Neuen Testament und zur Hermeneutik* (Munich: Kaiser, 1965), pp. 138-60.

Ellis, E.E., 'Paul and his Opponents: Trends in the Research', in *Christianity, Judaism and Other Greco-Roman Cults* (ed. J. Neusner; Leiden: Brill, 1975), I, pp. 264-98.

Ellwein, E. (ed.), *D. Martin Luthers Epistel-Auslegung: 3 Band, Die Briefe an die Epheser, Philipper, und Kolosser* (Göttingen: Vandenhoeck & Ruprecht, 1973).

Euler, K.F., *Die Verkündigung vom leidenden Gottesknecht aus Jes. 53 in der griechischen Bibel* (BWANT, 66; Stuttgart: Kohlhammer, 1934).

Ewald, H., *Die Sendschreiben des Apostels Paulus* (Bücher des Neuen Bunden, 3.1; Göttingen, 1857).

Exler, F.X.J., 'The Form of the Ancient Greek Letter: A Study in Greek Epistolography' (PhD thesis, Catholic University of America, 1923).

Fascher, E., '*Dynamis Theou*: Eine Studie zur urchristlichen Frömmigkeit', *ZTK* (1938), pp. 82-108.

Fee, G.D., 'Χάρις in 2 Corinthians 1.15: Apostolic Parousia and Paul–Corinth Chronology', *NTS* 24 (1978), pp. 533-38.

Feuillet, A., 'Mort du Christ et mort du chrétien d'après les épîtres pauliniennes', *RB* 66 (1959), pp. 481-513.

Fitzmyer, J.A., 'The Aramaic Background of Philippians 2.6-11', *CBQ* 50 (1988), pp. 478-83.

—'To Know Him and the Power of his Resurrection (Phil. 3.10)', in *Mélanges bibliques en hommage au R.P. Béda Rigaux* (ed. A. Descamps and A. de Halleux; Gembloux: Duculot, 1970), pp. 411-25.

Forestell, J.T., 'Christian Perfection and Gnosis in Philippians 3.7-16', *CBQ* 18 (1956), pp. 123-36.

Francis, F.O., 'The Form and Function of the Opening and Closing Paragraphs of James and 1 John', *ZNW* 61 (1970), pp. 110-26.

Frend, W.H.C., *Martyrdom and Persecution in the Early Church: A Study of a Conflict from the Maccabees to Donatus* (Oxford: Basil Blackwell, 1965).

Fridrichsen, A., 'ἰσόψυχος = ebenbürtig, solidarische', *Symbolae Osloenses* 18 (1938), pp. 42-49.

Friedrich, G., *Der Brief an die Philipper*, in *Die kleineren Briefe des Apostels Paulus* (NTD, 8; Göttingen: Vandenhoeck & Ruprecht, 1968), pp. 92-130.

—'Der Brief eines Gefangenen: Bemerkungen zum Philipperbrief', in *Auf das Wort kommt es an: Gesammelte Aufsätze zum 70. Geburtstag* (Göttingen; Vandenhoeck & Ruprecht, 1978), pp. 224-35.

Froitzheim, F., *Christologie und Eschatologie bei Paulus* (FB, 35; Würzburg: Echter, 1979).

Fuchs, E., 'Andacht über Phil. 2.12-18', in *idem, Zum hermeneutischen Problem in der Theologie: Die existenziale Interpretation: Gesammelte Aufsätze* (Tübingen: Mohr, 1959), I, pp. 320-22.

Funk, R.W., 'The Apostolic Parousia: Form and Significance', in *Christian History and Interpretation: Studies Presented to John Knox* (ed. W.R. Farmer, C.F.D. Moule and R.R. Niebuhr; Cambridge: Cambridge University Press, 1967), pp. 249-68.

—*Language, Hermeneutic, and Word of God: The Problem of Language in the New Testament and Contemporary Theology* (New York: Harper & Row, 1966).

—*Parables and Presence: Forms of the New Testament Tradition* (Philadelphia: Fortress Press, 1982).

Furnish, V.P., 'The Place and Purpose of Philippians 3', *NTS* 10 (1963), pp. 80-88.

—*Theology and Ethics in Paul* (Nashville: Abingdon, 1968).

Gaar, A. (ed.), *Clavis Patrum Latinorum* (Sacris Erudiri, 3; Steenbruges: Abbey of St Peter, 1961).

Gärtner, B., 'Suffering', *NIDNTT*, III, pp. 719-26.

Gaffin, R.B., Jr, 'The Usefulness of the Cross', *WTJ* 41 (1978–79), pp. 228-46.

Gager, J.G., Jr, 'Functional Diversity in Paul's Use of End-Time Language', *JBL* 89 (1970), pp. 325-37.

—'Some Notes on Paul's Conversion', *NTS* 27 (1981), pp. 697-704.

Garland, D.E., 'Philippians 1.1-26: The Defense and Confirmation of the Gospel', *RevExp* 77 (1980), pp. 327-36.

George, A.R., *Communion with God in the New Testament* (London: Epworth, 1953).

Georgi, D., *The Opponents of Paul in Second Corinthians* (Philadelphia: Fortress Press, 1986).

Gibbs, J.G., 'The Cosmic Scope of Redemption according to Paul', *Bib* 56 (1975), pp. 13-29.

—'The Relation between Creation and Redemption according to Phil. 2.5-11', *NovT* 12 (1970), pp. 270-83.

Giglioli, A., ' "Mihi enim vivere Christus est"; Congettura al testo di Phil. 1.21', *RivB* 16 (1968), pp. 305-15.

Glombitza, O., 'Der Dank des Apostels: Zum Verständnis von Philipper 4.10-20', *NovT* 7 (1964), pp. 135-41.

—'Mit Furcht und Zittern: Zum Verständnis von Phil. 2.12', *NovT* 3 (1959), pp. 100-106.

Gnilka, J., 'Die antipaulinische Mission in Philippi', *BZ* 9 (1965), pp. 258-76.

—*Der Philipperbrief* (HTKNT, 10.3; Freiburg: Herder, 1968).

Goodspeed, E.J., *Problems of New Testament Translation* (Chicago: University of Chicago Press, 1945).

Grässer, E., Review of J. Gnilka, *Der Philipperbrief*, *TLZ* 95 (1970), pp. 503-506.

Grant, R.M., *Gnosticism and Early Christianity* (New York: Columbia, 2nd edn, 1966).

Grayston, K., *The Letters of Paul to the Philippians and to the Thessalonians* (CBC; Cambridge: Cambridge University Press, 1967).

Groussouw, W., 'L'espérance dans le Nouveau Testament', *RB* 61 (1954), pp. 508-32.

Grube, G.M.A., *A Greek Critic: Demetrius on Style* (The Phoenix, Sup. Vol., 4; Toronto: University of Toronto Press, 1961).

Grundmann, W., *Der Begriff der Kraft in der neutestamentlichen Gedankenwelt* (BWANT, 60; Stuttgart: Kohlhammer, 1932).

Güttgemanns, E., *Der leidende Apostel und sein Herr: Studien zur paulinischen Christologie* (FRLANT, 90; Göttingen: Vandenhoeck & Ruprecht, 1966).

Guibert, J. de, 'Sur l'emploi d'ἔλπις et de ses synonymes dans le Nouveau Testament', *RSR* 4 (1913), pp. 565-69.

Gundry, R.H., *SŌMA in Biblical Theology, with Emphasis on Pauline Anthropology* (SNTSMS, 29; Cambridge: Cambridge University Press, 1976).

Gunther, J.J., *St Paul's Opponents and their Background: A Study of Apocalyptic and Jewish Sectarian Teachings* (NovTSup, 35; Leiden: Brill, 1973).

Hafemann, S.J., *Suffering and the Spirit: An Exegetical Study of 2 Cor. 2.14–3.3 within the Context of the Corinthian Correspondence* (WUNT, 2.19; Tübingen: Mohr, 1986).

Hamerton-Kelly, R.G., 'A Girardian Interpretation of Paul', *Semeia* 33 (1985), pp. 65-81.

Hansen, G.W., *Abraham in Galatians: Epistolary and Rhetorical Contexts* (JSNTSup, 29; Sheffield: JSOT Press, 1989).

Hawthorne, G.F., *Philippians* (WBC; Waco, TX: Word Books, 1983).

Hay, D.M., *Glory at the Right Hand: Psalm 110 in Early Christianity* (SBLMS, 18; Nashville: Abingdon, 1973).

Heitmüller, W., *Taufe und Abendmahl bei Paulus: Darstellung und religionsgeschichtliche Beleuchtung* (Göttingen: Vandenhoeck & Rurpecht, 1903).

—*Taufe und Abendmahl im Urchristentum* (RVDCG, 22/23; Tübingen: Mohr, 1911).

Hendriksen, W., *Exposition of Philippians* (Grand Rapids: Baker Book House, 1968).

Henry, P., 'Kénose', *DBSup*, V, pp. 7-161.

Herklots, H.G.G., *The Epistle of St Paul to the Philippians: A Devotional Commentary* (London: Lutterworth, 1947).

Hermann, I., *Kyrios und Pneuma: Studien zur Christologie der paulinischen Hauptbriefen* (SANT, 2; Munich: Kösel, 1961).

Hickling, C.J.A., 'Centre and Periphery in the Thought of Paul', in *Studia Biblica 1978. III. Papers on Paul and Other New Testament Authors* (ed. E.A. Livingstone; JSNTSup, 3; Sheffield: JSOT Press, 1980), pp. 199-214.

—'Paul's Reading of Isaiah', in *Studia Biblica 1978. III. Papers on Paul and Other New Testament Authors* (ed. E.A. Livingstone; JSNTSup, 3; Sheffield: JSOT Press, 1980), pp. 215-23.

Hielmann, W., 'Die Leidensmystik des hl. Paulus in ihrem Zusammenhand mit dem Gedanken des mystischen Leibes Christi', *TGl* 31 (1939), pp. 597-605.

Hoffmann, P., *Die Toten in Christus* (Munster: Aschendorff, 1966).

Holl, K., 'Die Vorstellung vom Märtyrer und die Märtyrerakte in ihrer geschichtlichen Entwicklung', in *idem, Gesammelte Aufsätze zur Kirchengeschichte. II. Der Osten* (Tübingen: Mohr, 1928), pp. 67-102.

Holladay, C.R., 'Paul's Opponents in Philippians 3', *ResQ* 12 (1969), pp. 77-90.

Holmberg, B., *Paul and Power: The Structure of Authority in the Primitive Church as Reflected in the Pauline Epistles* (Philadelphia: Fortress Press, 1980).

Holsten, C., *Das Evangelium des Paulus* (2 vols.; Berlin: Reimer, 1880, 1898).

Holtz, T., 'Zum Selbstverständnis des Apostels Paulus', *TLZ* 91 (1966), pp. 321-30.

Holtzmann, H.J., *Lehrbuch der neutestamentlichen Theologie* (2 vols.; D.A. Jülicher and W. Bauer; Tübingen: Mohr, 2nd edn, 1911).

Holzmeister, U., ' "Gaudete in Domino semper" (Phil. 4.4-9)', *VD* 4 (1924), pp. 358-62.

—' "Viscera Christi" (Phil. 1.8)', *VD* 16 (1936), pp. 161-65.

Hooker, M.D., 'Interchange and Atonement', *BJRL* 60 (1978), pp. 462-81.

—'Interchange and Suffering', in *Suffering and Martyrdom in the New Testament: Studies Presented to G.M. Styler by the Cambridge New Testament Seminar* (ed. W. Horbury and B. McNeil; Cambridge: Cambridge University Press, 1981), pp. 70-83.

—'Interchange in Christ', *JTS* 22 (1971), pp. 349-61.
—'Philippians 2.6-11', in *Jesus und Paulus: Festschrift für Werner George Kummel zum 70 Geburtstag* (ed. E.E. Ellis and E. Grässer; Göttingen: Vandenhoeck & Ruprecht, 1975), pp. 151-64.
Houlden, J.L., *Paul's Letters from Prison: Philippians, Colossians, Philemon and Ephesians* (PNTC; Harmondsworth: Penguin Books, 1970).
Huby, J., *Saint Paul: Les épîtres de la captivité (Colossiens, Philémon, Ephésians, Philippiens)* (VS, 8; Paris: Beauchesne, 1947).
Hübner, H., 'Der Galaterbrief und das Verhältnis von antiker Rhetorik und Epistolographie', *TLZ* 109 (1984), pp. 241-50.
Hunter, A.M., *Paul and his Precedessors* (London: SCM Press, 2nd rev. edn, 1961).
Hunzinger, C.-H., 'Die Hoffnung angesichts des Todes im Wandel der paulinischen Aussagen', in *Leben Angesichts des Todes: Beiträge zum theologischen Problem des Todes: Helmut Thielicke zum 60 Geburtstag* (ed. B. Lohse and H.P. Schmidt; Tübingen: Mohr, 1968), pp. 69-98.
Hurd, J.C., Jr, 'Paul Ahead of his Time: 1 Thess. 2.13-16', in *Anti-Judaism in Early Christianity*. I. *Paul and the Gospels* (ed. P. Richardson with D. Granskou; SCJ, 2; Waterloo: Wilfrid Laurier University, 1986), pp. 21-36.
—'Pauline Chronology and Pauline Theology', in *Christian History and Interpretation: Studies Presented to John Knox* (ed. W.R. Farmer, C.F.D. Moule and R.R. Niebuhr; Cambridge: Cambridge University Press, 1967), pp. 225-48.
—'The Sequence of Paul's Letters', *CJT* 14 (1968), pp. 189-200.
Jeremias, J., 'Beobachtungen zur Gedankenführung in den paulinischen Briefen', in *Studia Paulina in honorem J. de Zwaan* (ed. J.N. Sevenster and W.C. van Unnik; Haarlem: Bohn, 1953), pp. 146-54.
Jewett, R., 'Conflicting Movements in the Early Church as Reflected in Philippians', *NovT* 12 (1970), pp. 362-90.
—'The Epistolary Thanksgiving and the Integrity of Philippians', *NovT* 12 (1970), pp. 40-53.
—*Paul's Anthropological Terms: A Study of their Use in Conflict Settings* (AGJU, 10; Leiden: Brill, 1971).
—'Romans as an Ambassadorial Letter', *Int* 36 (1982), pp. 5-20.
Johanson, B.C., *To All the Brethren: A Text-Linguistic and Rhetorical Approach to 1 Thessalonians* (CBNT, 16; Stockholm: Almqvist & Wiksell, 1987).
Johnson, G., 'The Life of Christians in the World (Phil. 1.1–2.4)', *CJT* 3 (1957), pp. 248-54.
Jouön, P., 'Notes philologiques sur quelques versets de l'épître aux Philippiens', *RSR* 28 (1938), pp. 89-93, 299-310.
Kabisch, R., *Die Eschatologie des Paulus in ihren Zusammenhangen mit dem Gesamtbegriff des Paulinismus* (Göttingen, 1893).
Käsemann, E., 'A Critical Analysis of Philippians 2.5-11', *JTC* 5 (1968), pp. 45-88.
—'Die Legitimität des Apostels: eine Untersuchung zu II Korinther 10-13', *ZNW* 41 (1942), pp. 33-71.
—'Philipper 2.12-18', in *Exegetische Versüch und Besinnungen* (Göttingen: Vandenhoeck & Ruprecht, 1960), I, pp. 293-98.
—Review of J. Kremer, *Was an den Leiden Christi noch mangelt*, *TLZ* 82 (1957), pp. 694-95.

Bibliography 211

Kamlah, E., 'Wie beurteilt Paulus sein Leiden? Ein Beitrag zur Untersuchung seiner Denkstruktur', *ZNW* 54 (1963), pp. 217-32.

Keck, L., *Paul and his Letters* (Philadelphia: Fortress Press, 1979).

Kelly, J.N.D., *A Commentary on the Pastoral Epistles: I Timothy, II Timothy, Titus* (BNTC; London: A. & C. Black, 1963).

Kelsey, D.H., *The Uses of Scripture in Recent Theology* (Philadelphia: Fortress Press, 1975).

Kennedy, G.A., *The Art of Rhetoric in the Roman World: 300 BC–AD 300* (Princeton: Princeton University Press, 1972).

—*Classical Rhetoric and its Christian and Secular Tradition from Ancient to Modern Times* (Chapel Hill: University of North Carolina Press, 1980).

—*History of Rhetoric. I. The Art of Persuasion in Greece* (Princeton: Princeton University Press, 1963).

—*A History of Rhetoric. III. Greek Rhetoric under Christian Emperors* (Princeton: Princeton University Press, 1983).

—*New Testament Interpretation through Rhetorical Criticism* (Chapel Hill: University of North Carolina Press, 1984).

Kilpatrick, T.B., 'Suffering', in *Encyclopedia of Religion and Ethics* (ed. J. Hastings; New York: Charles Scribner's Sons, 1924), XII, pp. 1-10.

Kim, S., *The Origin of Paul's Gospel* (WUNT 2.4; Tübingen: Mohr, 1981).

Kirchgässner, A., 'Der Christ im Leiden: Sinndeutung des Leidens nach dem Apostel Paulus', *TTZ* 57 (1948), pp. 278-86.

Kirsch, J.P., *Die Lehre von der Gemeinschaft der Heiligen im christlichen Altertum: Eine dogmengeschichtliche Studie* (FCLD, 1.1; Mainz, 1900).

Klawiter, F.C., 'The Role of Martyrdom and Persecution in Developing the Priestly Authority of Women in Early Christianity: A Case Study of Montanism', *CH* 49 (1980), pp. 251-61.

Kleinknecht, K.T., *Der leidende Gerechtfertigte: Die alttestamentlich-jüdische Tradition vom 'leidenden Grechten' und ihre Rezeption bei Paulus* (WUNT, 2.13; Tübingen: Mohr, 1984).

Klijn, A.F.J., 'Paul's Opponents in Philippians 3', *NovT* 7 (1965), pp. 278-84.

Koester, H., *Introduction to the New Testament* (2 vols.; Philadelphia: Fortress Press; Berlin: de Gruyter, 1982).

—'The Purpose of the Polemic of a Pauline Fragment (Philippians 3)', *NTS* 8 (1962), pp. 317-32.

Koskenniemi, H., *Studien zur Idee und Phraseologie des griechischen Briefes bis 400 n. Chr.* (Helsinki: Suomalaien Tiedeakatemie, 1956).

Krause, B., *Leiden Gottes—Leiden des Menschen: Eine Untersuchung zur Kirchlichen Dogmatik Karl Barths* (CTMB, 6; Stuttgart: Calwer, 1980).

Kremer, J., ' "Die Gemeinschaft seiner Leiden" (Phil. 3.10). Meditation über den Sinn des Leidens im Leben der Christen nach den Aussagen des Apostels Paulus', *BK* 23 (1968), pp. 13-16.

—*Was an den Leiden Christi nocht mangelt: Eine interpretationsgeschichtliche und exegetische Untersuchung zu Kol. 1.24b* (BBB, 12; Bonn: Hanstein, 1956).

Krötke, W., Review of B. Krause, *Leiden Gottes—Leiden des Menschen*, *TLZ* 107 (1982), pp. 615-17.

Kümmel, W.G., *Introduction to the New Testament* (trans. H.C. Kee; Nashville: Abingdon, 1975).

—*The New Testament: The History of the Investigation of its Problems* (trans. S.M. Gilmour and H.C. Kee; Nashville: Abingdon, 1972).

Kuiper, G.J., Review of R.P. Martin, *Carmen Christi, BO* 27 (1970), pp. 94-96.

Lampe, G.W.H., 'Martyrdom and Inspiration', in *Suffering and Martyrdom in the New Testament: Studies Presented to G.M. Styler by the Cambridge New Testament Seminar* (ed. W. Horbury and B. McNeil; Cambridge: Cambridge University Press, 1981), pp. 118-35.

Landgraf, A.M., *Einführung in die Geschichte der theologischen Literatur der Frühscholastik unter dem Gesichtspunkte der Schulenbildung* (Regensburg: Gregorius, 1948).

Larcher, F.R. (trans.), *Commentary on Saint Paul's Epistle to the Galatians* (intro. R.T.A. Murphy; Aquinas Scripture Series, 1; Albany: Magi, 1966).

Lausberg, H., *Elemente der literarischen Rhetorik: Eine Einführung für Studierende der klassischen, romanischen, englischen and deutschen Philologie* (2 vols.; Munich: Hueber, 1984 [1963]).

—*Handbuch der literarischen Rhetorik: Eine Grundlegung der Literaturwissenschaft* (2 vols.; Munich: Hueber, 1960).

Leaney, A.R.C., 'The Eschatological Significance of Human Suffering in the OT and the Dead Sea Scrolls', *SJT* 16 (1963), pp. 286-96.

Lee, G.M., 'Philippians 1.22-23', *NovT* 12 (1970), p. 361.

LeGrelle, G., 'La plénitude de la parole dans la pauvreté de la chair d'après Col. 1.24', *NRT* 81 (1959), pp. 232-50.

Leivestad, R., 'Ταπείνος-Ταπεινόφρων', *NovT* 8 (1966), pp. 36-47.

Lemme, L., 'Leiden', *RPTK*, XI, pp. 360-63.

Leon-Dufour, X., *Resurrección de Jesús y mensaje pascual* (trans. R.S. Costoyas; BEB, 1; Salamanca: Sígueme, 1973).

Levie, J., 'Le chrétien citoyen du ciel (Phil. 3.20)', in *Studiorum Paulinorum Congressus Internationalis Catholicus, 1961* (AnBib, 17-18; Rome: Pontifical Biblical Institute, 1963), II, pp. 81-88.

Lightfoot, J.B., *The Apostolic Fathers* (5 vols.; London: Macmillan, 1889).

—*Biblical Essays* (London: Macmillan, 1893).

—*Saint Paul's Epistle to the Philippians: A Revised Text with Introduction, Notes and Dissertations* (London: Macmillan, 12th edn, 1896).

Lilla, S.R.C., *Clement of Alexandria: A Study in Christian Platonism and Gnosticism* (Oxford Theological Monographs; Oxford: Oxford University Press, 1971).

Lincoln, A.T., *Paradise Now and Not Yet: Studies in the Role of the Heavenly Dimension in Paul's Thought with Special Reference to his Eschatology* (SNTSMS, 43; Cambridge: Cambridge University Press, 1981).

Lipsius, R.A., *Die Briefe an die Galater, Römer, Philipper* (HKNT, 2.2; Freiburg: Mohr, 2nd rev. edn, 1893).

Locher, A. (ed.), *Marii Victorini Afri Comentarii in epistulas Pauli ad Galatas, ad Philippenses, ad Ephesios* (Bibliotheca scriptorum graecorum et romanorum teubneriana; Leipzig: Teubner, 1972).

Lohmeyer, E., *Die Briefe an die Philipper, an die Kolosser und an Philemon* (MeyerK, 9; Göttingen: Vandenhoeck & Ruprecht, 1964 [1930]).

—*Kyrios Jesus: eine Untersuchung zu Phil. 2.5-11* (Darmstadt: Wissenschaftliche Buchgesellschaft, 1961 [1928]).

Bibliography 213

Lohse, E., *Märtyrer und Gottesknecht: Untersuchungen zur urchristlichen Verkündigung vom Sühntod Jesu Christi* (FRLANT, 46; Göttingen: Vandenhoeck & Ruprecht, 2nd edn, 1963).

Longenecker, R.N., *Paul: Apostle of Liberty* (Grand Rapids: Baker Book House, 1976 [1964]).

Lopez, F.E., 'En torno a Fil. 3.12', *EstBib* 34 (1975), pp. 121-23.

Lüdemann, G., *Paul, Apostle to the Gentiles: Studies in Chronology* (trans. F.S. Jones; Philadelphia: Fortress Press, 1984).

—*Paulus der Heidenapostel*. II. *Antipaulinismus im frühen Christentum* (FRLANT, 130; Göttingen: Vandenhoeck & Ruprecht, 1983).

Lüdemann, H., *Die Anthropologie des Apostels Paulus und ihre Stellung innerhalb seiner Heilslehre* (Kiel: Universitäts, 1872).

Lührmann, D., *Das Offenbarungsverständnis bei Paulus und in paulinischen Gemeinden* (WMANT, 16; Neukirchen–Vluyn: Neukirchener Verlag, 1965).

Lyons, G., *Pauline Autobiography: Toward a New Understanding* (SBLDS, 73; Atlanta: Scholars Press, 1985).

Mackay, B.S., 'Further Thoughts on Philippians', *NTS* 7 (1960–61), pp. 161-70.

Malherbe, A.J., 'Ancient Epistolary Theorists', *OJRS* 5 (1977), pp. 3-77.

—*Moral Exhortation, A Greco-Roman Sourcebook*(Lec; Philadelphia: Westminster, 1986).

—*Paul and the Thessalonians: The Philosophic Tradition of Pastoral Care* (Philadelphia: Fortress Press, 1987).

Mansoor, M. (ed. and trans.), *The Thanksgiving Hymns* (Studies on the Texts of the Desert of Judah, 3; Grand Rapids: Eerdmans, 1961).

Martin, J., *Antike Rhetorik: Technik und Methode* (Handbuch der Altertumswissenschaft; Munich: Beck, 1974).

Martin, R.P., *Carmen Christi: Philippians 2.5-11 in Recent Interpretation and in the Setting of Early Christian Worship* (Grand Rapids: Eerdmans, 2nd edn, 1983).

—*The Epistle to the Philippians: An Introduction and Commentary* (Grand Rapids: Eerdmans, 1975 repr. [1959]).

—*Philippians* (NCBC; Grand Rapids: Eerdmans, 1985 [1976]).

Martyn, J.L., 'Epistemology at the Turn of the Ages: 2 Corinthians 5.16', in *Christian History and Interpretation: Studies Presented to John Knox* (ed. W.R. Farmer, C.F.D. Moule and R.R. Niebuhr; Cambridge: Cambridge University Press, 1967), pp. 269-87.

Mearns, C.L., 'The Identity of Paul's Opponents at Philippi', *NTS* 33 (1987), pp. 194-204.

Meeks, W.A., 'The Social Context of Pauline Theology', *Int* 36 (1982), pp. 266-77.

Meinhold, P., 'Episkope–Pneumatiker–Märtyrer: Zur Deutung die Selbstaussagen des Ignatius von Antiochien', in *Studien zu Ignatius von Antiochien* (VIEGM, 97; Wiesbaden: Steiner, 1979).

Ménard, J.E., 'La lettre de Pierre à Philippe', in *Gnosis: Festschrift für Hans Jonas* (ed. B. Aland; Göttingen: Vandenhoeck & Ruprecht, 1979), pp. 449-63.

—Review of R.P. Martin, *Carmen Christi*, *RHR* 175 (1969), pp. 215-18.

Mengel, B., *Studien zum Philipperbrief: Untersuchungen zum situativen Kontext unter besonderer Berücksichtigung der Frage nach der Ganzheitlichkeit oder Einheitlichkeit eines paulinischen Briefes* (WUNT 2.8; Tübingen: Mohr, 1982).,

Metzger, B.M., *A Textual Commentary on the Greek New Testament* (London: United Bible Societies, 1971).

Meyer, H.A.W., *Critical and Exegetical Handbook to the Epistles to the Philippians and Colossians* (trans. J.C. Moore; Edinburgh: T. & T. Clark, 1875).

Michael, J.H., *The Epistle of Paul to the Philippians* (London: Hodder & Stoughton, 1958 [1928]).

Michaelis, W., *Der Brief des Paulus an die Philipper* (THNT; Leipzig: Deichert, 1935).

—'Teilungshypothesen bei Paulusbriefen', *TLZ* 14 (1958), pp. 321-26.

Michel, O., 'Leiden, III: Im Neuen Testament', *RGG*, III, pp. 297-300.

Moffatt, J., *An Introduction to the Literature of the New Testament* (New York: Charles Scribner's Sons, 3rd edn, 1918).

Moule, C.F.D., Review of R.P. Martin, *Carmen Christi*, *JTS* 19 (1968), pp. 648-51.

Moule, H.C.G., *The Epistle to the Romans* (Grand Rapids: Baker Book House, 1981 [1890]).

Müller, J.J., *The Epistles of Paul to the Philippians and to Philemon* (NICNT, 11; Grand Rapids: Eerdmans, 1955).

Mullins, T.Y., 'Formulas in New Testament Epistles', *JBL* 91 (1972), pp. 380-90.

Munck, J., *Paul and the Salvation of Mankind* (London: SCM Press, 1959).

Murphy-O'Connor, J., 'Christological Anthropology in Phil. 2.6-11', *RB* 83 (1976), pp. 25-50.

—'Philippiens (Epître aux)', *DBSup*, VII, pp. 1211-33.

—Review of J. Gnilka, *Der Philipperbrief*, *RB* 76 (1969), pp. 276-78.

Musurillo, H. (ed.), *The Acts of the Christian Martyrs* (Oxford: Clarendon Press, 1972).

Nauck, W., 'Freude im Leiden: Zum Problem einer urchristlichen Verfolgungstradition', *ZNW* 46 (1955), pp. 68-80.

Neill S., *The Interpretation of the New Testament 1861-1961* (London: Oxford University Press, 1966).

Neyrey, J.H., 'The Form and Background of the Polemic in 2 Peter', *JBL* 99 (1980), pp. 407-31.

Nickelsburg, G.W.E., *Resurrection, Immortality, and Eternal Life in Intertestamental Judaism* (HTS, 26; Cambridge, MA: Harvard University Press, 1972).

Niebuhr, H.R., *Christ and Culture* (New York: Harper & Row, 1956 [1951]).

Nielsen, H.K., 'Paulus' Verwendung des Begriffes δύναμις: Eine Replik zur Kreuzestheologie', in *Die paulinischen Literatur und Theologie* (ed. S. Pedersen; ThS, 7; Århus: Aros; Göttingen: Vandenhoeck & Ruprecht, 1980), pp. 137-58.

Nissen, J., 'The Problem of Suffering and Ethics in the New Testament', in *Studia Biblica, 1978*. III. *Papers on Paul and Other New Testament Authors* (ed. E. Livingstone; JSNTSup, 3; Sheffield: JSOT Press, 1980), pp. 277-87.

Nowak, E., *Le chrétien devant la souffrance: Etude sur la pensée de Jean Chrysostome* (TH, 19; Paris: Beauchesne, 1973).

O'Brien, P.T., *Introductory Thanksgivings in the Letters of Paul* (NovTSup, 49; Leiden: Brill, 1977).

O'Daly, G.J.P., 'Time as "Distentio" and St Augustine's Exegesis of Philippians 3.12-14', *REA* 23 (1977), pp. 265-71.

Ogara, F., '"Dominus prope est" (Phil. 4.4-7)', *VD* 17 (1937), pp. 353-59.

—' "Socios gaudii mei omnes vos esse" (Phil. 1.6-11)', *VD* 15 (1935), pp. 324-30.

Ollrog, W.-H., *Paulus und seine Mitarbeiter: Untersuchungen zu Theorie und Praxis der paulinischen Mission* (WMANT, 50; Neukirchen-Vluyn: Neukirchener Verlag, 1979).

Omanson, R.L., 'A Note on the Translation of Philippians 1.3-4', *BT* 29 (1978), pp. 244-45.

—'A Note on the Translation of Philippians 1.12', *BT* 29 (1978), pp. 446-48.
O'Neill, J.C., 'Did Jesus Teach that his Death Would be Vicarious as well as Typical?', in *Suffering and Martyrdom in the New Testament: Studies Presented to G.M. Styler by the Cambridge New Testament Seminar* (ed. W. Horbury and B. McNeil; Cambridge: Cambridge University Press, 1981), pp. 9-27.
Pagels, E.H., 'Gnostic and Orthodox Views of Christ's Passion: Paradigms for the Christian's Response to Persecution?', in *The Rediscovery of Gnosticism: Proceedings of the International Conference on Gnosticism at Yale, New Haven, Connecticut, March 28-31, 1978: Volume One: The School of Valentinus* (ed. B. Layton; NumSup, 41; Leiden: Brill, 1980), pp. 262-68.
—*The Gnostic Gospels* (New York: Random House, 1979).
—*The Gnostic Paul: Gnostic Exegesis of the Pauline Letters* (Philadelphia: Fortress Press, 1975).
Palmer, D.W., 'To Die is Gain: Philippians 1.21', *NovT* 17 (1975), pp. 203-18.
Panikulam, G., *Koinōnia in the New Testament: A Dynamic Expression of Christian Life* (AnBib, 85; Rome: Pontifical Biblical Institute, 1979).
Parker, T.H.L., *Calvin's New Testament Commentaries* (London: SCM Press, 1971).
Patte, D., *Paul's Faith and the Power of the Gospel: A Structural Introduction to the Pauline Letters* (Philadelphia: Fortress Press, 1983).
—*What is Structural Exegesis?* (GBSNTS; Philadelphia: Fortress Press, 1976).
Paulsen, H., *Studien zur Theologie des Ignatius von Antiochien* (FKD, 29; Göttingen: Vandenhoeck & Ruprecht, 1978).
Pearson, B.A., 'Jewish Elements in Gnosticism and the Development of Gnostic Self-Definitions', in *Jewish and Christian Self-Definition* (ed. E.P. Sanders; London: SCM Press, 1980), I, pp. 151-60.
Perkins, P., *Resurrection: New Testament Witness and Contemporary Reflection* (Garden City: Doubleday, 1984).
Perler, O., 'Typologie der Leiden des Herrn in Melitons *Peri Pascha*', in *KYRIAKON: Festschrift Johannes Quasten* (ed. P. Granfield and J.A. Jungmann: Münster: Aschendorff, 1970), I, pp. 256-65.
—'Das vierte Makkabäerbuch, Ignatius von Antiochen, und die ältesten Martyrerberichte', *RArchC* 25 (1949), pp. 47-72.
Pesch, R., 'Zur Theologie des Todes', *BibLeb* 10 (1969), pp. 9-16.
Peter, H., *Der Brief in der römischen Literatur: Literargeschichtliche Untersuchungen und Zusammenfassungen* (Hildesheim: Olms, 1965 [1901]).
Pfitzner, V.C., *Paul and the Agon Motif: Traditional Imagery in the Pauline Literature* (NovTSup, 16; Leiden: Brill, 1967).
Pfleiderer, O., *The Influence of the Apostle Paul on the Development of Christianity* (trans. J.F. Smith; The Hibbert Lectures, 1885; New York: Charles Scribner's Sons, 1885).
Plank, K.A., *Paul and the Irony of Affliction* (SS, 16; Atlanta: Scholars Press, 1987).
Pobee, J.S., *Persecution and Martyrdom in the Theology of Paul* (JSNTSup, 6; Sheffield: JSOT Press, 1985).
Polhill, J.B., 'Twin Obstacles in the Christian Faith: Philippians 3', *RevExp* 77 (1980), pp. 359-72.
Pollard, T.E., 'The Integrity of Philippians', *NTS* (1966–67), pp. 57-66.
Priero, G., 'Didici... sufficiens esse (ἔμαθον... αὐρτάρκης εἶναι): Nota a Phil. 4.11', *RivBib* 10 (1962), pp. 59-63.

Proudfoot, C.M., 'The Apostle Paul's Understanding of Christian Suffering' (PhD thesis, Yale University, 1956).
—'Imitation or Realistic Participation? A Study of "Suffering with Christ"', *Int* 17 (1963), pp. 140-60.
Quinn, J.D., 'Seven Times He Wore Chains', *JBL* 97 (1978), pp. 574-76.
Rahner, K., 'On Martyrdom', in *idem*, *On the Theology of Death* (trans. C.H. Henkey; New York: Herder, 1961), pp. 89-127.
Rahtjen, B.D., 'The Three Letters of Paul to the Philippians', *NTS* 6 (1959-60), pp. 167-73.
Rathke, H., *Ignatius von Antiochien und die Paulusbriefe* (TU, 99; Berlin: Akademie, 1967).
Reicke, B.I., 'Caesarea, Rome and the Captivity Epistles', in *Apostolic History and the Gospel: Biblical and Historical Essays Presented to F.F. Bruce* (ed. W.W. Gasque and R.P. Martin; Exeter: Paternoster Press, 1970), pp. 277-86.
—'Unité chrétienne et diaconie: Phil. 2.1-11', in *Neotestamentica et Patristica: Eine Freundesgabe Herrn Professor Dr Oscar Cullmann* (NovTSup, 6; Leiden: Brill, 1962), pp. 203-12.
Reitzenstein, R., *Hellenistic Mystery-Religions: Their Basic Ideas and Significance* (trans. J.E. Steely; PTMS, 15; Pittsburgh: Pickwick, 1978).
Rey, B., *Creados en Cristo Jesús: La nueva creación según san Pablo* (AcBib, 10; Madrid: FAX, 1968).
—'Vie de foi et vie filiale selon saint Paul', *MSR* 39 (1982), pp. 3-18.
Riesenfeld, H., 'La descente dans la mort', in *Aux sources de la tradition chrétienne: Mélanges offerts à M. Maurice Goguel à l'occasion de son soixante-dixième anniversaire* (BTh; Neuchatel: Delachaux & Niestlé, 1950).
Robinson, J.A.T., *The Body: A Study in Pauline Theology* (SBT; London: SCM Press, 1952).
Robinson, J.M. (ed.), *The Nag Hammadi Library in English* (Philadelphia: Fortress Press, 1985).
Roetzel, C., *The Letters of Paul: Conversations in Context* (Atlanta: John Knox, 1975).
Rolla, A., 'La cittadinanza greco-romana e la cittadinanza celeste di Filippesi 3.20', in *Studiorum Paulinorum Congressus Internationalis Catholicus, 1961* (AnBib, 17-18; Rome: Pontifical Biblical Institute, 1963), II, pp. 75-80.
Rowley, H.H., *Submission in Suffering and Other Essays on Eastern Thought* (Cardiff: University of Wales, 1951).
Rumscheidt, H.M., 'The Need of the Evangelical Church: An Illustration in Karl Barth's Theology', *JTSA* 57 (1986), pp. 4-16.
Ruppert, L., *Der leidende Gerechte: Eine motivgeschichtliche Untersuchung zum Alten Testament und zwischentestamentlichen Judentum* (FB, 5; Würzburg: Echter, 1972).
Sanders, B., 'Imitating Paul: 1 Cor. 4.16', *HTR* 74 (1981), pp. 353-63.
Sanders, E.P., *Paul and Palestinian Judaism: A Comparison of Patterns of Religion* (London: SCM Press, 1977).
—*Paul, the Law, and the Jewish People* (Philadelphia: Fortress Press, 1983).
—'Paul on the Law, his Opponents, and the Jewish People in Philippians 3 and 2 Corinthians 11', in *Anti-Judaism in Early Christianity. I. Paul and the Gospels* (ed. P. Richardson with D. Granskou; SCJ, 2; Waterloo: Wilfrid Laurier University, 1986), pp. 75-90.
—'R. Akibah's View of Suffering', *JQR* 63 (1972-73), pp. 332-51.

Sanders, J.T., *The New Testament Christological Hymns: Their Historical and Religious Background* (SNTSMS, 15; Cambridge: Cambridge University Press, 1971).

—'The Transition from Opening Epistolary Thanksgiving to Body in the Letters of the Pauline Corpus', *JBL* 81 (1962), pp. 348-62.

Sanders, J.A., *Suffering as Divine Discipline in the Old Testament and Post-Biblical Judaism* (Colgate Rochester Divinity School Bulletin, Special Issue, 28; Rochester: Colgate Rochester Divinity School, 1955).

Sass, G., *Apostelamt und Kirche: Eine theologische-exegetische Untersuchung des paulinischen Apostelbegriffs* (FGLP, 9; Munich: Chr. Kaiser Verlag, 1939).

—'Zur Bedeutung von δοῦλος bei Paulus', *ZNW* 40 (1941), pp. 24-32.

Satake, A., 'Apostolat und Gnade bei Paulus', *NTS* 15 (1968–69), pp. 96-107.

Schade, H.H., *Apokalyptische Christologie bei Paulus: Zusammenhang von Christologie und Eschatologie in den Paulusbriefen* (GTA, 18; Göttingen: Vandenhoeck & Ruprecht, 1981).

Schlatter, A., *Paulus, der Bote Jesu: Eine Deutung seiner Briefe an die Korinther* (Stuttgart: Calwer, 1962 [1934]).

—*Die Theologie des Apostel* (Stuttgart: Calwer, 1977 [1922]).

Schmid, J., 'Kol. 1.24', *BZ* 21 (1933), pp. 330-44.

—Review of J. Gnilka, *Der Philipperbrief*, *TRev* 65 (1969), pp. 459-61.

Schmithals, W., *The Office of Apostle in the Early Church* (trans. J.E. Steely; Nashville: Abingdon, 1969).

—*Paul and the Gnostics* (trans. J.E. Steely; Nashville: Abingdon, 1972).

Schmitz, O., *Die Christusgemeinschaft des Paulus im Licht seines Genitivegebrauchs* (NF, 2; Gütersloh: Bertelsmann, 1924).

Schneider, C., *Geistesgeschichte des antiken Christentums* (2 vols.; Munich: Beck, 1954).

Schneider, J., *Die Passionsmystik des Paulus: Ihr Wesen, ihr Hintergrund, und ihr Nachwirkungen* (UNT, 15; Leipzig: Hinrichs, 1929).

Schoedel, W.R., *Ignatius of Antioch: A Commentary on the Letters of Ignatius of Antioch* (Hermeneia; Philadelphia: Fortress Press, 1985).

Schubert, P., 'Form and Function of the Pauline Letters', *JR* 19 (1939), pp. 365-77.

—'Form and Function of the Pauline Thanksgiving' (Chicago: University of Chicago Libraries, 1937).

—*Form and Function of the Pauline Thanksgivings* (BZNW, 20; Berlin: Töpelmann, 1939).

Schütz, J.H., *Paul and the Anatomy of Apostolic Authority* (SNTSMS, 26; Cambridge: Cambridge University Press, 1975).

Schweitzer, A., *The Mysticism of the Apostle Paul* (trans. W. Montgomery; New York: Seabury, 1968 [1931]).

—*Paul and his Interpreters: A Critical History* (trans. W. Montgomery; London: A. & C. Black, 1912).

Schweizer, E., *Lordship and Discipleship* (SBT, 28; London: SCM Press, 1960).

—'Paul's Christology and Gnosticism', in *Paul and Paulinism: Essays in Honour of C.K. Barrett* (ed. M.D. Hooker and S.G. Wilson; London: SPCK, 1982), pp. 115-23.

—'Der zweite Thessalonicherbrief ein Philipperbrief?', *TZ* 1 (1945), pp. 90-105, 286-89.

Scott, E.F., 'The Epistle to the Philippians: Introduction and Exegesis', *IB*, XI, pp. 3-129.

Scroggs, R., Review of R.P. Martin, *Carmen Christi*, *Int* 22 (1968), pp. 351-52.

Seidensticker, P., *Paulus, der verfolgte Apostel Jesu Christi* (SBS, 8; Stuttgart: Katholisches, 1965).

Selwyn, E.G., *The First Epistle of St Peter* (London: Macmillan, 2nd edn, 1947).

Siegert, F., *Argumentation bei Paulus: Gezeigt an Rom 9–11* (WUNT, 34: Tübingen: Mohr, 1985).

Smalley, B., *The Study of the Bible in the Middle Ages* (Notre Dame, IN: University of Notre Dame Press, 1964).

—'The Exposition and Exegesis of Scripture, 3: The Bible in the Medieval Schools', in *The Cambridge History of the Bible*. II. *The West from the Fathers to the Reformation* (Cambridge: Cambridge University Press, 1969), pp. 197-220.

Smyth, H.W., *Greek Grammar* (rev. G.M. Messing; Cambridge, MA: Harvard University Press, 1956).

Souter, A., *The Earliest Latin Commentaries on the Epistles of St Paul: A Study* (Oxford: Clarendon Press, 1927).

—*The Text and Canon of the New Testament* (London: Gerald Duckworth, 2nd edn, 1954).

Spicq, C., 'ὑπομονή, patientia', *RSPT* 19 (1930), pp. 95-106.

Staab, K., *Briefe des Apostels Paulus: Die Briefe an die Epheser, Philipper, Kolosser und Thessalonicher* (Echter, 4; Würzburg: Echter, 1968).

—*Pauluskommentare aus der griechischen Kirche, aus Katenenhandschriften* (NA, 15; Münster: Aschendorff, 1933).

Stählin, G., ''Ασθενής κτλ.', *TDNT*, I, p. 491.

Stagg, F., 'The Mind of Christ Jesus: Philippians 1.27–2.18', *RevExp* 77 (1980), pp. 337-47.

Stambaugh, J.E., and D.L. Balch, *The New Testament in its Social Environment* (LEC; Philadelphia: Westminster, 1986).

Stanley, D.M., ' "Become Imitators of Me": The Pauline Conception of Apostolic Tradition', *Bib* 40 (1959), pp. 859-77.

—*Christ's Resurrection in Pauline Soteriology* (AnBib, 13; Rome: Pontifical Biblical Institute, 1961).

—'The Theme of the Servant of Yahweh in Primitive Christian Soteriology and its Transposition by St Paul', *CBQ* 16 (1954), pp. 385-425.

Stauffer, E., 'Märtyrertheologie und Täuferbewegung', *ZKG* third series, 52 (1933), pp. 545-609.

—*New Testament Theology* (trans. J. Marsh; London: SCM Press, 1955).

Steen, H.A., 'Les clichés épistolaires dans les lettres sur papyrus grècques', *Classica et Medievalia* 1 (1938), pp. 119-76.

Stoops, R.F., Jr, 'If I Suffer . . . : Epistolary Authority in Ignatius of Antioch', *HTR* 80 (1987), pp. 161-78.

Stowers, S.K., *Letter Writing in Greco-Roman Antiquity* (LEC, 5; Philadelphia: Westminster Press, 1986).

—*The Diatribe and Paul's Letter to the Romans* (SBLDS, 57; Chico, CA: Scholars Press, 1981).

Strimple, R.B., 'Philippians 2.5-11 in Recent Studies: Some Exegetical Conclusions', *WTJ* 41 (1979), pp. 247-68.

Stuhlmacher, P., 'Achtzehn Thesen zur paulinischen Kreuzestheologie', in *Rechtfertigung: Festschrift für Ernst Käsemann zum 70. Geburstag* (ed. J. Friedrich, W. Pöhlmann and P. Stuhlmacher; Tübingen: Mohr; Göttingen: Vandenhoeck & Ruprecht, 1968), pp. 509-25.

—*Historical Criticism and Theological Interpretation of Scripture: Toward a Hermeneutic of Consent* (trans. R.A. Harrisville; Philadelphia: Fortress Press, 1977).

—'Zur paulinischen Christologie', *ZTK* 74 (1977), pp. 449-63.

Bibliography 219

Suhl, A., *Paulus und seine Briefe: Ein Beitrag zur paulinischen Chronologie* (SNT, 11; Gütersloh: Mohn, 1975).

Sutcliffe, E.F., *Providence and Suffering in the Old and New Testaments* (London: Nelson, 1953).

Swain, L., *The People of the Resurrection.* I. *The Apostolic Letters* (Good News Studies, 15; Wilmington, DE: Michael Glazier, 1986).

Swartley, W.M., 'The *Imitatio Christi* in the Ignatian Letters', *VC* 27 (1973), pp. 81-103.

Sykutris, J., 'Epistolographie', *RE* Sup. V, pp. 185-220.

Talbert, C.H., 'The Problem of Pre-Existence in Phil. 2.6-11', *JBL* 86 (1967), pp. 141-53.

Tannehill, R.C., *Dying and Rising with Christ: A Study in Pauline Theology* (BZNW, 32; Berlin: Töpelmann, 1967).

Theissen, G., *Psychologische Aspekte paulinischer Theologie* (FRLANT, 131; Göttingen: Vandenhoeck & Ruprecht, 1983).

Thiering, B., 'Suffering and the Asceticism at Qumran, as Illustrated in the Hodayot', *RevQ* 8 (1974), pp. 393-405.

Thornton, L.S., *The Common Life in the Body of Christ* (Westminster: Dacre, 1941).

Thraede, K., *Grundzüge griechisch-römischer Brieftopik* (Zetemata, 48; Munich: Beck, 1970).

Trudinger, L.P., 'A Further Brief Note on Colossians 1.24', *EvQ* 45 (1973), p. 37.

Tuñí, J.O., 'Pau i Jesus: La vida de Jesus i la vida de Pau', *RCT* 12 (1987), pp. 29-54.

Urbach, E.E., *The Sages: Their Concepts and Beliefs* (2 vols.; trans. I. Abrahams; Jerusalem: Magnes Press, 1979).

Vincent, M.R., *A Critical and Exegetical Commentary on the Epistles to the Philippians and to Philemon* (ICC; Edinburgh: T. & T. Clark, 1961 [1897]).

Vitti, A., ' "Comprehensus sum a Christo Jesu" (Phil. 3.12)', *VD* 9 (1929), pp. 353-59.

Vogel, C.J. de, 'Reflexions on Phil. 1.23-24', *NovT* 19 (1977), pp. 262-74.

Volkmann, R., *Die Rhetorik der Griechen und Römer in systematischer übersicht* (Hildesheim: Olms, 1963 [1885]).

Walter, N., 'Die Philipper und das Leiden: Aus den Anfangen einer heidenchristlichen Gemeinde', in *Die Kirche des Anfangs: Festschrift für Heinz Schürmann zum 65. Geburtstag* (ed. R. Schnackenburg, J. Ernst and J. Wanke; Leipzig: St Benno, 1977), pp. 417-34.

Watson, D.F., 'A Rhetorical Analysis of Philippians and its Implications for the Unity Question', *NovT* 39 (1988), pp. 57-88.

Weinrich, W.C., *Spirit and Martyrdom: A Study of the Work of the Holy Spirit in Contexts of Persecution and Martyrdom in the New Testament and Early Christian Literature* (Washington, DC: University Press of America, 1981).

Wendland, H.D., *Der zweite Korintherbrief* (NTD, 2; Göttingen: Vandenhoeck & Ruprecht, 1933).

White, J.L., 'The Ancient Epistolography Group in Retrospect', *Semeia* 22 (1982), pp. 1-14.

—'Epistolary Formulas and Clichés in Greek Papyrus Letters', in *Society of Biblical Literature 1978 Seminar Papers* (ed. P.J. Achtemeier; SBLSPS, 14; Missoula, MT: Scholars Press, 1978), II, pp. 289-319.

—*The Form and Function of the Body of the Greek Letter: A Study of the Letter-Body in the Non-Literary Papyri and in Paul the Apostle* (SBLDS, 2; Missoula, MT: Scholars Press, 2nd edn, 1972).

—'Introductory Formulae in the Body of the Pauline Letter', *JBL* 90 (1971), pp. 91-97.

—*Light from Ancient Letters* (Facets and Foundations; Philadelphia: Fortress Press, 1986).
—'Saint Paul and the Apostolic Letter Tradition', *CBQ* 45 (1983), pp. 433-44.
Whiteley, D.E.H., *The Theology of St Paul* (Oxford: Basil Blackwell, 2nd edn, 1974).
Wichmann, W., *Die Leidenstheologie, eine Form der Leidensdeutung im Spätjudentum* (BWANT, 53; Stuttgart: Kohlhammer, 1930).
Wikenhauser, A., *Pauline Mysticism: Christ in the Mystical Teaching of St Paul* (trans. J. Cunningham; New York: Herder, 1960).
Wikenhauser, A., and J. Schmid, *Introducción al Nuevo Testamento* (trans. C.R. Garrido; BHSE, 36; Barcelona: Herder, rev. edn, 1978).
Wiles, M.F., *The Divine Apostle: The Interpretation of St Paul's Epistles in the Early Church* (Cambridge: Cambridge University Press, 1967).
Wilmart, D.A., 'Le commentaire sur les Psaumes imprimé sous le nom de Rufin', *RBen* 31 (1914–19), pp. 258-76.
Wilson, W.E., 'The Development of Paul's Doctrine of Dying and Rising Again with Christ', *ExpTim* 42 (1930–31), pp. 562-65.
Windisch, H., *Paulus und Christus: Ein biblisch-religionsgeschichtlicher Vergleich* (UNT, 24; Leipzig: Hinrichs, 1934).
Wrede, W., *Paulus* (RVDCG, 1.5-6; Tübingen: Mohr, 2nd edn, 1907 [1905]).
Wuellner, W., 'Where is Rhetorical Criticism Taking Us?', *CBQ* 49 (1987), pp. 448-63.
Yates, R., 'Paul's Affliction in Asia: 2 Corinthians 1.8', *EvQ* 53 (1981), pp. 241-45.
Zerwick, M., *Biblical Greek* (ed. J. Smith; Scripta Pontificii Instituti Biblici, 114; Rome: Pontifical Biblical Institute, 1963).
Ziesler, J.A., *The Meaning of Righteousness in Paul: A Linguistic and Theological Inquiry* (SNTSMS, 20; Cambridge: Cambridge University Press, 1972).

INDEXES

INDEX OF REFERENCES

OLD TESTAMENT

Genesis		88.4 LXX	143	52.13	162, 163
8.1	18	104.26 LXX	143	52.14	162
		104.42 LXX	143	53	40, 162, 170
Exodus		109.1 LXX	184	53.1-12	170
14.31	143	119.36	51	53.2	162
20.20	181	119.80	51	53.3	162
		119.116	51	53.4-12	170
Numbers				53.7-8	162
12.7	43	Proverbs		53.8	162, 177
		25.21	187	53.11	162, 163
Joshua				53.12	39, 162, 177
14.7	143	Isaiah			
		3.17	102	Jeremiah	
2 Kingdoms LXX		26	199	7.25	143
7.5	143	41.3-5	162, 163	25.4	143
		42.1	57	26.27	143
4 Kingdoms LXX		45	162		
18.12	143	45.23	162	Daniel	
		48.20	143	9.8	143
Job		49.1	68	9.10	143
1.8	143	49.3	162, 163	12	199
13.16	154, 168	49.4	162, 163		
		49.5	162, 163	Amos	
Psalms		49.6	57	3.7	143
8.7 LXX	184	49.24-25	162		
25.3	51	50.4-6	57	Malachi	
27.9	143	52	162	3.24	143
43	25	52.11	163		

APOCRYPHA

Wisdom		2 Maccabees		24.22	51
10.2	53	15.11	39	31.28	188
1-6	199			40.18	188
		Sirach		51.18	51
		6.12	184		

NEW TESTAMENT

Matthew		6	36	16.19-20	184
7.6	198	6.1-23	200	16.19	170
11.25	22	6.4	32	16.20	82, 111,
16.26	180	6.5	179		115, 116,
		6.8	60		136
Mark		6.24	32	16.22	82
4.14-20	123, 155	6.25	32	16.25-27	82
10.43	39	7.1	77, 79		
12.44	187	7.4	45	1 Corinthians	
16.12	102	7.25	116	1.1	75, 186, 144
		8.11	32	1.2	75
Luke		8.14	112	1.4-9	76, 105
21.4	187	8.17	21, 38, 39	1.4	105, 145
		8.19-25	154	1.7	187
Acts		8.32	170	1.8	105
5.41	52	8.34	184	1.9	106
9.1–13.12	150	8.38	183	1.10	77, 115
14.22	183	8.39	183	1.17	102
16.1	142	9.22	142	1.18	48, 102, 186
16.12-15	150	11.25	48, 37, 79	2.6	186
16.16-40	150	11.29	183	3.1	86
17.14	142	11.33-36	116	3.6	56
20.19	188	12.1	115	3.10	56
23.1	102	12.20	187	4.6	102, 112
24.4	185	13.4	112	4.9-13	43, 45
		13.6	176	4.11	187
Romans		15.8	171, 198	4.14-21	80, 110, 111
1.1-7	122	15.13	82	4.14-15	56, 80, 109
1.1	75, 137, 142	15.14-33	80, 110, 111	4.14	148
1.5	186, 170	15.14-15	80, 109, 110	4.15	148
1.8-13	80, 110, 111	15.16	171	4.16	80, 115
1.8-10	76, 145	15.17	171	4.17	109, 110
1.9-10	105	15.18	170	4.19	110
1.9	109, 105	15.19	48	5.3	93
1.13	77, 79, 107	15.26	122	6.13-15	32
1.15	79	15.27	176	7.26-28	43
2.12	112	15.30	115	7.29	129
2.13	79	15.33	111, 115,	7.31	102
2.19-20	198		116, 136	8.8	187
3.22	79	16.1-2	82	9.19-23	68
3.23	187	16.16-19	100	10.1	77, 79
4.25	170	16.16	82	11.1	112
5.17	183	16.17-19	82, 200	11.21	187
5.18	183	16.17	102, 115,	11.33-34	114
5.21	183		183	11.34	187

Index of References

12.3	77, 79	4.12	39	13.20	82	
12.24	187	4.18	102, 183	*Galatians*		
15	164	5.1	163, 183, 184, 186	1.1-5	121, 122	
15.1	77, 79			1.1	75, 140	
15.3-5	170	5.14-15	115	1.3-4	104	
15.10	164	6.1	115, 164	1.6-10	121	
15.14	31.164	6.4-5	43	1.6-7	77	
15.25	184	6.10	52	1.9	77	
15.27-28	184	6.13	56, 112	1.10	140, 142	
15.31	40	7.4	52, 154	1.11–2.14	123	
15.32	42	7.46	186	1.11-12	77, 123	
15.40	103, 184	8.1	77, 79	1.11	77, 79, 107	
15.45	45	8.2	158	1.12–2.14	123	
15.49	45	8.14	187	1.13–2.14	123	
15.58	164	8.18–9.3	109	1.13–2.1	150	
16.1-12	111	8.22	109	1.13-14	77	
16.5	110	9.3-5	110	1.15-16	68	
16.11	209	9.5	109	1.15	79	
16.15	115	9.8	188	1.21	150	
16.17	177, 187	9.12	176, 187	2.1–3.21	21, 126	
16.20	82	9.13	122	2.1	150	
16.21	82	10.1-2	93, 111	2.2	161	
16.22	82	10.1	185	2.7-9	198	
		10.10-11	93	2.11	79	
2 Corinthians		11.5	187	2.15-21	125	
1.1	75, 110, 142	11.7	61, 103, 187, 188	2.17	108	
1.3-5	106			2.19	45	
1.4-5	39, 43	11.9	177, 187	2.20	32	
1.4-7	190	11.13	102	3.1–4.31	126	
1.5-7	52	11.14	102	3.1-5	126	
1.5-6	40, 55	11.15	102	3.1	79	
1.5	38	11.23-30	177	3.3	158	
1.6	27	11.23-29	158	3.4	24	
1.7	105	11.25-30	43	3.6-14	126	
1.8	77, 79, 107	12.2	150	3.15-18	126	
1.11	106	12.9	54	3.26–4.11	126	
1.20	112	12.10	38, 55	4.1	163	
2.8	77	12.11	187	4.12-20	80, 110, 126	
2.14	146, 148	12.14	110	4.13-14	43	
3.1	146, 148	12.18	109, 115	4.19	56	
3.8	115	12.21	61, 103, 187	4.21-31	126	
3.12	154	13.1	110	4.26	184, 187	
3.18	45, 146, 148	13.2	93	5.1–6.10	91	
4.5	140	13.9	52	5.2	80, 109	
4.7-12	45	13.10	93	5.10	80, 110	
4.10-12	43	13.11	82, 111, 120, 136	5.11	103	
4.10-11	39, 40, 55			5.24	45	
4.10	146, 148	13.13	82			

6.1	102, 183	1.3-11	130, 76,	1.12	58, 61, 64,
6.2	39		101, 105,		77, 107,
6.6	123, 155		106, 116,		124, 149,
6.11-18	136		117, 121,		187
6.11	82		122, 137,	1.13-14	124, 149,
6.12-17	82		155, 159,		159
6.12	103		165, 192	1.13	122, 146,
6.14-17	45	1.3-7	30, 105		148, 149
6.14	103	1.3-6	121, 145	1.14	56, 63, 107,
6.17	40, 43, 129	1.3-4	104, 105,		123, 124,
			122, 145		149, 151,
Ephesians		1.3	104, 105,		155
1.1	75, 140, 142		147	1.15–2.18	107, 111,
1.3-14	76	1.4	61, 104,		116, 117,
1.3	106		145, 156		126
1.15-17	106	1.5–1.7	119, 194	1.15-18	107, 108,
1.20-23	105	1.5	105, 106,		117, 121,
1.22	184		121-23, 137,		124, 125,
2.5	32		145, 146,		133, 137,
2.8	108		150, 176,		250, 165
2.11	198		187, 189,	1.15-17	107, 108,
2.16	103		192, 193		200
3.1	39, 41	1.6	106, 145	1.15	124, 158
3.2	146	1.7	36, 51, 64,	1.16	124, 151
3.8	146		106, 121,	1.17	151, 158,
3.13	39, 111		122, 137,		193
3.20-21	116		145, 146,	1.18-2.18	14, 101,
4.1	115		148, 149,		102, 107,
4.2	188		158, 159,		111
4.14	183		165, 176,	1.18-26	108, 117,
5.1	112		187, 189,		126, 137,
5.6	164		192, 193		152, 153,
6.10	129	1.8	106, 121		159, 165,
6.21-22	77, 79, 109,	1.9-11	105, 122		169, 174,
	115	1.9-10	121		194, 196
		1.9	106, 122,	1.18-20	108, 117,
Philippians			147, 187		152, 155
1.1–3.1	63, 98, 137	1.11	165, 189	1.18	24, 64, 102,
1.1–2.30	98, 116,	1.12–4.20	107, 113		107, 108,
	117, 140	1.12–2.18	109		109, 111,
1.1–2.4	94	1.12–2.2	27		116, 153,
1.1-2	104, 120,	1.12-26	48, 50, 98,		154
	165, 192		119, 154,	1.19-20	54
1.1	40, 50, 140,		157	1.19	108, 126,
	142, 164-66,	1.12-14	53, 61, 64,		152, 154,
	174, 176,		77, 107,		155, 165,
	194		124, 149		168
1.2	141, 165	1.12-18	153, 188	1.20	21, 26, 43,

Index of References

	52, 60, 126,		114, 127,	2.4		19, 102,
	152, 154,		147, 184			113, 183
	155, 163,	1.28–2.18	98, 127, 128	2.5-11		31, 103,
	165, 193		137			119, 170,
1.21-26	117, 126,	1.28-30	53, 157, 168			176
	152-55, 193	1.28-29	39	2.5-8		31
1.21-25	20	1.28	30, 102,	2.5		102, 109,
1.21	23, 27, 102,		103, 113			111, 113,
	108, 153,	1.29-30	20, 103,			127, 147,
	160, 182		137, 157,			165, 187
1.22-24	126		158, 160,	2.6-11		13, 32, 109,
1.22	102, 108,		193			112, 113,
	155, 156,	1.29	23, 23, 28,			135, 160-69,
	189		38, 43, 52,			173-75, 177,
1.23	62, 152, 156		56, 101,			180, 183,
1.23-26	171		150, 157,			184, 188,
1.23	62, 152, 156		158, 165,			195
1.24-26	163		166, 176	2.6-8		22, 23, 193
1.24	64, 152,	1.30	61, 103,	2.6-7		166
	155, 156		113, 150,	2.6		19, 27, 31,
1.25-26	61, 108,		157, 160,			102, 112-14,
	126, 155,		166, 187			162, 165,
	156	2.1–3.21	125			174
1.26-28	188	2.1-18	157	2.7-8		114, 157,
1.26	102, 108,	2.1–11	32, 64, 103,			166, 184
	165, 187		114, 117,	2.7		102, 106,
1.27–2.18	103, 108,		122, 123,			112, 113,
	113, 114,		127, 135,			144-46, 162,
	117, 119,		160, 169,			163-66, 168,
	126, 127,		170, 172			174
	129, 135,	2.1-8	31	2.8		27, 28, 102,
	157, 164,	2.1-4	103, 119,			103, 113,
	165, 168,		143			127, 162,
	169, 174,	2.1-2	137			163, 165,
	188, 190,	2.1	102, 108,			176, 177,
	195		116, 127,			186, 187
1.27–2.16	50		161, 187	2.9-30		128
1.27–2.11	127	2.2-3	147, 174	2.9-11		109, 114,
1.27-30	48, 108,	2.2	64, 102,			163, 165,
	117, 127,		103, 108,			166, 178,
	135, 157,		109, 113,			184
	158, 160,		147, 161,	2.9		27, 31, 109,
	161, 168,		165, 188			112, 162,
	169, 170	2.3-15	169			165, 187
1.27-29	53, 159	2.3	103, 147,	2.10-11		103, 162
1.27-28	103		165, 188	2.10		112, 113,
1.27	58, 93, 102,	2.4-11	170			165, 184
	108, 113,	2.4-5	127, 134	2.11–3.21		112, 127

Ref	Pages	Ref	Pages	Ref	Pages
2.11	103, 113, 165	2.21	186, 174	3.2-3	130
2.12-28	161	2.22	144, 145, 164-66, 174	3.2	98, 100, 103, 130, 178, 199, 200
2.12-18	103, 114, 117, 123, 127, 135, 168-72	2.23	109, 128		112
		2.24	64, 80, 110, 111, 117, 171	3.3-7	112
2.12	93, 109, 111, 127, 128, 165, 195	2.25-30	109-11, 117, 173, 196	3.3-4	130, 134, 181
		2.25-26	109, 128	3.3	
2.13	50, 155	2.25	110, 165, 175, 176	3.4-8	130
2.14-18	108			3.4-6	130, 131, 133, 137, 178
2.14-16	101, 169	2.26	110		
2.14-15	108	2.27	110, 128, 165, 176, 177	3.4	112
2.14	127			3.5-6	59
2.16-18	171			3.6	131
2.16	103, 164, 165	2.28	101, 108, 110, 111	3.17–4.7	127
2.17-18	108, 114, 171, 176	2.29-30	110	3.7-16	119
		2.29	108	3.7-11	130, 133, 179, 182
2.17	18, 40, 43, 53, 55, 61, 64, 102, 103, 108, 109, 111, 157, 176, 193	2.30	39, 128, 165, 176, 177, 187	3.7-8	59, 133, 134
				3.7	102, 165
		3.1–4.7	107, 111, 115, 117, 129, 135, 136, 196	3.8-11	112, 133-35, 182
				3.8-10	179
2.18	102, 103, 108, 109, 111	3.1–4.1	101	3.8	44, 103, 112, 134, 135, 165, 177, 179, 182
		3.1-21	50, 102		
		3.1-16	98, 111, 114, 115, 117, 129, 133, 137, 165, 178		
2.19–4.7	14				
2.19-30	13, 27, 107, 109, 111, 116, 117, 119, 128, 165, 173, 176, 193	3.1-11	103, 115, 117	3.9	102, 134, 135, 163, 165, 179, 182
				3.10-12	18
		3.1-6	119, 136	3.10-11	44, 178-80
2.19-24	83, 173, 174, 196	3.1	98, 100, 101, 102, 108, 111, 115, 129, 187	3.10	19, 21, 25, 28, 39-41, 44, 47, 49, 51, 52, 56, 59, 67, 102, 103, 134, 135, 165, 179-82, 193
2.19-23	80, 109, 111, 117				
2.19	64, 109, 110, 118, 174	3.2–4.3	101		
		3.2-4.1	98, 99		
2.20-22	110, 128	3.2-11	98, 129, 179, 200	3.11	32, 103
2.20	102, 147, 165, 174,	3.2-4	129, 133,	3.12–3.19	200

Index of References

3.12-16	68, 103, 112, 117, 129, 134	3.20	102, 103, 112, 113, 165,	4.10	136, 188, 192, 193 77, 102,
3.12-15	47	3.21	21, 31, 32,		106, 108,
3.12-13	103		45, 62, 102,		116, 137,
3.12	112, 116, 134, 135, 182		103, 112-14, 165, 183, 184, 186,	4.11-14	147, 165, 187, 188 188
3.13-16	112, 115, 182	4.1-20	188, 193 50, 136	4.11-13 4.11	137, 188 116, 187,
3.13-14	23, 182	4.1-9	136		188
3.13	102, 112, 135, 182	4.1-7	112, 114, 115, 117,	4.12	56, 61, 102, 103, 165,
3.14	102, 135, 165, 182,	4.1-3	136, 185 114	4.13	187 19, 137
	183	4.1	102, 112,	4.14-15	187, 189
3.15-16	135		114, 127,	4.14	56, 61, 102,
3.15	102, 112, 147, 165, 186	4.2-9 4.2-7	184 98, 122 63	4.15-20	111, 116, 188 116, 117
3.16	103, 112, 116	4.2-3 4.2	112, 115 115, 147	4.15-17 4.15-16	189 137, 150,
3.17–4.7	98, 111-13, 115, 117, 129, 135-37, 165, 183	4.3 4.4-9 4.4-6 4.4-5	115 186 115 115, 185	4.15	189, 190, 193 102, 108, 136, 189
3.17–4.1	113	4.4	31, 64, 101,	4.17	102, 116,
3.17-21	61, 112, 114, 115, 117, 136	4.5	112, 115, 187 112, 115	4.18-19 4.18	137, 189 137, 189 28, 102,
3.17-19	30, 31, 200	4.6	112, 154		103, 117,
3.17-18	184	4.7	111, 115,		187, 190
3.17	102, 103, 112, 113, 165, 183, 200	4.8-20	165, 185 14, 107, 115-17, 121, 136, 137	4.19-20 4.19 4.20	116 61, 150, 165, 190 116, 137,
3.18-21	112, 130	4.8-15	116, 119		161
3.18-19	119, 197	4.8-14	117	4.21-23	63, 98, 116,
3.18	18, 19, 112, 113.165,	4.8-9	101, 115, 116		117, 120, 137, 192
	186, 193, 197	4.8	111, 136, 187	4.21 4.23	165 82, 116
3.19	102, 103, 113, 165, 184, 186	4.9 4.10-20	136, 187 98, 99, 101, 102, 122,	*Colossians* 1.1	75, 140, 142
3.20-21	112, 136, 178, 183, 184	4.10-14	136, 165, 188, 196 65, 116,	1.2 1.3-8 1.3	104 76 105, 145

1.3-4	106	2.13	106	3.16		82, 116
1.9-12	106	2.14-16	150, 198	3.17		82
1.13-20	105	2.14	112, 158,	3.18		82
1.20	103		160	4.1		122
1.21-29	105	2.17–3.13	80, 110			
1.24	39-41, 43,	2.17–3.8	110	*1 Timothy*		
	52, 55, 177,	2.17-19	80, 109	3.3		185
	186, 187	2.17	93	3.16		178
2.1	77, 79, 112	2.18	150	6.1		112
2.5	93	2.19-20	80	6.6		188
2.8	164	3.1-2	109	6.9		102
2.14	103	3.1	142			
2.18	188	3.2-5	110	*2 Timothy*		
2.23	188	3.2	110, 142,	1.9		183
3.1	184		150	2.5		53
3.10	112	3.3-4	110	2.10		39
3.12	188	3.5	110, 164	2.11		39
3.22-23	163	3.6	110	2.12		38
3.27	112	3.7	115	4.6		53
4.7-9	77, 79.109,	3.10	187	4.7		53
	111, 115	3.14	53			
4.16	82	3.19-20	106	*Titus*		
4.17-18	82	4.1	115	1.1		140, 142
4.18	82	4.10	115	1.11		102
6.12	112	4.13	77, 79	3.2		185
6.16	112	5.14	115			
		5.23-24	82	*Philemon*		
1 Thessalonians		5.23	102, 136	1–2		175
1.1	104	5.25	82	4–6		76
1.2-10	76, 106	5.26	82	4		104, 105
1.2	104, 105,	5.27	82	7		77
	145	5.28	82	8–14		77
1.3	123, 159	5.32	116	8–10		115
1.5	148			17–22		111
1.6	52, 112,	*2 Thessalonians*		18		108
	123, 155,	1.1	142	19		80, 82, 109
	158, 159	1.3-12	76, 105	20		112, 115
1.9	24	1.3	106	21		80, 110
1.10	105	1.4-5	159	21–22		80
2.1-20	142, 145	1.5	158	22		110
2.1-6	154	1.6	39			
2.1	24, 77, 79,	1.11	123, 183	*1 Peter*		
	107, 116,	2.1-3	150	1.1		184
	164	2.3-10	43	1.10		183
2.2	142, 150	2.3	102	2.1		184
2.7	56, 148	2.13	106	2.18		185
2.12	32, 127	3.1	48, 111, 129	2.21-25		170
2.13-16	100	3.12	115, 122	2.21		183

4.13	52	3.17	185	11.13	184
4.15	27	4.10	188		
4.17–18	39			Revelation	
5.5	188	Jude		1.1	140-142
5.6	187, 188	1	140	4–5	178
				14.4-5	170
2 Peter		Hebrews		14.4	170
1.1	140	1.8-13	178	14.5	170
		3.1	183	22.15	108
James		6.12	112		
1.1	140	10.32–33	24		

PSEUDEPIGRAPHA

Apocalypse of James		Jubilees		Martyrdom of Polycarp	
4.38–6.18	20	23	199	1.2	19
				14.1-2	53
Assumption of Moses		3 Maccabees			
10	199	4.1	52	Odes of Solomon	
				29.2	51
2 Baruch		4 Maccabees			
30	199	1.18-23	52	Psalms of Solomon	
30.2	199	6.10	53	3	199
31	199	8	199		
		9.22	104	Testament of Benjamin	
1 Enoch		9.23	53	3.5	39
10	199	10.20–21	52	10	199
22	199	11.20	53		
92.3	199	13.15	53	Testament of Judah	
108	99	17.12	53	25.199	

JOSEPHUS

Antiquities		War	
2.99	52	2.164-65	132

EARLY CHRISTIAN LITERATURE

Ignatius		9.2	18	Trall.	
Rom.				5.2	170
2.2	18	Eph.			
4.2	18, 170	1.2	170	Pol.	
4.3	18, 170	3.1	18	6.1	53
5.1-2	18	7.1.	198		
5.3	18	10.3	170	1 Clement	
6.2	18			16.1-17	170
6	18			38	177

Index of References

Eusebius		
Hist. Eccl.		
1.23	19	
1.41	19	
2.2	19	
5.1.10	170	
5.1.23	170	
5.1.41	56	
5.2.2	170	

Polycarp
Philippians
3.2	97, 99
9.1	19
11	100
12.3	19

Theodoto
Exerpta ex
| 22.1-2 | 20 |

Epistula ad Rheginum
| 44.17-21 | 20 |

Martyrdom of Carpus, Papylys, Agathonice
3.6	19
22.1-2	20
44.17-21	20

Clement of Alexandria
Paedagogus
| 1.62 | 20 |
| 100.1 | 20 |

Origen
Contra Celsum
| 3.75 | 20 |
| 86 | 20 |

Victorinus
Marii Victorini Afri Comentarii in epistulas Pauli ad Galatas, ad Philippenses, ad Ephesios
| 1203a-b | 21 |
| 122b | 21 |

Jerome
Commentarii in Epistolam ad Philippenses
| PL 30.845c | 22 |
| PL 30.849b | 22 |

John Chrysostom
In epistolam ad Philippenses commentarius
PG 62.184	24
PG 62.185	24
PG 62.187	24
PG 62.109	24
PG 62.198	24
PG 62.200-201	24
PG 62.266	24

Tertullian
Adversus Marcionem
| 5.20 | 21 |

OTHER ANCIENT LITERATURE

Epictetus
Dissertations
| 3.23 | 43 |

Ps. Demetrius
On Style
4.223	84
4.224	84
4.226	84
4.227	84
4.229	84
4.231	84
4.235	84

Aristotle
On Rhetoric
1.2 (1356b1)	85, 126
1.3 (1358b 10-20)	85, 120
3.14 (1415a 23-24)	86, 88
3.13	86

Ps. Aristotle
Rhet. ad Alex.
1421b10	20
1436a34-39	88
1438a4-6	88
1438a22	88, 123
1438a33	88
1438b29-1439b2	89
1439b4-1439b14	90
1439b11-13	136
1436a33-1438a1	88

Cicero
Inv.
1.15.20-18.26	86
1.15.20-21	87
1.15.20	86, 87
1.15.21	87
1.16.21	87
1.16.22	121
1.16.23	88, 121
1.19.27	88
1.20.28	88
1.20.29	88
1.20–21.29	88
1.22.31–23.33	125
1.22.31	124
1.24.34–41.77	89
1.24.34–25.36	89
1.24.34	89, 90
1.26.37–28.43	89
1.29.44	90
1.32.53	186
1.32.54	156
1.34.57–41.77	126

Function of Suffering in Philippians 231

1.34.57	156	1.9.14	88	4.3.1–9	125	
1.42.78	90	2.48-49	129	4.4.1	90, 125	
1.42.79	90			4.5.1–28	125	
1.43.78	90	Quintilian		4.5.1	90	
1.51.96	130	*Inst.*		5	90	
1.51.97	128	3.6.4.	86	5.pr.4	89	
1.52.98	91	3.8.6	121	5.9.1	89	
1.53.100-		3.8.12	119	5.9.9	87	
105	129	3.8.13	120	5.9.12	89	
1.53.100	91, 136	3.8.22	125	5.10.11	89	
1.53.106	91	3.8.26	125	5.10.23-31	89	
1.54.104-		3.8.27	125	5.10.32-52	89	
105	129	3.8.34	126	5.11.1-2	89	
1.55.108	137	3.8.36	126	5.11.3	89	
1.56.109	137	3.8.49	166	5.11.6	89, 90	
		3.8.50	166	5.11.7	91	
Cicero		3.8.51	166	6.1.1	91	
Letters		4.1	86	6.1.2	91	
2.4.1	85	4.2.21	88	6.1.9-12	91	
		4.2.31	88	6.1.12	137, 189	
Ps. Cicero		4.2.36-39	88	6.2.8-17	92	
Rhet. Her.		4.2.40-51	88	6.2.11	92	
1.2.2		4.2.52-60	88	6.2.14	92	
1.2.3	86	4.2.64	88	6.2.18	92	
1.3.5	87	4.2.116	24, 88			

INDEX OF AUTHORS

Ahern B.M. 43, 44
Aland, K. 100
Antin, P. 154
Aune, D.E. 92, 95, 119, 120
Austin, J.L. 176

Bailey, C. 78
Bammel, E. 150
Barclay, W. 32
Barth, K. 57-63, 65, 68, 69, 122, 134, 141, 146, 147, 171, 178, 179, 199
Baumbach, G. 185, 201
Baumeister, T. 43, 158
Baumert, N. 168
Baur, F.C. 199, 200
Beare, F.W. 33, 44, 45, 101, 122, 134, 143, 157, 161, 176, 182, 183, 187, 198, 200
Becker, J. 112, 143, 1785
Beker, J.C. 45, 94
Benoit, P. 100, 130, 163, 185
Bertram, G. 153
Best, E. 43, 142, 143
Betz, H.D. 90, 94, 95, 119, 120-23, 125, 126, 136, 181, 200
Beyschlag, K. 19, 26
Biser, E. 186
Bjerkelund, C.J. 127, 136, 161
Black, C.C. 95, 119, 120, 124
Black, D.A. 176, 177
Black, D.L. 158
Bligh, J. 161
Booth, W. 154
Boüttger, P.C. 146, 186
Bonhoeffer, D. 62
Bonnard, P. 60, 61, 168
Bornkamm, G. 44, 98, 200

Bousset, W. 36
Bouttier, M. 60-62, 148, 155, 156, 168
Brown, S. 69
Brox, N. 43
Bruce, F.F. 100
Bünker, M. 95
Bultmann, R. 36, 44, 60, 161

Caird, G.B. 148, 157, 159
Calvin, J. 28-30, 58, 59, 154
Carrez, M. 160, 184
Cerfaux, L. 52, 162, 163, 166, 170
Chadwick, H. 72, 98
Collange, J.F. 46, 48, 56, 60, 63, 64, 69, 103, 113, 127, 130, 153, 156, 159-61, 163, 167, 169-72, 174, 177, 183, 185, 188, 200
Colombas, G.M. 25
Culpepper, R.A. 47, 98, 111, 164, 174, 175, 177

Dacquino, P. 186
Dalton, W.J. 100, 101, 1113, 183
Davies, W.D. 42, 44
De Boer, M.C. 41, 45, 48
Deidun, T.J. 127, 138
Deissmann, A. 36-38, 43, 72, 73, 82, 83, 118
Delling, G. 153
De Lubac, H. 79
Denis, A.-M. 154
Denton, D.R. 154
Dewailly, L.M. 105, 122, 123, 147
Dibelius, M. 36, 38, 55, 122, 130, 134, 152, 161, 171, 175, 176, 183
Doty, W. 73, 75, 76, 80, 81, 82, 84, 94, 110, 115, 140

Index of Authors

Dunn, J.D.G. 162
Dupont, J. 155

Ellis, E.E. 47, 189, 200
Evans, D. 176
Ewald, H. 100
Exler, F.X.J. 73, 74, 821, 116

Feuillet, A. 61
Fitzmeyer, J.A. 160
Forestell, J.T. 33, 45, 180
Francis, F.O. 106
Frend, W.H.C. 25, 39
Fridrichsen, A. 174
Friedrich, G. 48, 60, 65, 65, 113, 134, 148, 179
Froitzheim, F. 57, 199
Funk, R.W. 80, 81, 93, 94, 107, 110, 111, 148, 155, 171
Furnish, V.P. 141, 168

Garland, D.E. 144
Georgi, D. 46
Giglioli, A. 153
Glombitza, O. 189, 190
Gnilka, J. 46-48, 63, 140, 142, 143, 147, 148, 152, 153, 155, 157, 164, 166, 167, 171, 172, 189, 190
Gottwald, N.K. 192
Grandmaison, L. de 180
Grant, R.M. 200
Grayston, K. 141, 147, 149, 154, 158, 163, 171
Grube, G.M.A. 85
Güttgemanns, E. 38-41, 55, 56, 69, 112, 191
Gundry, R.H. 112, 150, 155
Gunther, J.J. 46

Hafemann, S.J. 160, 190
Hamerton-Kelly, R. 171
Hansen, G.W. 94, 121-23, 125
Hawkes, T. 65
Hawthorn, G.F. 99, 100, 122, 127, 140, 142, 143, 148, 149, 161, 169-71, 175, 177, 180, 183, 198, 199, 201
Hay, D.M. 178

Henry, P. 163
Herklots, H.G.G. 149
Hoffmann, P. 150
Holladay, C.R. 46, 129
Holsten, C. 35, 188
Holtz, T. 40, 55
Holtzmann, H.J. 36
Hooker, M.D. 101, 180, 186
Houlden, J.L. 141, 144, 148, 158, 177
Howard, G. 162
Huby, J. 43, 134, 179, 180
Hunter, A.M. 161, 162
Hunzinger, C.-H. 153

Jewett, R. 46-48, 52, 63, 95, 106, 107, 122, 123, 155, 156, 168, 174, 183, 185, 199, 200
Johanson, B.C. 95
Johnson, G. 94
Jouön, P. 134, 152, 174, 179, 181, 184

Kabisch, R. 42
Käsemann, E. 54-56, 67, 69, 161, 191
Kamlah, E. 40, 55
Keck, L. 94
Kelly, J.N.D. 40
Kelsey, D.H. 176
Kennedy, G.A. 94, 95, 119, 120, 124
Kim, S. 44, 45, 186
Kleinknecht, K.T. 134, 160, 179
Klijn, A.F.J. 198
Koester, H. 46-48, 63, 184, 186, 200
Koskenniemmi, H. 73
Krause, B. 58
Kremer, J. 38, 177
Krötke, W. 58
Kümmel, W.G. 42, 47, 190, 200

Lampe, G.W.H. 53, 59
Landgraf, A.M. 26
Lausberg, H. 86, 87-90, 93, 121, 123
Leipoldt, J. 99
Léon-Dufour, X. 44, 167
Lightfoot, J.B. 19, 31, 32, 97, 99, 100, 101, 105, 123, 131, 145, 152, 153, 156, 158, 164, 173, 176, 199, 200

Lilla, S.R. 20
Lincoln, A.T. 46, 48, 112
Lipsius, R.A. 122, 136, 147, 172, 175, 176, 178, 183, 188, 189, 198
Lohmeyer, E. 50-54, 69, 112, 113, 141, 142, 144, 148, 156, 158, 161, 163, 167, 172, 183
Lohse, E. 41, 53
Lüdemann, H. 35
Lührmann, D. 55
Luther, M. 30, 58, 59
Lyons, D. 95, 1120, 131

Mackay, B.S. 99, 100, 101, 124
Malherbe. A.J. 83, 84, 91, 93, 150
Malina, B.J. 192
Martin, J. 86-88, 142, 144, 146, 157, 178, 180
Martin, R.P. 99, 160, 161, 163
Meinhold, P. 18
Ménard, J.E. 161, 162
Michael, J.H. 32, 123, 145, 146, 148, 149, 158, 160, 163, 168, 171, 172
Michaelis, W. 64
Michel, O. 39
Mitton, C.L. 99
Moffatt, J. 99
Moule, H.C.G. 171
Müller, J.J. 46, 149, 166, 171, 189, 190
Mullins, T.Y. 73, 75, 76, 78, 84, 104, 115
Murphy-O'Connor, J. 100, 160, 162, 163, 166, 167, 181
Musurillo, H. 19

Neill, S. 35
Neyrey, J.H. 132, 181
Niebuhr, H.R. 20
Norden, E. 113
Nowak, E. 24

O'Brien, P.T. 122, 145, 146
O'Daly, G.J.P. 23
Ollrog, W.-H. 173
Omanson, R.L. 105, 145

Pagels, E.H. 20, 25

Panikulam, G. 45, 122, 130, 145, 147, 161, 183
Parker, T.H.L. 29
Patte, D. 65-70, 167-69, 193, 194
Pearson, B.A. 200
Pesch, R. 41, 156
Pfitzner, V.P. 18, 135, 182
Pfleiderer, O. 35
Plank, K.A. 95, 192
Pobee, J.S. 52, 53, 149
Polhill, J.B. 44
Pontet, M. 22
Priero, G. 188
Proudfoot, C.M. 43, 44

Quasten, J. 21

Rahtjen, B.D. 97-99
Reicke, B.I. 160-161
Reitzenstein, R. 36˙
Rey, B. 161
Richler, P.J. 192
Riesenfeld, H. 164
Roetzel, C. 115
Rolla, A. 184
Rumscheidt, H.M. 57, 62

Sanders, B. 41
Sanders, E.P. 45
Sanders, J.T. 76, 105, 107, 166
Sass, G. 39, 40, 142-44
Schade, H.H. 161, 162, 170
Schenkel, D. 200
Schelkle, K. 43
Schlatter, A. 18
Schmid, J. 99
Schmithals, W. 46-48, 63, 182, 199, 200
Schmitz, O. 3638-41
Schneider, J. 38, 55
Schoedel, W.R. 18
Schubert, P. 76, 93, 107
Schütz, J.H. 44, 45
Schweitzer, A. 18, 34-37, 42-44, 47-52, 55, 191
Schweizer, E. 163, 164, 170
Scroggs, R. 161
Selwyn, E.G. 19

Sheehan, T. 58
Siegert, F. 94, 95
Smalley, B. 27, 28
Souter, A. 99
Staab, K. 100, 122, 153, 164
Stählin, G. 54
Stambaugh, J. 158
Stanley, D.M. 67, 117, 167
Stauffer, E. 38-40, 51
Steen, H.A. 79, 84, 104, 105, 108, 109, 115, 181
Stoops, R.F. 18
Stowers, S.K. 93-95
Strange, E. 100
Strecker, G. 113
Strimple, R.B. 161, 162
Stuhlmacher, P. 41, 61
Swartley, W.M. 18
Sykutris, J. 78, 83
Syncellus, G. 97
Talbert, C.H. 16
Tannehill, R. 45, 184
Tejera, V. 192
Theissen, G. 68
Thompson, G.H.P. 39
Thraede, K. 83

Trudinger, L.P. 183
Turri, J.O. 167, 168
Urbach, E.E. 132

Victorinus, M. 21, 34
Vincent, M.R. 36-38, 48, 99, 101, 121, 134, 141, 143, 146, 152, 154, 157, 158, 171, 175, 179, 183, 186, 199
Vitti, A. 182
Volkmann, R. 86, 88

Walter, N. 123, 155, 157
Watson, D.F. 86, 95, 120, 121, 123, 125, 126, 128, 130, 136
Weinrich, W.C. 56, 57, 68, 69, 168
Wendland, H.D. 54
White, J.L. 72-82, 84, 84, 107-11, 173
Wikenhauser, A. 38, 99, 197
Wiles, M.F. 25
Wilmart, D.A. 26
Windisch, H. 39-41, 46, 55, 56, 68
Wrede, W. 42
Wuellner, W. 94

JOURNAL FOR THE STUDY OF THE NEW TESTAMENT

Supplement Series

5   THE PEOPLE OF GOD
    Markus Barth
6   PERSECUTION AND MARTYRDOM IN THE THEOLOGY OF PAUL
    John S. Pobee
7   SYNOPTIC STUDIES:
    THE AMPLEFORTH CONFERENCES OF
    1982 AND 1983
    Edited by C.M. Tuckett
8   JESUS ON THE MOUNTAIN:
    A STUDY IN MATTHEAN THEOLOGY
    Terence L. Donaldson
9   THE HYMNS OF LUKE'S INFANCY NARRATIVES
    THEIR ORIGIN, MEANING AND SIGNIFICANCE
    Stephen Farris
10 CHRIST THE END OF THE LAW:
    ROMANS 10.4 IN PAULINE PERSPECTIVE
    Robert Badenas
11 THE LETTERS TO THE SEVEN CHURCHES OF ASIA
    IN THEIR LOCAL SETTING
    Colin J. Hemer
12 PROCLAMATION FROM PROPHECY AND PATTERN:
    LUCAN OLD TESTAMENT CHRISTOLOGY
    Darrell L. Bock
13 JESUS AND THE LAWS OF PURITY:
    TRADITION HISTORY AND LEGAL HISTORY IN MARK 7
    Roger P. Booth
14 THE PASSION ACCORDING TO LUKE:
    THE SPECIAL MATERIAL OF LUKE 22
    Marion L. Soards
15 HOSTILITY TO WEALTH IN THE SYNOPTIC GOSPELS
    Thomas E. Schmidt
16 MATTHEW'S COMMUNITY:
    THE EVIDENCE OF HIS SPECIAL SAYINGS MATERIAL
    Stephenson H. Brooks
17 THE PARADOX OF THE CROSS IN THE THOUGHT OF ST PAUL
    Anthony Tyrrell Hanson
18 HIDDEN WISDOM AND THE EASY YOKE:
    WISDOM, TORAH AND DISCIPLESHIP IN MATTHEW 11.25-30
    Celia Deutsch

19 JESUS AND GOD IN PAUL'S ESCHATOLOGY
    L. Joseph Kreitzer
20 LUKE:
    A NEW PARADIGM (2 Volumes)
    Michael D. Goulder
21 THE DEPARTURE OF JESUS IN LUKE–ACTS:
    THE ASCENSION NARRATIVES IN CONTEXT
    Mikeal C. Parsons
22 THE DEFEAT OF DEATH:
    APOCALYPTIC ESCHATOLOGY IN 1 CORINTHIANS 15 AND ROMANS 5
    Martinus C. de Boer
23 PAUL THE LETTER-WRITER
    AND THE SECOND LETTER TO TIMOTHY
    Michael Prior
24 APOCALYPTIC AND THE NEW TESTAMENT:
    ESSAYS IN HONOR OF J. LOUIS MARTYN
    Edited by Joel Marcus & Marion L. Soards
25 THE UNDERSTANDING SCRIBE:
    MATTHEW AND THE APOCALYPTIC IDEAL
    David E. Orton
26 WATCHWORDS:
    MARK 13 IN MARKAN ESCHATOLOGY
    Timothy J. Geddert
27 THE DISCIPLES ACCORDING TO MARK:
    MARKAN REDACTION IN CURRENT DEBATE
    C. Clifton Black
28 THE NOBLE DEATH:
    GRAECO-ROMAN MARTYROLOGY
    AND PAUL'S CONCEPT OF SALVATION
    David Seeley
29 ABRAHAM IN GALATIANS:
    EPISTOLARY AND RHETORICAL CONTEXTS
    G. Walter Hansen
30 EARLY CHRISTIAN RHETORIC AND 2 THESSALONIANS
    Frank Witt Hughes
31 THE STRUCTURE OF MATTHEW'S GOSPEL:
    A STUDY IN LITERARY DESIGN
    David R. Bauer
32 PETER AND THE BELOVED DISCIPLE:
    FIGURES FOR A COMMUNITY IN CRISIS
    Kevin Quast
33 MARK'S AUDIENCE:
    THE LITERARY AND SOCIAL SETTING OF MARK 4.11-12
    Mary Ann Beavis

34 THE GOAL OF OUR INSTRUCTION:
   THE STRUCTURE OF THEOLOGY AND ETHICS
   IN THE PASTORAL EPISTLES
   Philip H. Towner
35 THE PROVERBS OF JESUS:
   ISSUES OF HISTORY AND RHETORIC
   Alan P. Winton
36 THE STORY OF CHRIST IN THE ETHICS OF PAUL:
   AN ANALYSIS OF THE FUNCTION OF THE HYMNIC MATERIAL
   IN THE PAULINE CORPUS
   Stephen E. Fowl
37 PAUL AND JESUS:
   COLLECTED ESSAYS
   Edited by A.J.M. Wedderburn
38 MATTHEW'S MISSIONARY DISCOURSE:
   A LITERARY CRITICAL ANALYSIS
   Dorothy Jean Weaver
39 FAITH AND OBEDIENCE IN ROMANS:
   A STUDY IN ROMANS 1–4
   Glenn N. Davies
40 IDENTIFYING PAUL'S OPPONENTS:
   THE QUESTION OF METHOD IN 2 CORINTHIANS
   Jerry L. Sumney
41 HUMAN AGENTS OF COSMIC POWER
   IN HELLENISTIC JUDAISM AND THE SYNOPTIC TRADITION
   Mary E. Mills
42 MATTHEW'S INCLUSIVE STORY:
   A STUDY IN THE NARRATIVE RHETORIC OF THE FIRST GOSPEL
   David B. Howell
43 JESUS, PAUL AND TORAH:
   COLLECTED ESSAYS
   Heikki Räisänen
44 THE NEW COVENANT IN HEBREWS
   Susanne Lehne
45 THE RHETORIC OF ROMANS:
   ARGUMENTATIVE CONSTRAINT AND STRATEGY AND PAUL'S
   DIALOGUE WITH JUDAISM
   Neil Elliott
46 THE LAST SHALL BE FIRST:
   THE RHETORIC OF REVERSAL IN LUKE
   John O. York
47 JAMES AND THE Q SAYINGS OF JESUS
   Patrick J. Hartin

48 TEMPLUM AMICITIAE:
   ESSAYS ON THE SECOND TEMPLE PRESENTED TO ERNST BAMMEL
   Edited by William Horbury
49 PROLEPTIC PRIESTS:
   PRIESTHOOD IN THE EPISTLE TO THE HEBREWS
   John M. Scholer
50 PERSUASIVE ARTISTRY:
   STUDIES IN NEW TESTAMENT RHETORIC
   IN HONOR OF GEORGE A. KENNEDY
   Edited by Duane F. Watson
51 THE AGENCY OF THE APOSTLE:
   A DRAMATISTIC ANALYSIS OF PAUL'S RESPONSES
   TO CONFLICT IN 2 CORINTHIANS
   Jeffrey A. Crafton
52 REFLECTIONS OF GLORY:
   PAUL'S POLEMICAL USE OF THE MOSES–DOXA TRADITION IN
   2 CORINTHIANS 3.12-18
   Linda L. Belleville
53 REVELATION AND REDEMPTION AT COLOSSAE
   Thomas J. Sappington
54 THE DEVELOPMENT OF EARLY CHRISTIAN PNEUMATOLOGY
   WITH SPECIAL REFERENCE TO LUKE–ACTS
   Robert P. Menzies
55 THE PURPOSE OF ROMANS:
   A COMPARATIVE LETTER STRUCTURE INVESTIGATION
   L. Ann Jervis
56 THE SON OF THE MAN IN THE GOSPEL OF JOHN
   Delbert Burkett
57 ESCHATOLOGY AND THE COVENANT:
   A COMPARISON OF 4 EZRA AND ROMANS 1–11
   Bruce W. Longenecker
58 NONE BUT THE SINNERS:
   RELIGIOUS CATEGORIES IN THE GOSPEL OF LUKE
   David A. Neale
59 CLOTHED WITH CHRIST:
   THE EXAMPLE AND TEACHING OF JESUS IN ROMANS 12.1–15.13
   Michael Thompson
60 THE LANGUAGE OF THE NEW TESTAMENT
   CLASSIC ESSAYS
   Edited by Stanley E. Porter
61 FOOTWASHING IN JOHN 13 AND THE JOHANNINE COMMUNITY
   John Christopher Thomas
62 JOHN THE BAPTIZER AND PROPHET:
   A SOCIO-HISTORICAL STUDY
   Robert L. Webb

63 POWER AND POLITICS IN PALESTINE:
   THE JEWS AND THE GOVERNING OF THEIR LAND 100 BC–AD 70
   James S. McLaren
64 JESUS AND THE ORAL GOSPEL TRADITION
   Edited by Henry Wansbrough
65 THE RHETORIC OF RIGHTEOUSNESS IN ROMANS 3.21-26
   Douglas A. Campbell
66 PAUL, ANTIOCH AND JERUSALEM:
   A STUDY IN RELATIONSHIPS AND AUTHORITY IN EARLIEST CHRISTIANITY
   Nicholas Taylor
67 THE PORTRAIT OF PHILIP IN ACTS:
   A STUDY OF ROLES AND RELATIONS
   F. Scott Spencer
68 JEREMIAH IN MATTHEW'S GOSPEL:
   THE REJECTED PROPHET MOTIF IN MATTHAEAN REDACTION
   Michael P. Knowles
69 RHETORIC AND REFERENCE IN THE FOURTH GOSPEL
   Margaret Davies
70 AFTER THE THOUSAND YEARS:
   RESURRECTION AND JUDGMENT IN REVELATION 20
   J. Webb Mealy
71 SOPHIA AND THE JOHANNINE JESUS
   Martin Scott
72 NARRATIVE ASIDES IN LUKE–ACTS
   Steven M. Sheeley
73 SACRED SPACE:
   AN APPROACH TO THE THEOLOGY OF THE EPISTLE TO THE HEBREWS
   Marie E. Isaacs
74 TEACHING WITH AUTHORITY:
   MIRACLES AND CHRISTOLOGY IN THE GOSPEL OF MARK
   Edwin K. Broadhead
75 PATRONAGE AND POWER:
   STUDIES ON SOCIAL NETWORKS IN CORINTH
   John Kin-Man Chow
76 THE NEW TESTAMENT AS CANON:
   A READER IN CANONICAL CRITICISM
   Robert Wall and Eugene Lemcio
78 THE FUNCTION OF SUFFERING IN PHILIPPIANS
   L. Gregory Bloomquist
79 THE THEME OF RECOMPENSE IN MATTHEW'S GOSPEL
   Blaine Charette